T0230740

GAME MAGIC

A Designer's Guide to Magic Systems in Theory and Practice

GAME MAGIC

A Designer's Guide to Magic Systems in Theory and Practice

JEFF HOWARD, Ph.D.

Assistant Professor of Game Development and Design
Dakota State University

CRC Press

Taylor & Francis Group
Boca Raton London New York

CRC Press is an imprint of the
Taylor & Francis Group, an **informa** business

AN A K PETERS BOOK

CRC Press
Taylor & Francis Group
6000 Broken Sound Parkway NW, Suite 300
Boca Raton, FL 33487-2742

First issued in hardback 2017

© 2014 by Taylor & Francis Group, LLC
CRC Press is an imprint of Taylor & Francis Group, an Informa business

No claim to original U.S. Government works

Version Date: 20140213

ISBN-13: 978-1-4665-6785-6 (pbk)
ISBN-13: 978-1-138-42775-4 (hbk)

Library of Congress Cataloging-in-Publication Data

Howard, Jeff, 1978-
  Game magic : a designer's guide to magic systems in theory and practice / Jeff Howard.
    pages cm
  Includes bibliographical references and index.
  ISBN 978-1-4665-6785-6 (paperback)
  1. Magic--Psychological aspects. 2. Magic tricks. I. Title.

GV1547.H86 2014
793.8--dc23   2014001353

Visit the Taylor & Francis Web site at
http://www.taylorandfrancis.com

and the CRC Press Web site at
http://www.crcpress.com

*Dedicated to Angela Behrends
and my parents, Lamar and Melissa Howard*

Contents

List of Figures

List of Tables

Thanks

Thanks to Giles Timms (gilestimms.com) for his fantastic, gorgeous illustrations and cover art. Thank you to everyone who read the book at various stages of writing and offered feedback, including Steve Graham, Andrew Plotkin, Joshua Madara, Matthew Weise, Denis Dyack, Matt Nelles, and Jeramy de Vos.

Thanks also to the students in the game design program at Dakota State University, especially the team who worked with me on *Arcana: A Ceremonial Magick Simulator* to put the ideas in this book into practice (Daryl Bunker, Landon Anker, Travis Till, Pat Gilmore). I owe a special debt of gratitude to the students in Game 492: Magic and Combat Systems and Game 492: Game Mechanics (Magic and Combat Systems), who helped me to work out the ideas in this book through discussion, practice, and prototyping.

The Author

Jeff Howard is Assistant Professor of Game Development and Design at Dakota State University, Madison, South Dakota, where he has practiced, studied, and taught game design since 2009. He plays a key role leading the narrative design focus in the game design program, in which he teaches classes in level design, game genres, game mechanics, and mythology. He is the author of *Quests: Design, Theory, and History in Games and Narratives* and contributed a chapter entitled "Howard's Law of Occult Design" to *100 Game Design Principles*. Howard has spoken about magic systems  at the Singapore-M.I.T. Gambit Game Lab and the Game Developer's Conference. He earned his Ph.D. and M.A. from the University of Texas at Austin, and his B.A. from the University of Tulsa, Oklahoma. He continues his work on his transmedia project *Arcana*, which includes *Arcana: A Ceremonial Magick Simulator* and *The Arcana Ritual Toolset*. His website, designingquests.com, will include resources related to this book. Howard can be contacted via Twitter: @gamemagicarcana.

Table of Recipes/ Code Snippets

Like any grimoire or cookbook, this book contains recipes, which are examples for how to implement game magic. These recipes consist of code snippets written in several programming languages associated with a variety of engines, software packages, and platforms. The recipes fall into a few major categories, listed below.

In many cases, I extrapolate from a particular language into pseudo-code (a language that resembles the syntax of programming languages but which is not actually tied to a particular language). The table below lists the name of the recipe, its author (when derived from a secondary source), and the language in which it is coded.

   I Inform7 (Tolti-Aph, Savoir-Faire/Damnatio)

  II Roguelikes (Angband and variants, C/C++)

 III Flash Actionscript

 IV Javascript, implemented in Unity (Arcana)

Proverbs of Game Magic

The central ideas of this book can be summarized in a few sentences that serve as proverbs and mottos.

- *Magic is system*: Any particular view of magic—whether historical, fictional, or invented from wholecloth—can be simulated as a system of rules and symbols.

- *Magic is ritual*: The systems of magic are frameworks for the performance of ritual, understood as a set of symbolic actions designed to alter reality or transform consciousness.

- *Magic is language*: The rules and symbols of a given magic system constitute a language, with a vocabulary and a grammar.

- *Magical language is coextensive with its world*: In order to function adequately in gameplay and in narrative, the language of magic must be coextensive with the world in which it exists. For every utterance possible in the language, there should be an aspect of the world that this utterance can describe and command.

- *Ritual language is multimodal*: The languages of ritual are multimodal and based on matrices of symbolic correspondences.

- *Reduce the gap of player performance*: To enhance player immersion and engagement with a magic system, reduce the gap between player action and character performance by allowing players to master some of the techniques and knowledge wielded by their characters.

- *Rituals are puzzles*: To reduce the gap of player performance, rituals can be simulated as puzzles or mini-games, based on the symbolic correspondences of a particular magical language.

- *Magical innovation is strengthened by historical knowledge*: In order to create innovative magic systems and avoid re-inventing the wheel, seek inspiration from the game magic, fictive magic, and occult magic of the past.

- *Procedural adaptation*: Fictive magic systems can be adapted into systems of rules by expressing the actions of magic-wielding characters as a set of procedures, a ritual protocol.

- *Magic is programming*: The underlying logic of a given magic system can be expressed through programming, which is itself a magical manipulation of symbolic languages to construct and alter a simulated reality.

- *Programming is logic*: The logical framework of a magic system is most important to a game designer, because game engines and associated languages become obsolete over time. At the same time, every design must be tested through implementation.

Epigraphs

"I must Create a System, or be enslav'd by another Man's."

**THE CHARACTER LOS IN *JERUSALEM*, BY THE
POET AND ENGRAVER WILLIAM BLAKE**

"'Magic,' says Gentle, 'is the first and last religion of the world.'
A religion of which—may I add?—play is surely the profoundest
ritual.'"

**INTRODUCTION TO THE RULEBOOK FOR
THE COLLECTIBLE CARD GAME *CLIVE
BARKER'S IMAJICA* BY CLIVE BARKER**

"Through the darkness of futures past, the magician longs to see.
One chants out between two worlds: fire walk with me."

THE ONE-ARMED MAN, *TWIN PEAKS*

CHAPTER 1

How to Use This Book

THIS BOOK IS A grimoire: a guidebook to the construction of magic systems that doubles as a compendium of arcane lore, encompassing the theory, history, and structure of magic systems in both games and human belief. The book thus combines the rigors of scholarly analysis with the strengths of a handbook for game design and a textbook of magic. The book is a cookbook, a compendium of recipes, a spellbook for weaving more potent and subtler magic in games. The text is intercut with examples of how to design and program magic systems written as snippets of pseudocode, with working examples downloadable from the book's website. The book will show how to set up tables of correspondences and spell components, and how to write a program integrating those components as part of game mechanics. It shows how to divide a simulated world into domains of influence (i.e. schools of magic like alteration, conjuration, and necromancy), and how to use specific rules systems to simulate powers within these realms.

Cookbooks need not be read cover to cover in a linear order, although this book is structured so that it can be read in this way. But, like a cookbook or a grimoire, this book can be dipped into or leafed through by designers at any point in order to inspire the creation of game magic. Some sections cross-reference other sections, emphasizing the dense web of interconnectedness across media that constitutes game magic. Carry the book with you, consulting it as an encyclopedia. Wield it as a compendium of spells and recipes to experiment with in your own sanctum or laboratory, or while braving the wilderness on your own game design quests.

1.1 WHO IS THIS BOOK FOR?

The book is intended for anyone interested in game design, magic, or the intersection of the two. More broadly, it is meant for people who would like to make their games richer and deeper, and for those who want a deeper and richer understanding of the history and structure of magic. Audiences include game designers, game developers, students, and occultists. The interdisciplinary nature of the book allows it to potentially reach a variety of audiences, and the main thread of the argument will be readable and interesting to all intended audiences.

Because of the multiple audiences reached by the book's interdisciplinary approach, symbols are used to signal sections that are especially relevant to particular audiences, such as game designers, technical readers, casual readers, mystical readers, and so on. For example, a particular symbol and color (such as a computer icon and a blue sidebar) could indicate that a section is especially of interest to technical readers, since the section might contain the concept of an array or relational databases.

1.2 A NOTE ON AUDIENCE, AND A SYMBOLIC KEY OF INTENDED AUDIENCES

Although the primary audience for this book is game designers, it will also be useful to a variety of other audiences: game design teachers, game design students, occultists, and readers of fantasy literature, to name a few. Some sections are directed at particular audiences more than others, and some sections may be unnecessary to some readers. A game designer will know that *World of Warcraft* is an MMO (massively multiplayer online role-playing game), but a reader of fantasy literature might not. An occultist will certainly know who Aleister Crowley is, but a game designer may not.

With a multiplicity of possible audiences in mind, I've prepared a pie graph (Figure 1.1) with symbols that stand for each of the book's main subject areas. Throughout the book, sidebars and callouts contain information on subjects that may be crucial to some audiences but unnecessary to others. Each symbol will designate that the sidebar contains crucial information for a particular audience. As shown in the figure, a book represents history, a joystick represents games, a computer represents technical knowledge, a pentagram represents occultism, and a dragon represents fantasy.

FIGURE 1.1 (See color insert.)   A Symbolic Key of Intended Audiences. (Pentagram image from Clickr.com)

1.3 TRIANGULATING GAME MAGIC

This book navigates, or more precisely triangulates, between three different types of magic. At the apex of the triangle is game magic, referring primarily to magic in videogames. This magic is often part of a magic system, though the book argues that magic systems (as conventionally defined) are only one way of simulating magic in games, and often not the most interesting or innovative way. Sometimes, simulating magic requires the invention of new forms of gameplay that fall outside of the lists of spells conventionally associated with game magic. The main goal of the book is to help game designers create better magic in videogames, so game magic is at the apex of the triangle. Figure 1.2 illustrates the triangle of game magic, occult magic, and fictive magic.

Game magic should not, does not, and perhaps cannot exist in a vacuum, uninfluenced by other media. Indeed, we as designers often fall into ruts of clichéd mechanics (such as spamming abilities until the magic user's mana pool runs out) because we are sometimes not aware of how we have been influenced. As Matthew Weise argued in his Game Developer's Conference 2013 talk "Getting a Team on Board with Narrative Design," we are unoriginal not when we are influenced, but when we are not influenced

FIGURE 1.2   Triangulating Game Magic. (Image by Giles Timms.)

by *enough* things. It is important, then, that the apex of game magic have two points at its base to balance it: fictive magic and occult magic.

As potential influences for game magic, there are two major traditions through which the human imagination has represented and theorized magic, which I call fictive magic and occult magic. Fictive magic refers to sorcery as represented in the literature of the fantastic, broadly conceived to include ancient mythology, medieval romance, and especially modern fantasy (such as the work of George R.R. Martin and Michael Moorcock). Fictive magic is one of the richest and most direct potential sources of inspiration for game magic. When discussing the literature of the fantastic, it is common to speak of the magic system of a given fantasy novel or series, referring to the techniques and metaphysical underpinnings of magic in a given fantasy universe. Many early game designers often directly adapted these fantastic magic systems as game mechanics in role-playing games, such as *Dungeons & Dragons*, which features a Vancian magic system of memorized spells in limited spell slots based on the *Dying Earth* series by fantasy author Jack Vance. Similarly, the concept of mana as a finite, exhaustible pool of spell energy so central to role-playing games derives directly from Larry Niven in his short story "The Magic Goes Away."

Without understanding the derivation of game mechanics from these fictional sources, many modern game designers treat Vancian and mana-based systems as inevitable and immutable, not recognizing a wealth of magical paradigms that could be derived from a vast range of imaginative visions, from Neil Gaiman's *Sandman* to Roger Zelazny's *Chronicles of Amber* to George R.R. Martin's *Game of Thrones*. Such works are a rich wellspring of potential inspiration for game magic. Yet the potential limitation of fictive magic as a source for game magic is that magic primarily serves narrative-based thematic ends in story. No matter how coherent world-building in a given story, readers can passively observe magic-using characters casting spells without having to actively participate in sorcerous mechanics. As long as a fictive magic system entertains readers, allowing them to suspend disbelief and perhaps stimulating their imaginations, the author does not ultimately have to worry about whether the readers could perform the magic in the story as a system. For game designers, coherence of magic as a system of practice is a primary concern. For this reason game magic can be effectively triangulated *between* fictive magic and another type of magic: occult magic.

Occult magic refers to human mystical practices amongst people who on some level believe that magic is real (such as voodoo or Western ceremonial magick).

"Magick" is a spelling of magic frequently used by occultists to distinguish genuine mystical practice from illusionism, stage magic, or charlatanry. The term was popularized by occultist Aleister Crowley, whose book *Magick* is a standard work on the topic. As the eleventh letter in the alphabet, "k" signifies the passage beyond the ten traditional branches of the kabbalistic tree of life and into the beyond of transcendence. Magick also sounds a bit romantically archaic, like medieval or Shakespearean English.

Whether magic is or is not real is of no import. As Aleister Crowley famously declares in *Liber O*, a book about the magical practice of traveling between planes in visions: "In this book it is spoken of the Sephiroth and the Paths; of Spirits and Conjurations; of Gods, Spheres, Planes, and many other things which may or may not exist. It is immaterial whether these exist or not. By doing certain things certain results will follow; students are most earnestly warned against attributing objective reality or philosophic validity to any of them." Occult magic is useful for game designers because when a group of people believes in the reality of contacting and manipulating mystical forces, they often invest intense energy into assuring that their magical system is coherent and workable. Occult magic consists of systems of interactive practice in the real world, involving imaginative voyages and quests into other dimensions that parallel those of gamers into virtual worlds. Regardless of whether or not occult magic is real, its coherent systems of performance and practice make it a useful source of inspiration for game designers. Occult magic allows us as designers to invest our games with a deep sense of authenticity and internal coherence, allowing us to remain agnostic about the metaphysical content of our games as long as it deepens and enriches players' experiences.

1.3.1 The Controversy of Occult Magic and Role-Playing Games

The investigation of occult magic in conjunction with game magic is likely to be controversial in some circles because of the condemnation of games, especially tabletop role-playing games like *Dungeons & Dragons*, as Satanic because they supposedly encourage ritualistic behavior. The attack on role-playing games by fundamentalist Christian groups reached a fever pitch in the 1980s, during the so-called Satanic panic, which also involved an attack on heavy metal music and other supposed threats to conservative morality. The comic books of Christian evangelist Don Chick, such as the infamous "Dark Dungeons," exemplify and perhaps unintentionally caricature this viewpoint, as they show a young girl named Debbie who is brainwashed into joining a Satanic coven through her playing of *Dungeons & Dragons*. The fundamentalist condemnation of role-playing games died down over the next few decades, though periodically it reemerges, as in Pat Robertson's recent condemnation of games that feature magic.

It is useful for game designers to be aware of such potential for controversy, which is the price of imaginative freedom. The goal of this book is to help game designers create rich, deeper, more engaging game magic by triangulating it in relation to fictive and occult magic. Such a goal is incompatible with Chick and Robertson's worldview (though perhaps not with early Christianity, which co-existed with ancient Roman and Greek mystical beliefs and magical practices). In the end, this book is not written for Don Chick or Pat Robertson. It is written for game designers.

CHAPTER 2

Magic Systems in Theory and Practice

A MAGIC SYSTEM IS ANY set of rules and symbols designed to rigorously simulate the alteration of reality through the will by way of metaphysical forces and entities. In order to simulate magic in a game, magic must be defined in part by rules. For example, a rule might specify that a player (or a computer) should roll two six-sided dice in order to calculate the amount of damage from a fire projectile. Another rule might demand that a player is unable to cast a spell if he has fewer than five mana points. A set of consistent, complete, internally consistent rules governing magic is part of a magic system.

But rules alone are not enough. Symbols are at the heart of magic. Whether a glowing pentagram or a circle of light, symbols help us to envision, to hear, and to feel magic. Without representational elements like words, images, sounds, and haptics, players have a hard time experiencing magic as anything other than a set of mathematical calculations. But *with* symbols, magic comes alive.

Magic is pervasive as a game mechanic and fictional construct within games, spanning across genres (role-playing game [RPG], MMORPG, adventure game, action-adventure, fighter, survival horror) and decades (from the 1974 first edition of *Dungeons & Dragons* to *World of Warcraft* and beyond).

Dungeons & Dragons was the first tabletop role-playing game, invented in 1974 by Dave Arneson and Gary Gygax as an outgrowth of their wargame, *Chainmail*. In *Dungeons & Dragons*, players take the role of questing adventurers, such as brave warriors and powerful mages.

World of Warcraft was one of the most popular Massively Multiplayer Online Role-Playing Games (MMORPG, or MMO for short), first released in 2004.

Magic is part of the very nature of why people play games: to simulate abilities that they do not possess in real life; to escape from the prison of the mundane to the realm of enchanted; to weave the chaotic forces of life into a rule-bound system that can be understood and, at least partially, controlled.

Game mechanics, the core interactions that constitute a game, are largely defined by rules. Rules are the actions that are or are not permitted, as well as requirements that must be satisfied in order to play the game.

2.1 PUTTING THE MAGIC BACK IN MAGIC SYSTEMS

Many videogames (probably thousands or tens of thousands) feature magic systems. Yet something has gone wrong with magic systems. All too often, they are not magical. Instead, the magic systems in many videogames are repetitive, dull, lacking in variety, and superficial.

RPGs, both multiplayer and single player, have the same shortcoming: players press a button on a tray of icons, then watch an animation fire, followed by a cooldown period, after which players press the same button again. This process of spamming a hotkey button or two, cued to one's most powerful spells, doesn't feel like magic. Far too many magic systems are simply rows of spell icons on which players click to cast a spell, followed by a cooldown period, after which players click the same icon again. This process makes magic seem like a chore or repetitive routine; there is nothing otherworldly about it. Moreover, this repetitive version of magic has no relationship to ritual or ceremony, i.e. the symbols through which an occult magician accesses otherworldly forces. Magic in myth and mysticism is a complex art of words, gestures, and colors, woven by skilled adepts whose every action shows their initiation into hidden mysteries. The adepts' gestures and words combine with ritualistic artifacts and ingredients in order to draw away the veil between the natural and supernatural worlds, invoking metaphysical forces.

The presence of metaphysical forces and entities distinguishes magic from other means of altering reality, such as medicine, engineering, or warfare. Of course, all of these enterprises could be conceived of as forms of magic. (The history of medicine in particular is closely tied up with alchemy.) Magic entails contact with forces and entities beyond the physical (the literal meaning of metaphysics). Forces include bonds of sympathy, the energy of other planes, the aura, and karma; entities include spirits, gods, and demons. Magic allows human beings to pull aside the veil between the ordinary world and another world beyond. Magic then offers the promise of putting these otherworldly forces to use in everyday life.

Yet in many magic systems, there are no mysteries or otherworldly forces. Frequently, magic consists primarily of projectiles of various elements—"magic" bullets of fire, water, earth, and air. These four elements, though derived originally from the ancient Greek shaman Empedocles—have been used so often and with so little depth in game magic systems that they spawn boredom, if not dread. The four elements certainly could be used as vehicles for metaphysical depth and enchantment, but in games they are usually flashy and physical: "vulgar," to use the terminology of *Mage: The Ascension*, "cantripped shenanigans of fire and light," as one mage scornfully observes in *The Elder Scrolls V: Skyrim*.

Reality is of such great complexity and variety that no four elements are sufficient to exhaust or classify it. The traditions of magic form a treasure trove of symbolic correspondences: planets, signs, sigils, and planes that number in the hundreds of thousands, not to mention all those signs that have not yet been invented.

At the current time, game magic is all too mundane not just in what aspects of reality are altered but in how they are altered, i.e. in the player's mode of input. Icons on quickbars with cooldown periods, or button-mashing, equally fail to convey a sense of magic because at the heart of magic is ritual. Ritual is the way that magicians put symbols into practice, drawing on a tradition of symbolic correspondences. In every way, rule system, interface, and symbol, magic systems could be more magical. The aim of this book is to help put the magic back into magic systems.

2.2 A HISTORY OF GAME MAGIC SYSTEMS

My solution is a three-pronged approach of game archeology (locating and analyzing the most innovative magic systems in games), studying the fictional magic systems on which many game mechanics are based, and investigating the actual occult systems that can provide inspiration for game designers.

An analysis of magic systems from a game historical perspective is useful in order to locate games that have featured spellcasting methods that are more immersive and richly meaningful than the average RPG. Game interfaces and mechanics tend to become homogenous over time due to familiarity and a desire to create low learning curves for both designers and players. However, there are many hidden gems from throughout the history of magic systems which occur either before the standard row of spell icons becomes well established or which work in deliberate opposition to this way of casting spells.

2.3 OCCULT MAGIC AND GAME MAGIC

While careful examination of game history can help re-energize magic systems from a formal and aesthetic perspective, depth of gameplay may require reaching outside of videogames and into the human ritual practices and metaphysical symbolism often referred to as the occult. In this context, occultism includes many mythological and ritualistic traditions, including Western ceremonial magic as well as tarot and voodoo, characterized by an attempt to conjure and control metaphysical forces. Game designers have tended to shy away from talking about the metaphysical aspect of magic systems because of the attack on *Dungeons & Dragons* in the 1980s by fundamentalist Christian groups due to its perceived occult content or ritualistic nature. Yet, because rituals are intended to be practiced rather than merely observed or read about, real ceremonial practices are often systematically organized in a way that lends them to being implemented digitally and interactively.

2.4 MAGICAL GRAMMARS

Medieval occultists acknowledged the grammatical structure of magic language when they dubbed magic books "grimoires," derived from the Middle French word for "grammar" (see Chapter 6, Section 6.14). They also acknowledged the alphabetical character of magic when they called individual acts of sorcery "spells." Magic books are grammars, and spells are spelling. Occultist Aleister Crowley suggests this underlying grammatical structure in *Magick*, when he writes that "ANY required Change may be effected by the application of the proper kind and degree of Force in the proper manner, through the proper medium to the proper object" (126). The application of force is the verb, while kind and degree serve the function of adjectives and adverbs. The proper medium plays the role of an indirect object, while the proper object is, as the phrase suggests, the direct object of a magical statement.

Throughout the long history of videogames, many innovative games have featured magical grammars, usually in the form of runes or symbols that can be combined to create spells. The word "grimoire" (pronounced "grim war") comes from the Middle English "grammarye," which means grammar, as in a set of syntactical rules for combining words into well-formed sentences. A grammar can also refer to a book containing these linguistic rules. The etymological connection between "grimoire" and "grammar" comes from a medieval distrust of learning whereby any schoolmaster carrying a grammatical handbook was perceived by the illiterate as a potential warlock. Grimoires also resemble grammars because grimoires contain the meaning of elaborate symbols and sigils as well as rules for combining these symbols in order to produce magical effects through ritual.

2.5 RITUAL AND SYMBOLIC CORRESPONDENCES

Rituals are complex multi-sensory productions involving the rule-based combination of gestures (tracing sigils), objects (wands and chalices), spatial configurations (temples and magic circles), auditory elements (chanting and music), and scents (incense). Such symbols are combined according to the principle of correspondences, through which elements stand by association for other elements. The literature of ceremonial magic is rife with tables of corresponding Tarot cards, Hebrew letters, astrological signs, musical notes, precious gems, and innumerable other elements. Such books include Aleister Crowley's *Liber 777* and its more recent expansion as Stephen Skinner's *Complete Magician's Tables*. The correspondences tabulated within these books are regarded by practitioners as deeply meaningful and intended to encode insights about the metaphysical structure of the universe (often by way of the kabbalistic tree of life, whose branches or sephiroth have lent their name to one famous RPG villain).

The Kabbalah (also spelled Cabbalah or Cabala) is a body of mysticism, Jewish in origin, which has heavily influenced occultist and New Age thought. Modern Kabbalah is often only tenuously related to traditional Jewish Kabbalah. One aspect of Kabbalah emphasizes the Tree of Life, a geometrical design representing the underlying reality of the universe through emanations from God represented as branches.

Aleister Crowley (1875–1947) was a British occultist whose central work *Magick* was highly influential on modern ideas about magic. Crowley preferred to spell magick with a *k* to distinguish mysticism from sleight of hand. The religion that Crowley invented, the Law of Thelema, emphasized the power of the will as a magical force.

2.6 RITUAL AND MULTIMODAL INPUT

Magicians express meaning in ritual through performative and participatory action, requiring the active involvement of magical practitioners with an understanding of its rules and symbol systems. As such, ceremonial magic is a precursor and analogue to games as interactive multimedia. Because these multimedia performances are intended to accomplish pragmatic or spiritual work, ritual in ceremonial magic is often referred to as a working or, in more modern English, an operation. Both these terms were frequently used by occultist Aleister Crowley, and later by graphic novelist Alan Moore to refer to his spiritually-purposed multimedia performances.

 Alan Moore is a graphic novelist, famous for creating highly sophisticated and literary comic books, such as *Watchmen*, *From Hell*, and *V for Vendetta*. Moore is also by his own account a practicing magician who uses shamanic and artistic techniques to construct performance art rituals that inspire his work.

The words "working" and "operation" also hearken to the tradition of opera (Italian for work), so named because the synergy of music, poetry, theatrical sets, and costuming is a work of art that is greater than the sum of its parts. The most superb magic systems and the games of which they are a part aspire toward the condition of opera, as in the magnificent cohesion of *Demon's Souls*. Indeed, scholars such as Marie-Laure Ryan regard Richard Wagner's imagined synaesthetic and fourth-wall-shattering future opera, called gesamtkunstwerk (German for "total art work"), as a foreshadowing of interactive multimedia. Graphic novelist and practicing magician Alan Moore elaborates on the relationship between magic and the multimodality of opera in an interview with Jay Babcock, in which Moore explains:

> Opera was entirely an invention of alchemy. The alchemists decided that they wanted to design a new art form that would be the ultimate artform. It would include all the other artforms: it would include song, music, costume, art, acting, dance. It would be the ultimate artform, and it would be used to express alchemical ideas. Monteverdi was an alchemist. You've only got to look at the early operas, and see just how many of them are about alchemical themes. *The Ring*. *The Magic Flute*. All of this stuff, there's often overt or covert alchemical things running through it all.

The idea of an art form that combines all the previous ones also resonates with the game company Silicon Knights' understanding of videogames as the Eighth Art, built upon the foundation of the previous seven. Not coincidentally, Silicon Knights' most celebrated game, *Eternal Darkness*, applies the principles of the Eighth Art through a magic system with multimodal input.

Unfortunately, games rarely take full advantage of this potential for multimedia input or feedback, instead restricting players to mouse or gamepad input accompanied by primarily auditory and visual feedback with a minor amount of haptics. However, the increasing prevalence of alternative input methods like tablets (iPad, Wii U) or motion control (Kinect, PlayStation Move) offers many opportunities for multimodal input that more closely simulate magic as a subtle art of multimodal ritual. The history of magic systems also presents several examples of games that allow players to cast spells using combinatorial grammars, alternative input methods, and sometimes a combination of grammar and alternative control scheme. By studying and understanding magic systems with these traits, game designers can imitate and improve upon their best features within new technological contexts.

In terms of combinatorial grammars with metaphysically meaningful correspondences, the highest example may be *Eternal Darkness: Sanity's Requiem*, a horror game in which players cast spells by placing runes along the points of geometric figures in order to express a given spell's meaning. For example, the combination of protect, self, and, intensify would create a buffing magical armor spell at a level of power influenced by the number of intensification runes (pargon) placed at the end of the spell. Players cast each spell under the aspect of three alignment runes that correspond to Lovecraftian Ancients, each of which is associated with a color that stands for a principle of humanity (body, mind, and sanity). These three Ancients and their associated runes and colors trump each other in a rock-paper-scissors mechanic, which players manipulate by imbuing weapons and protective spells with a particular color of magic designed to overcome monsters of the opposed (and weaker) color. Spells in *Eternal Darkness* are philosophical propositions with narrative context and magical force: for example, Xel'otath's green rune trumps Ulyaoth's blue rune because the dissolution of sanity erodes the mind. If the enemy chooses the Xel'otath rune on a given playthrough, then a cutscene shows Chattur'gha defeating Xel'otath, since in the game a healthy body can ultimately overcome the subtleties of sanity. The rock-paper-scissors mechanics of tokens that trump each other are thus enacted in the overarching mythological narrative of the game. Figure 2.1 is a chart of the runes in *Eternal Darkness*.

FIGURE 2.1   The Runes of *Eternal Darkness*. (Image by Matt Holland. Used with permission.)

This particular lineage of games with combinatorial grammars, of which *Eternal Darkness* is a high point, starts with an early first-person dungeon crawling RPG *Dungeon Master* in which players combined strings of runes in order to cast spells (see Chapter 4, Section 4.5). These runes allow for the discovery of new spells through trial-and-error experimentation, enacted in real-time combat that adds both a cerebral and a dexterity-based challenge to the system. Despite these technical innovations, *Dungeon Master* lacked an overarching meaning to its systems beyond flavor text within the game's manual. Figure 2.2 is a screenshot of the rune interface in *Dungeon Master*.

Ultima Underworld and *Ultima Underworld II* extend the lineage of Dungeon Master, in which players collect rune stones in order to piece together, through trial and error, spells governed by a magical grammar. This magic system has precedents in the virtue system of Britannia, based on a set of correspondences between three principles of Truth, Love, and Courage and their combinations to form eight virtues, each of which was attributed to a dungeon, a town, a character class, and a color based on permutations of three primary tints. The magic system of the

FIGURE 2.2   Runes in *Dungeon Master.* (Image by Faster Than Light Games.)

FIGURE 2.3   Runes in *Ultima Underworld.* (Image by Origin Systems and Electronic Arts.)

early *Ultima* games was, to a limited extent, based on runes and syllables typed in a text parser, as well as the combination of alchemical reagents.

Building on the runes, *Ultima Underworld* added a grammatically based combinatorial system as well as a first-person interface hearkening back to *Dungeon Master.* The occurrence of first-person interfaces with grammatically based magic systems suggests that both features serve the larger goal of immersion—allowing the player to actively take the role of spell-caster through the mechanic of combining magic words and the visual perspective from the eyes of the caster. Figure 2.3 shows the rune interface in *Ultima Underworld.*

These twin features of magical grammar and first-person interface gain the third element of a gestural interface to form a triad of immersive magic-casting in *Arx Fatalis*, a dungeon crawl by Arkane studios originally pitched as the third *Ultima Underworld*, in which players cast spells by tracing combinations of runes in the air with colored light. Figure 2.4 is a screenshot of gestural casting in *Arx Fatalis*. (This method of spellcasting

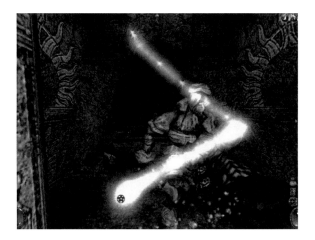

FIGURE 2.4   Gestural Spellcasting in *Arx Fatalis.*

The Pentagrams

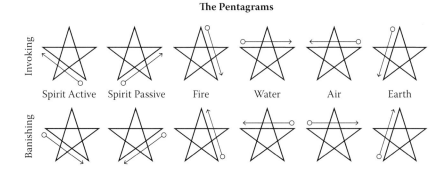

FIGURE 2.5   Pentagrams for Invoking and Banishing. (Image by the Golden Dawn. In public domain because of age.)

resembles and may originate within certain occultist traditions, such as the Lesser Ritual of the Pentagram of the Order of the Golden Dawn, in which ceremonial magicians traced combinations of pentagrams in various configurations and with appropriate implements in order to banish or invoke spiritual presences.) Figure 2.5 shows the various gestures associated with the Invoking and Banishing Rituals of the Pentagram in the Golden Dawn System. A more immersive but less combinatorial approach appears in *Black and White*, Peter Molyneux's famed strategic simulation of godhood, which deliberately eliminates a heads-up display (HUD) in order to allow players godlike control over a disembodied hand that traces symbols over its domain in order to cast miracles. Molyneux's game is

FIGURE 2.6   Gestural Casting in *Black & White.*

sometimes referred to as the first gestural interface, in part because a later patch enabled players to control gestures with a P5 Virtual Reality glove, adding another level of physical immersion. Figure 2.6 shows gestural casting in *Black & White.*

2.7 RITUALS AS PUZZLES

At its heart, game magic as represented in games like *Black & White* and *Eternal Darkness* is a puzzle. A puzzle, broadly conceived, is a cognitive challenge—anything that, in the terms of game designer Jesse Schell— causes the player to *"stop and think"* (208). In order to evoke the experience of a magician wielding an arcane art, game magic must make players stop and think. But game magic can be a puzzle in a more specific sense: a complex set of symbolic, re-configurable parts that must be deciphered and shifted around until the player achieves a solution. A Rubik's cube is a puzzle. The rune and color combinations of *Eternal Darkness* are puzzles. The musical magic spells of the LucasArts adventure game *Loom* are puzzles. The magical gestures of *Black & White* are puzzles. The rituals of the MMO *The Secret World*, discussed at length in this book's section on MMO magic, are puzzles.

Systems of magical practice are games that can generate many puzzles in the form of rituals, just as chess gives rise to chess problems. The ritual implements, such as candles, wands, and skulls, are the pieces of the game. The ritual environment, such as a temple or an altar, is the board. Many possible rituals can be constructed out of a particular set of pieces and environments, just as the pieces of a chess board can be re-arranged to create or solve many possible problems. For example, a traditional temple of ceremonial magic has a circle on the floor with a design, but the design could be a pentagram, hexagram, octagram, or nonogram. Similarly, the circle may contain a Tau cross of ten squares representing the kabbalistic tree of life, but the magician could stand on any of the ten squares, depending on the particular force to which the ritual is consecrated. If the altar has candles, the candles could be of various colors, numbers, and sizes. Each re-configuration has a different metaphysical significance and (the magician hopes) a different effect on reality.

The spells of game magic are special kinds of puzzles in that they have more than one solution, require players to master symbols, and have metaphysical significance.

Puzzles are typically defined as having only one solution (an optimal strategy in game theory terms, as defined by Jesse Schell), but Raph E. Koster argues that games aspiring to the condition of art would be ambiguous puzzles that "lend themselves to interpretation" and therefore have multiple solutions (147). Espen Aarseth in *Cybertext* distinguishes between the configurative function by which a player interacts with a game, re-arranging and configuring its elements, and the interpretative function, by which a reader imaginatively transforms a text (64). As I argue in *Quests*, the interpretative and configurative functions can be bridged if the re-arrangements that the player makes also have meaning and significance (xiv). If the parts of a puzzle are symbols (tarot, planetary sigils, runes), then these re-configurations will necessarily also double as statements in the symbolic language. For example, if the faces of a Rubik's cube were inscribed with runes instead of colored squares, each re-arrangement of the cubes would result in a different set of arcane messages. (One could speak, tongue in cheek, of a Runik's Cube.) Not all of the messages implied in the cube would be meaningful (unless the cube had been very carefully designed), but some of them would. In the same way, not every combination of the runes in *Eternal Darkness* yields a working spell, but enough spells can be discovered to reward combinatorial exploration. Because puzzles entail deciphering and manipulation of symbols, puzzles map naturally onto magic understood as the configuration of symbolic correspondences.

If the symbols that players re-configure in a puzzle are metaphysically charged, then the manipulations of the puzzle can have metaphysical significance. One fictional example of a metaphysically significant puzzle is the Lament Configuration, which recurs throughout the extended *Hellraiser* mythos. The Lament Configuration is an elaborate puzzle box that can be re-configured in many patterns, one of which opens a gateway to another hellish dimension. Barker implies that the secret of the box is the metaphysical ideas and forces encoded in its physical movements, as when he describes the box as "products of the Chinese taste for making metaphysics of hard wood" (1–2). As if inspired by *Hellraiser*, the celebrated tablet game *The Room* allows players to unlock metaphysically charged puzzleboxes inside of puzzleboxes in much the way that I suggested would be possible in my 2010 talk at the Workshop on Integrated Design in Games entitled "*Demonik* and the Ludic Legacy of Clive Barker."

Clive Barker (1952–present) is a transmedia artist who writes, directs, paints, supervises game design, and works in a variety of other media.

Hellraiser is a transmedia franchise that begins with Clive Barker's short story "The Hellbound Heart" and the 1987 horror film *Hellraiser*, and now extends to many sequels, comic books, and a novel-in-progress called *The Scarlet Gospels*.

If game magic is defined as any set of rules and symbols designed to evoke the experience of performing magic, then many games that do not have a formal magic system in the sense of a discrete list of spells may nevertheless have game magic. Many occult-themed action-adventure and survival horror games include puzzles in which players must configure talismans, runes, or gems in order to activate (or interfere with) a dark ritual. One example is *Silent Hill 2* (particularly on the secret "Rebirth" ending of the second playthrough, in which protagonist James prepares a ritual to resurrect his wife by acquiring the Book of Lost Memories, the Book of Crimson Ceremony, the Obsidian Goblet, and the White Chrism). Another example is *Haunting Ground*, in which Fiona performs many occult-tinged alchemical operations, including a mechanism for producing new artifacts that is based on the colored sephiroth of the kabbalistic tree of life (Figure 2.7).

It is no coincidence that so many ritualistic puzzles are based around language and alphabets, such as kabbalistic diagrams, runes, and glyphs.

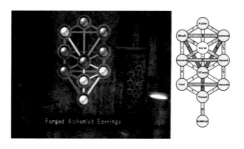

FIGURE 2.7 The Tree of Life in *Haunting Ground*.

These puzzles confirm that at a deep level magic systems are fundamentally linguistic. In order to construct rituals as performative, symbolic puzzles, the overall language of a given world's magic needs to first exist as a framework for gameplay. By examining the history and structure of the languages of game magic, designers can create a richer relationship between game systems and game worlds.

CHAPTER 3

From Exemplary Game Magic Systems to Code Recipes

3.1 MAGIC SYSTEMS AND LANGUAGE

At its heart, a magic system is a language. This is true of fictional, game, and occult systems alike, though the nature of the medium and purpose defines the character of the language. Various systems can be more and less explicit and self-aware of their linguistic status, but they are always fundamentally linguistic. Because magic systems are languages, they have both vocabularies and grammars: a set of symbols and rules for combining them. The simplest grammatical structure is the verb: do this action, cause this change—such as damage or heal. Most magic systems allow the user to target a particular entity, which becomes the direct object—as in "damage goblin" or "heal paladin." Many magic systems also feature adverbs, often pertaining to temporal duration (specifying how long a verb should be in effect) or spatial location (expressing the range over which the verb should apply).

In addition to vocabularies, many magic systems are structured around alphabets, including symbols such as runes, glyphs, and sigils, though these symbols are rarely phonetic alphabets in the sense of representing primarily sounds. Magic alphabets tend to be ideogrammatic in that each symbol stands for an idea. These symbols may also stand for sounds, allowing for magical effects to be unleashed through speech in the form of incantations or writing in the form of inscriptions. Yet, at their heart, these symbols stand essentially and primarily for ideas.

The letters in magical alphabets stand for ideas because magic involves the manipulation of the deepest forces of the universe. One classic example of such a magical alphabet are the twenty-two Hebrew letters, which magicians influenced by the Kabbalah use to represent a vast confluence of cosmic forces refracted through an array of intricate correspondences, including tarot cards, colors, and numbers. These twenty-two letters carry an immense amount of profound mystical symbolism with them, and they have influenced a variety of games, including the *Persona* series, *Vagrant Story*, and the story mode of the author's own game, *Arcana: A Ceremonial Magick Simulator*.

But the Hebrew alphabet is not the only magical alphabet that can symbolize profound ideas. Traditional witch Andrew Chumbley's sorcerer's alphabet is an example of a deeply original, personal, and sometimes bizarre set of ideogrammatically-charged letters which Chumbley distributed over a larger sigil representing the paths connecting the letters and the portals of mystical experience that each path could open (see Chapter 6, Section 6.15.1) The tendency to distribute magical characters spatially in larger designs such as paths, trees, magic circles, sigils, and voodoo vevés ties into the idea that occult magical languages tend to be part of rituals expressed through acts that involve the movement of consecrated objects in sacred space (see Chapter 6, Section 6.11). Early modern and contemporary occultists like Cornelius Agrippa and Andrew Chumbley no doubt tend toward an ideogrammatic understanding of magical alphabets in part because some of the ancient alphabets on which magic draws are ideogrammatic, including ancient Egyptian hieroglyphics.

In the traditions of Afro-Caribbean magic sometimes known as voodoo, a vevé or vever is a symbolic design representing a given spirit or group of spirits, called loa. Voodoo practitioners sometimes draw vevés on the ground with chalk or colored sand.

The language of magic needs more verbs. It is a common complaint about games that they lack sufficient verbs. The argument originates in game designer Chris Crawford and is reiterated by Jesse Schell, and by Matthew Weise and Geoffrey Long in their game verbs workshop. Many magic systems tie magical abilities into a single "cast" verb that can activate multiple spells, yet these spells often devolve down into a few actions: attack, heal, buff, debuff, hide. But grimoires and other classic magical texts teach us that ritual action involves more than spontaneous bursts of energy. Instead, rituals involve lighting candles, burning incense, reciting incantations, and walking in circles. The addition of a "use" verb can allow players to perform ritual actions upon objects, so that by clicking on a candle the player can light it, or by clicking on a cup the player can fill it with wine or blood. Adding "pick up" and "put down" as verbs allows for a broader range of ritual actions, such as placing a candle or a tarot card on a slot. *Arcana* uses this methodology, building an elaborate system of ritual divination through the verbs "pick up" and "put down."

Yet, generic "use" verbs are an inadequate solution to the problem of ritual magic, since while these verbs may *represent* other actions like burning incense, generic "use" verbs do not *simulate* separate actions, nor is there any challenge to figuring out what to do with a given object. Ritual puzzles can certainly be built around activating a particular set of objects in a particular order, often encoding a symbolic meaning (many of the ritual puzzles in *The Secret World* follow this pattern), yet a richer set of verbs would make for more immersive magic systems. To understand how to create sophisticated magical languages, it can help to turn to the most word-centric game genre: text-based interactive fiction, where text parsers meet mystical incantations.

3.2 INTERACTIVE FICTION AND *ENCHANTER*

The first magic word in interactive fiction is "XYZZY" in *Adventure*, a.k.a. *Colossal Cave Adventure* (1976). XYZZY is a teleportation spell that returns the player from the cave to the brick building near the trail, thereby saving him trouble when he inevitably becomes lost. *Adventure* is a realistic simulation of the Mammoth Cave system in Kentucky with the addition of fantasy elements, so the XYZZY spell is an isolated magical incantation rather than a part of a fully developed system.

Infocom's *Enchanter* trilogy (consisting of *Enchanter*, *Sorcerer*, and *Spellbreaker*) builds on the foundation of XYZZY to develop a fully coherent and highly imaginative system of magic words. In *Enchanter*, the overriding metaphors are writing and speech, as befits an interactive fiction driven by a text parser. Spells are incantations in a magical language consisting of verbs (e.g. frotz, blorb, rezrov, nitfol, and gnusto). Once again, the invention of a magical language runs counter to the guideline in *Dungeons & Dragons* that players do not need to learn any special words even though their characters chant incantations. The fictional mode of casting spells is also singularly appropriate to the way that the player interacts with the game. Spells are cast through simple verb-noun phrases (e.g. rezrov chest, gnusto scroll), just as players perform other actions in the game world (e.g. enter shack, examine mountain).

As in *Adventure*, the player types commands into a text parser, but in *Enchanter* there is an entire magical vocabulary in addition to the English one used to execute mundane actions. The use of the magical language takes advantage of the constraints of interactive fiction to create a seamless relationship between player and character actions. Because interactive fiction is driven by a text parser, players are only able to interact with the game's world by typing brief commands, typically consisting of a verb and a noun phrase (e.g. "open oven," "fill jug with water," "examine egg"). Therefore, the magic in the game consists of a set of enchanted verbs, such as "frotz" (create light). By combining these magic words with appropriate nouns, the player can work a range of miraculous effects in the simulated world. For example, "frotz jug" will transform a jug into a glowing light source. Like *Dungeons & Dragons*, *Enchanter* also features a Vancian system, in which the player must gnusto (transcribe) spells into the spell book from scrolls, then memorize spells to have them ready. The range of spells is reminiscent of *Advanced Dungeons & Dragons*, though the interest of spells often consists less in their immediate effects and more in their emergent ramifications within a deeply simulated world.

The full vocabulary of *Enchanter* consists of sixteen words: Frotz, Blorb (protect in a lockbox), Rezrov (unlock and open), Nitfol (speak in the tongues of beasts), Krepf (repair damage), Exex (speed up), Zifmia (summon), Vaxum (make friendly), Cleesh (transform into a frog or toad), Kulcad (dispel magic), Ozmoo (save from artificial death), Melbor (protect from evil), Filfre (make gratuitous fireworks), Gondar (extinguish fire), Izyuk (fly), and Guncho (banish to another plane).

Zifmia is particularly interesting in that many beings can be summoned, each with intriguing effects, including the Implementers (deities of several Infocom fictions who are metafictional stand-ins for the programmers of the games). The Terror and Belboz can also be summoned, even though summoning the Terror is self-destructive and summoning Belboz is unnecessary. Indeed, one of the strengths of *Enchanter* is that its spells, while designed to help the player to solve puzzles, actually allow for a variety of emergent behaviors due to the simulation and world-modeling of the game. Cleesh allows the player to attempt to turn any living being into a toad, even though this transformation is entirely unnecessary to completing the game. Krepf can potentially repair any broken object, even though the player is only required to repair the shredded scroll in order to complete the game.

While many of these spells have equivalents in *Dungeons & Dragons* and are clearly based on this game, the rich world modeling of interactive fiction (IF) in comparison to many RPGs allows spells to be put to a wide variety of uses outside of combat. Indeed, one of these spells is tied to combat through systems of numerical damage. Hence, Vaxum (which is essentially the equivalent of Charm Person from *Dungeons & Dragons*) becomes more than just a way to neutralize an enemy, but rather opens up new and amusing social interactions with guards, a dragon, and an adventurer.

Game designers can draw a conclusion from the magical language of *Enchanter*: a magic system will be most robust when its underlying conceptual language has an effect on a dynamic, cohesive world. When a given spell can only affect one aspect of the world (such as combat with a particular enemy, or the solution to a specific puzzle), the interest of that spell is limited. But when a spell can alter many aspects of a given world, then the spell can function in dynamic and sometimes unexpected ways, unanticipated by designers. These emergent spell behaviors are at the heart of magic's unpredictability, which in turn is at the core of what makes magic magical. The construction of a magic system is, like many aspects of game design, largely an exercise in world-building.

In addition to linguistic elements, *Enchanter* and other interactive fiction games often contained feelies (toy-like elements like wheels, stones, badges, and books included with a game). These objects heightened the games' sense of magic because the feelies evoked arcane artifacts, appealing to the sense of touch, giving weight and solidity to enchantment. The philosophy of including feelies goes directly against the general idea, articulated in the *Dungeons & Dragons* manual, that players do not need any special artifacts and the accompanying distance between player and character performance of magic.

The *Enchanter* trilogy put a premium on player immersion in magic, through its magical language, its feelies, and its escalating difficulty that simulates a beginning mage's gradual initiation into the arcane arts. An examination of the *Enchanter* page at the Zork Library, where all of the feelies and associated documentation for the *Enchanter* trilogy have been collected, shows an overt and intentional increase in difficulty from part one to part three, a movement from "standard" to "advanced" to "expert" difficulty as labeled on the front of the box. In another intro document, expert difficulty is described as "real diehards seeking the ultimate challenge in interactive fiction." This ramping up in difficulty resembles the movement from *Wizardry I* to *Wizardry IV* (the most magic-centric and diabolical of the titles), which was labeled an expert scenario. The implication of these early games is that magic is difficult, not just for character but also for player. Initiation into its secrets involves not just a title or arbitrary number of experience points, accumulated through time expenditure and grinding, but sharpened cognitive faculties and mastery of a body of knowledge.

3.3 STEVE JACKSON'S *SORCERY!* AND GAMEBOOKS

In the same year as *Enchanter*, Steve Jackson's *Sorcery!* series of choose-your-own adventure style books adds a unique twist on the idea of the magical languages and immersive feelies by using the gamebook format to simulate a wizard's spellbook. *Sorcery!* is a part of the popular *Fighting Fantasy* series, a British gamebook in which readers take the role of an adventurer whose journeys are narrated in second person, allowing readers to turn to particular pages in order to make choices about what will happen in the book's narrative. *Sorcery!*, intended as an adult, sophisticated version of the genre, went to great lengths to simulate the experience of Vancian magic, in which the magician must memorize spells from a spellbook (see Chapter 7, Section 7.2 and Chapter 8, Section 8.6). *Sorcery!* required the use of a separate, physical spellbook with spell descriptions, names, and three-letter abbreviations that players were urged to study and memorize before embarking on their adventure. The spellbook is explained to be too heavy and valuable to be carried on the adventure, thus requiring memorization. When facing challenges and associated choices during the adventure, readers would sometimes have the option to cast a spell by choosing from a short list of spell abbreviations without names. Only a player who had carefully studied and memorized spells in the spellbook would reliably be able to choose an appropriate spell for a given challenge, especially since some of the abbreviations were false, non-existent spells that would penalize the player if chosen. The *Sorcery!* books draw effectively on the gamebook format to give players the tactile sense experience of holding and using a spellbook.

In 2013, an iOS version of the first *Sorcery!* book, *The Shamutanti Hills*, was adapted by Inkle Studios, bringing new levels of richness to the gamebook's magic system. The game's fiction explains that the spells available to the player character are now correlated with the alignments of particular constellations in locations at specific times. In gameplay terms, the spellcasting interface becomes a starry background with three apertures that can be aligned with letters floating in the stars in order to spell a given spell abbreviation. This new interface and its associated fiction helps to explain why only certain spells are available at a particular choice juncture by representing this limitation astrologically. The touch-based sliding of letters and stars is also deeply immersive and even a little awe-inspiring as it allows players to feel as if they are tapping astral energies. Since the player's spellbook is accessible at all times through an icon, the iPad version of *Sorcery!* removes the constraint of requiring players to memorize spells before their adventure.

3.4 MODERN MAGICAL IF

Emulating early examples like *Enchanter* and *Sorcery!*, Graham Nelson's modern text adventure *The Reliques of Tolti-Aph* is an excellent first recipe or example of a magic system, implemented in the Inform7 programming language for creating interactive fictions. *The Reliques* is an old-school role-playing game in the style of *Dungeons & Dragons* with a fully implemented Vancian magic system.

The source code is available for *The Reliques* and illustrates the basics of creating a Vancian magic system. The advantage of Inform7 source code is that it is written in natural English and is therefore relatively transparent and easy to understand (though not always easy to write, since one of the characteristics of programming languages that makes them resemble magic incantations is their exacting nature).

RECIPE 1: DEFINING SPELLS IN A VANCIAN SYSTEM
(FROM NELSON'S *RELIQUES*, INFORM7)

CHAPTER 2 - MAGIC

SECTION 2(A) - THE PHENOMENON OF MAGIC

```
A spell character is a kind of value.
The spell characters are offensive, defensive, healing and
   arcana.
A valency is a kind of value.
The valencies are targeted and untargeted.

A spell is a kind of value.
The spells are defined by the Table of Enchantments.[1]
```

First, the code defines spell characters, which refer to schools of magic (offensive, defensive, healing, and arcana). Then, the value of valency is defined with two possible values, targeted and untargeted. Valency refers to the way that the spell is attached.

Next, spells themselves are defined as values, described in a table. Spells in the table have a name, a nature (which is synonymous with spell character), a cost, a requirement, an emission, a valency, a duration, a duration timer, and a usage count. In this example, the requirement column is synonymous with the material component from the *Dungeons & Dragons* magic system. The cost refers to strength, indicating that this spell system is actually a hybrid of a Vancian system and a mana-based system. *Reliques* presents the player with a difficult resource management problem, since spells are powered by his own health. The duration timer and usage count columns are deliberately left blank with only the placeholder value of "a number," since both of these values will be set by the code during runtime.

RECIPE 2:   A TABLE OF SPELLS (FROM NELSON'S *RELIQUES*, INFORM7)

"Table of Enchantments

spell	nature	cost	requirement	emission	targeting	duration	duration timer	usage count
detect trap	defensive	1	air	"diffuse blue light"	untargeted	--	a number	a number
memorise	arcana	3	air	"a glowing symbol"	targeted	--		
fashion staff	arcana	2	wood	"woodpulp"	untargeted	--		
know nature	arcana	1	air	"probing rays"	targeted	--		
make sanctuary	arcana	8	clay	"rainbow walls"	untargeted	--		

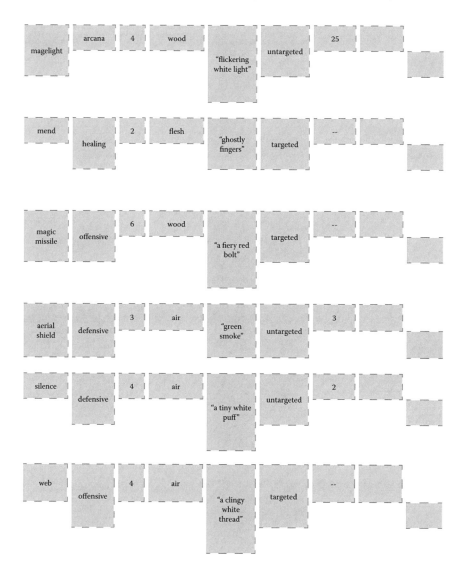

magelight	arcana	4	wood	"flickering white light"	untargeted	25		
mend	healing	2	flesh	"ghostly fingers"	targeted	--		
magic missile	offensive	6	wood	"a fiery red bolt"	targeted	--		
aerial shield	defensive	3	air	"green smoke"	untargeted	3		
silence	defensive	4	air	"a tiny white puff"	untargeted	2		
web	offensive	4	air	"a clingy white thread"	targeted	--		

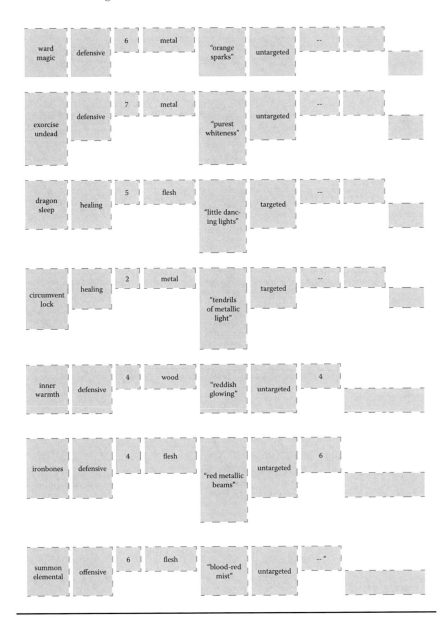

ward magic	defensive	6	metal	"orange sparks"	untargeted	--		
exorcise undead	defensive	7	metal	"purest whiteness"	untargeted	--		
dragon sleep	healing	5	flesh	"little dancing lights"	targeted	--		
circumvent lock	healing	2	metal	"tendrils of metallic light"	targeted	--		
inner warmth	defensive	4	wood	"reddish glowing"	untargeted	4		
ironbones	defensive	4	flesh	"red metallic beams"	untargeted	6		
summon elemental	offensive	6	flesh	"blood-red mist"	untargeted	-- "		

The next section, entitled "The Capacity for Magic," implements the Vancian aspects of the system. First, the code defines memorisation (the British spelling of memorization) as a relationship between members of two types of objects: people (who memorize spells) and spells (which are memorized). The code then expresses the relationship of memorization through the verb "to know." The next few functions allow the player to list currently memorized spells, either independently or as part of the inventory of carried objects. The inclusion of memorized spells in the inventory is significant, suggesting the primary use of spells in interactive fiction as virtual objects for the purpose of solving puzzles.

RECIPE 3:   CODING VANCIAN MEMORIZATION (FROM
            NELSON'S *RELIQUES,* INFORM7)

SECTION 2(B) - THE CAPACITY FOR MAGIC

```
Memorisation relates various people to various spells. The
  verb to know (he knows, they know, he knew, it is known)
  implies the memorisation relation.
Understand "spells" as listing spells. Listing spells is an
  action applying to nothing. Carry out listing spells: reel
  off the spells. [1]
After taking inventory: reel off the spells; continue the
  action.
To reel off the spells:
say "You have the following spells committed to memory:[line
  break]";
repeat through the Table of Enchantments in cost column
  order: [2]
let this spell be the spell entry;
if the player knows this spell:
say " [this spell] ([nature of this spell]): cost [cost of
  this spell] strength";
unless the requirement of this spell is air, say ", requires
  [requirement of this spell]";
say "[line break]"."
```

The next functions of Nelson's simple magic system define the action of casting. Players will perform magic in *Reliques* by typing "cast [x spell]." In *Reliques*, spells alter reality some of the time by affecting people (keeping in mind Nelson's own section heading that "monsters are people, too.") The casting action itself takes two parameters: a spell and a visible thing. Grammatically, the spell is the direct object, while the target is the indirect object. If the player does not specify a target, then the target (second noun) is the room in which the spell takes place.

RECIPE 4: CODING THE SPELLCASTING ACTION (FROM NELSON'S *RELIQUES,* INFORM7)

SECTION 2(D) - THE CASTING ACTION

Affectedness relates various people to various spells. The
  verb to be affected by implies the affectedness
  relation. [1]
Casting it at is an action applying to one spell and one
  visible thing. Rule for supplying a missing second noun
  while casting: change the second noun to the location. [2]
Understand "cast [spell]" or "[spell]" as casting it at.
Understand "cast [spell] on/at [something]" or "[spell]
  [something]" as casting it at.
The current spell focus is an object which varies. [3] Before
  casting, change the current spell focus to the location.
Check casting (this is the can't cast what you don't know
  rule): [4]
if the player does not know the spell understood, say "You
  do not know the mystery of that enchantment." instead.
Check casting (this is the can't cast on the wrong sort of
  target rule):
if the targeting of the spell understood is targeted:
if the second noun is a room, say "That enchantment must be
  cast at something." instead;
otherwise:
unless the second noun is a room, say "That enchantment
  cannot be cast at anything." instead.
Check casting (this is the can't cast without strength rule):
if the strength of the player <= the strength cost of the
  spell understood to the player, say "You are weak, and
  have not sufficient strength of mind." instead.
Check casting (this is the can't cast at yourself rule):
if the player is the second noun, say "It is a cardinal rule
  of magic that no mage may cast an enchantment upon
  himself." instead.
Check casting (this is the can't cast without required
  materials rule):
let the stuff be the requirement of the spell understood;
unless the stuff is air:
if the player is carrying something (called the focus) which
  is made of the stuff,
change the current spell focus to the focus;
otherwise say "To weave that enchantment, you must have
  something made of [stuff] in your hands." instead.
Check casting (this is the can't magically attack a warded
  person rule):
if the nature of the spell understood is offensive and the
  second noun is a person:
let the intended victim be the second noun;

if the intended victim knows ward magic, say "With a
  contemptuous wave of orange sparks, [the intended victim]
  cancels your [spell understood] incantation." instead.[5]
Effect is a rulebook.[6]
The current spell outcome is an indexed text which varies.
  To record outcome (eventual message - text): change the
  current spell outcome to eventual message.
The current spell event is a rule which varies. To record
  event (eventual rule - rule): change the current spell
  event to eventual rule.
This is the no spell event at all rule: stop.
Carry out casting:
record outcome "but then nothing obvious happens";
record event the no spell event at all rule;
change the strength of the player to the strength of the
  player minus the strength cost of the spell understood to
  the player;
increase the usage count of the spell understood by 1;
if the usage count of the spell understood is less than 3[7]:
award cost of the spell understood points;
award cost of the spell understood points;
if the cost of the spell understood is at least 5 and the
  current spell focus is something, remove the current spell
  focus from play;
consider the effect rulebook.
Report casting:
say "As you intone the words of the [spell understood]
  spell,";
if the current spell focus is something:
say "[the current spell focus]";
unless the player is holding the current spell focus, say
  "vanishes as it";
say "releases";
otherwise:
say "your fingers release";
say emission of the spell understood;
unless the second noun is a room, say "at [the second noun]";
say ", [current spell outcome]";
if the player is affected by the spell understood:
if duration of the spell understood is greater than 0:
say ", which will last for [duration of the spell understood
  in words] turn[s]";
change the duration timer of the spell understood to the
  duration of the spell understood;
increase the duration timer of the spell understood by 1;
say ".";
consider the current spell event.
Every turn:
repeat through the Table of Enchantments:
let the remaining effect be the duration timer entry;

```
decrease the remaining effect by 1;
if the remaining effect > = 0, change the duration timer
  entry to the remaining effect;
if the remaining effect is 0:
now the player is not affected by the spell entry;
say "(The [spell entry] spell wears off.)".[8]
Understand "xyzzy" and "plugh" as a mistake ("Nobody
  believes those old children's stories about a colossal
  cave with magic words any more. Magic's something you
  spend years and years learning.").
```

This code block begins with a series of checks that ascertain whether a player fulfills or does not fulfill a given precondition of casting a spell. The checks include whether the player has sufficient strength, the required spell focus, is casting the spell at a legal target rather than herself or a magically protected opponent, and has memorized the spell. These checks do not permit a player to cast spells unless she fulfills all of the preconditions, and the checks are therefore rules in the classic game mechanic sense of specifying allowed and disallowed actions. Inform7 allows Nelson to name these checks as rules: the "can't cast what you don't know rule" (essential to Vancian magic), the "can't cast on the wrong sort of target rule," the "can't cast without strength rule," the "can't cast at yourself rule," the "can't cast without required materials rule," and the "can't magically attack a warded person rule." This pattern of checking spellcasting preconditions through rules appears over and over again in the code for magic systems, and it can be analyzed as a design pattern independent of its implementation in any particular language or technology. It is significant that Inform7 stores such rules in rulebooks and (according to Nelson's own code comments) replicates the organization of tabletop RPG manuals in its spell tables. Code is an implementation of the logic underlying design patterns, which can be expressed rigorously on paper or in diagrams.

While *Reliques* is a deliberately retro throwback to the mechanics of early *Dungeons & Dragons* magic, there are several recent works of interactive fiction with innovative magic systems, often in the form of magical grammars as befits the games' status as text adventures.

These works include Graham Nelson's *Balances* (a sequel to the *Enchanter* trilogy), David Fisher's *Suveh Nux, Savoir-Faire, Damnatio Memoriae, Words of Power, The Colder Light*, and *Augmented Fourth*. *Savoir-Faire*, a classic work of interactive fiction by Emily Short, features a magic system called Lavori d'Aracne (the labors of Arachne, named after the Greek spider goddess in a reference to the linkages of spiderwebs) in which players link objects to other objects such that objects exchange properties and effects. Players make links normally (so that an effect applied to the first object is automatically applied to the second), twist a link (so that effects applied to one object are reversed for the second), or reverse link (to mingle two objects' properties). In a "Philosophical Explanation of Linking," Short offers alternate metaphysical rationales for linking through Platonic idealism and the philosopher Berkeley's vision of objects as ideas in God's mind. *Damnatio Memoriae* is a prequel to *Savoir-Faire*, using the same magic system but in an ancient Roman setting rather than an eighteenth century European one (and written in the Inform7 programming language rather than the previous Inform6).

Suveh Nux is a room escape game in which a player must master a magical grammar to manipulate objects in order to escape from a vault. Players learn the game's nouns by pointing at objects while holding a teardrop-shaped gem, much as a new speaker of a language might query the names of objects by pointing at them in the presence of a native speaker. Players acquire the game's magical verbs from a book of spells, in which entries describing the game's world encode the verbs as acrostics (word puzzles in which the first letters of each line spell a message). *Suveh Nux* playfully references early magical languages in interactive fiction, as when typing "xyzzy" (the magic word from *Adventure*) yields a joke about the word's unpronounceability, or typing the magic words from *Enchanter* creates "a strange sensation of being in entirely the wrong universe." By experimenting with various verb-noun combinations, as well as occasional adverbs, players gradually learn how to escape from the room. The title *Suveh Nux* derives from the in-game words for "negate darkness." Nouns in the game's language pertain to words inside the vault, which effectively becomes a microworld, i.e. a heavily constrained space that allows a language to be modeled efficiently. Nouns include agri (shelf), amutasl (parchment), imoentar (cage), ami (self), fierno (door), tolanisu (floor), amunisu (ceiling), nisu-ewa (west wall), nisu-esa (east wall), and nisu-so (south wall). Verbs include suveh (negate) and aveh (create).

The Colder Light features combinatorial, rune-based magic through an interface based on hyperlinks rather than a text parser that nonetheless avoids choice of your own adventure format. *Augmented Fourth* has a musical magic system rendered through text (as the name, which refers to a musical interval).

3.4.1 The Text-Based Rituals of *Hadean Lands*

The insight that rituals can double as puzzles is at the heart of another piece of contemporary interactive fiction: acclaimed author Andrew Plotkin's work in progress, *Hadean Lands*. In this experimental interactive fiction, players perform alchemical rituals on an abandoned magical spaceship. Plotkin's approach to magic is partially influenced by my own ideas about magic systems as delivered at the M.I.T. Gambit Game Lab in April 2010. Plotkin explains:

> The first notions for *this* game came to me during a lecture that Jeff Howard gave at MIT's game design lab. Jeff was visiting from Dakota State University, where he teaches, and he was talking about the use of magic in videogames. He's trying to build an immersive game interface that encompasses many modalities of ritual magic: colors, sounds, gesture, tarot symbolism, and so on.

That idea merged in my mind with a quote from *Taltos*, a fantasy novel by Steven Brust:

> If a witch could teleport (a thing that seems impossible, but I could be wrong), it would involve hours of preparation, rituals, chanting, and filling all the senses with the desired result until the spell would work in a blinding explosion of emotional fulfillment.
>
> That's exactly right. The magic that I present shouldn't feel like pushing a button or walking through a door. I work in text, so I don't *literally* have colors or Tarot images on the screen, but I should be able to use the text interface to conjure—as it were—the same effect.

Plotkin embraces the idea of magic as complex and multimodal, built around elaborate preparations and rituals that weave together all of the senses. Moreover, Plotkin's implementation of magic is simultaneously inspired by alchemical and occultist rituals and by the imaginative fantasy of Steven Brust, whose *Taltos* is part of the larger *Jhereg* series. These ideas of magic were well-received by Plotkin's already devoted audience: *Hadean Lands* received more than $31,000 from a Kickstarter initiative.

As Plotkin has continued to work on *Hadean Lands* and provide progress updates on his Kickstarter page, the relationship between puzzle and ritual has become clearer, with Plotkin building what he calls a "ritual engine" and a set of programmatic tests to make sure that each ritual can be successfully performed by players. Plotkin describes his own ritual engine as a state machine, a programming term for a machine comprised of a set of distinct states and the events that can trigger movement from one state to another. Plotkin has also been mapping *Hadean Lands* using a self-designed tool called Plotex, designed to diagram plots (understood in the abstract sense of progression through the game rather than story *per se*). He has also mapped *Enchanter,* the classic interactive fiction about spellcasting, using PlotEx. Both Plotkin's state machine and his use of PlotEx demonstrate the strength of a designer who understands the high-level goals of a multimodal, ritualistic magic system and concrete, rigorous programming techniques for implementing such a system.

To give a concrete example, the instructions for one of *Hadean Land*'s rituals reads as follows:

> FOR THE CLEANSING OF BRASS TARNISH: Prepare an atmosphere of fiery principles. Place a brass token within the bound, and seal it. Speak a word of essential nature, so that the properties of brass may be evoked. Compound the atmosphere with a resinous note. Then intone the Lesser Phlogistical Saturation to complete the token's investment. Place token directly on tarnished item. Scrawled at the bottom, in a more familiar handwriting: "Resinous note—wave the rosemary, swabbie."

In order to perform this ritual, the player must open a vial of ginger oil, thereby creating "an atmosphere of fiery principles." He must then put a brass pin, the "token" of the instructions, onto the desk, and speak the sealing word in order to seal the token. Next, he must speak the word of essential nature. Next, he must wave a sprig of rosemary in order to add the "resinous note" to the atmosphere. Finally, he must speak the Lesser Phlogistical Saturation in order to charge the brass pin, which he can then place on the brass calipers in order to polish them and remove their rust. Because the *Hadean Lands* teaser is a work of interactive fiction, the player technically only interacts with the game through a text parser, but the descriptions vividly evoke smell, sight, and touch. Plotkin deliberately chooses intense, memorable sensations, such as the burning smell of ginger oil, in order to create correspondences that players can deduce (such as the association of ginger oil with fire). Moreover, the player receives feedback on the successful or unsuccessful progress of the ritual through various sensory output, such as changes in the atmosphere or a glowing light surrounding the bounds of the workbench. The text-based format of interactive fiction, both classic and contemporary, helps designers to see clearly the relationship between mechanics and world by omitting the layer of graphics that could otherwise obscure game systems. Another early game genre, the roguelike, helps designers see and modify game systems even more directly through the stark medium of ASCII graphics.

 Roguelikes are a subgenre of role-playing game named after the game Rogue. Roguelikes are defined by graphics made of ASCII art (keyboard characters, such as @ and *), permadeath (in which a player character is permanently dead when vanquished, without the ability to return to a save state), and procedurally generated levels (in which levels of a dungeon are created at runtime through algorithms rather than being pre-planned).

3.5 FROM ROGUELIKES TO RECIPES

There is an understanding among the still-active roguelike community that playing these games leads to deciphering their underlying source code and, eventually, modding roguelikes. This is perhaps more often the case in roguelikes than in other types of games because the underlying structures are less obscured by layers of graphics and sound, which are largely lacking in favor of ASCII characters only. Playing a roguelike in its ASCII form is like seeing into the Matrix, learning to think systemically rather than superficially. "The Beginner's Guide to Roguelikes in C/C++" praises this aspect of roguelikes as "the right level of abstraction," explaining wittily "you're not playing an interactive novel, but on the other hand, you're not worried about alpha blending, frustrum culling or sprite animations." The guide then heralds the achievements possible through the abstraction associated with roguelike development that are difficult or impossible in big-budget, graphically intensive commercial development, including producing efficiently producing mechanics for "a necromancer with an army of thousands of ressurected [sic] dead in tow." Roguelikes emphasize what the guide calls dynamic content, produced procedurally and at runtime rather than statically before the game runs.

Through roguelikes, one learns to think systemically and in terms a computer can understand. As the *Nethack* wiki explains, "You may dive into the very sourcecode, looking to explain that one-in-a-thousand shot you just pulled off. You will probably learn some C, and possibly get into heated debates about the merits of pseudorandom number generators, expected returns, inconsistencies between competing mythologies, and the ethics of exploiting bugs." As an example of seeing into the matrix, Andrew Doull's vast, multi-part blog series on designing magic systems in roguelikes is a deep, challenging reflection on game magic. On Roguelikebasin.com, two programmers (Juho Snellman and Sean Middleditch) have also contributed primers on how to program magic systems in C and/or C++. Each author explores multiple approaches, finally arriving at their own favored strategy.

In "Programming Roguelike Magic," Snellman at first explores the method of hard-coding spells individually. To hard-code a spell means to write a unique piece of code in the form of a function for it. The programmer could then write a switch-case statement, a function meant to switch between the various spells based on the player's input, such as pressing a spell number, with each number being a case. Snellman's pseudocode for this approach is:

RECIPE 5:   A SWITCH-CASE STATEMENT FOR
            SELECTING SPELLS (SNELLMAN, C)

```
switch (spell_num)
{
  case SPELL_FIREBALL:
   cast_fireball(y, x);
  break;
  case SPELL_MAGICMISSILE:
   cast_magicmissile(y, x);
  break;
  case SPELL_HEALSELF:
   cast_healself();
  break;
}
```

Snellman calls this a "first-time approach," inflexible and repetitive in that it requires the programmer to repeat long stretches of code for spells that are not particularly different from one another.

Snellman then offers a second approach, which is built around combinable and extensible spell properties. For example, any spell would have the properties of effect, area, and targets. All of these properties could be stored in a struct (a data structure for aggregating multiple objects into one object). The effect property in particular is stored as a function pointer. When spells are initialized, each property is defined for a given spell, as in Snellman's example below.

RECIPE 6:   FUNCTIONS FOR HEALING AND
            FIREBALL SPELLS (SNELLMAN, C)

```
int spell_init(void)
{
  /* a heal-player spell */
  /* The function pointer can be assigned to using the name of
```

```
     the function without the parenthesis at the end*/
  spells[0].ef = spell_effect_heal;         /* Correct way */
  /* spells[0].ef = spell_effect_heal(); */ /* Wrong way */
  spells[0].area = AREA_SQUARE;
  spells[0].target = TARGET_SELF;

  /* a fireball spell */
  spells[1].ef = spell_effect_fire;
  spells[1].area = AREA_BIGSQUARE; /* Well, it's almost a
    ball ;) */
  spells[1].target = TARGET_VISIBLE;

  return 0;
}
```

There are also functions for each spell effect, specifying what properties such as spell_effect_heal and spell_effect_fire should do, such as adding hitpoints to players and monsters, or drawing an ASCII character to represent fire and subtracting hitpoints from the target. Finally, there is a function for casting the spell, which acquires the spell's target and then applies the spell effect to the relevant squares on the game grid.

Roguelike programmer Sean Middleditch advocates a similar approach that defines spells as classes, with subclasses for spell effects that define die rolls and modifiers as arguments. Middleditch's overall approach is data-driven in that he sets up a basic data structure for spells by defining a class, then pulls in data from a hard-coded spell table. (Middleditch also observes that an expansion of the approach could involve bringing in data from a text file, an approach currently used in my game *Arcana*.) His example data structures and casting functions are as follows.

RECIPE 7:   DEFINING DATA STRUCTURES FOR SPELL
            EFFECTS (MIDDLEDITCH, C)**

```
enum ESpellEffectType {
     kEffectNone,
     kEffectHeal,
     kEffectDamage,
     kEffectTickle,
     kEffectCreateObject,
};
```

** Used with permission of Sean Middleditch.

```
#define NUM_SPELL_EFFECT_PARAMS 5
struct SpellEffect {
    enum ESpellEffectType type;
    int params[NUM_SPELL_EFFECT_PARAMS];
};

#define NUM_SPELL_EFFECTS 5
struct Spell {
    char* name;
    int mpCost;
    int level;
    struct SpellEffect effects[NUM_SPELL_EFFECTS];
};

void CastSpell (const struct Spell* spell, struct Actor*
  source, struct Actor* target) {
    int effectIndex;
    PrintLog("%s cast%s on%s", source->name, spell->name,
      target->name);
    for (effectIndex = 0; effectIndex < NUM_SPELL_EFFECTS &&
    spell->effects[effectIndex].type ! = kEffectNone; ++
      effectIndex) {
    const struct SpellEffect* effect =
      &spell->effects[effectIndex];
    switch (effect->type) {
      case kEffectHeal:
            Heal(target, effect->params[0] + source-
              >level * effect->params[1]);
            break;
      case kEffectDamage:
            Damage(target, effect->params[0] + source-
              >level * effect->params[1]);
            break;
      case kEffectCreateObject:
            CreateObjectAt(effect->params[0],
              target->position);
            break;
      }
}
}
}
```

Doull's approach to designing and implementing magic systems diverges from Snellman and Middleditch's approaches, emphasizing unique abilities that are programmed through individual code paths. Doull eloquently explains:

> As a programmer, your intuition is ultimately to try to re-use your code where ever possible. But as a game designer, of the magic systems, you want to ensure that each ability uses at least some unique code path.

That is, each ability in your game must in some way be a hack. It can be a small hack (fire burns, cold freezes) or a large hack (the recent implementation of a Find Familiar spell required a complete monster progression system to be interesting), but it should ensure that each ability is different, and therefore affects the game play in some unique way. Extend the ability idea as far as you can (cold freezes water, allowing you to cross rivers and block swimming monsters from attacking you) and then push yourself a little to see where it takes you. Don't obsess with trying to make the code clean and regular: it's the abilities that the player has that keep them empowered and playing, and suspension of disbelief should trump any reduction in code complexity.

A hack, in Doull's terminology, is a workaround, a unique piece of code designed to function in a particular situation rather than to efficiently cover all cases. Doull is arguing that each ability needs to have unique mechanics associated with it, either through secondary effects (such as an element affecting the environment in a particular way that no other element does, rather than all elements simply doing varying amounts of damage against different enemies). Doull's approach emphasizes not only secondary and tertiary consequences, but also an entire subsystem to allow a summoned familiar to level up and grow. Earlier in his blog entries, Doull gives another example of unique subsystems when he discusses how druidic spells can affect the weather in his game *Unangband*, necessitating the programming of entire sub-systems to represent the weather.

The source code for many roguelikes is open-source, meaning that it can be freely downloaded, examined, and modified under the terms of various licenses, such as the GNU License 2.0. Members of the roguelike community have even coined the term "source-diving" to refer to the activity of studying sourcecode in order to understand it and possibly modify it. As the *Nethack* wiki page for source diving explains, "Source diving is the action of examining the sourcecode of NetHack. A person who practices source diving is called a source diver. The source code is freely available for anyone, unlike in most commercial programs." By source-diving into the code that drives the magic systems of roguelikes, game developers can understand how a particular game's brand of game magic is constructed and modify these systems or develop one's own.

The magic of roguelikes comes in many flavors corresponding to the settings of various games. The magic of *Nethack*, a classic roguelike, is rather vanilla, since it primarily adapts or copies *Dungeons & Dragons* spells like cone of cold and magic missile. *Nethack* does, however, model a very real and unfortunate aspect of human cognition: forgetfulness. As each turn elapses, the player character's knowledge of spells degrades.

RECIPE 8: MODELING SPELL FORGETFULNESS (*NETHACK*, C)

```
/* called from moveloop() */
void
age_spells()
{
    int i;
    /*
     * The time relative to the hero (a pass through move
     * loop) causes all spell knowledge to be decremented.
     * The hero's speed, rest status, conscious status etc.
     * does not alter the loss of memory.
     */
    for (i = 0; i < MAXSPELL && spellid(i) ! = NO_SPELL; i++)
        if (spellknow(i))
            decrnknow(i);
    return;
}
```

Angband, another classic roguelike whose name derives from Tolkien lore, also has a fairly standard set of spells. On the other hand, *Angband* variants *Zangband*, as well as offshoots *Cthangband* (set in H.P. Lovecraft's Dreamlands) and *Hellband* (set in a version of hell inspired by sources such as Dante's *Inferno*) all have unique schools of magic with unusual spells whose mechanics reflect their flavor in intriguing ways. Of the *Angband* variants, *Zangband* begins the move toward more complex magic systems with a variety of schools. *Angband* has only two schools of magic: Arcane and Divine, the equivalents of wizardly and priestly magic in *Dungeons & Dragons*. In contrast, *Zangband* has seven schools of magic, called realms. The game's designer himself, Topi Ylinen, acknowledges that these seven realms originate in the strategy game *Master of Magic*. In the "History" file of *Cthangband*, Ylinen explains that his "strong addiction to the Civilization style fantasy strategy game 'Master of Magic' inspired him to write a new magic system." The *Zangband* help files also offer a highly self-reflective analysis of the game's magic system by Ylinen:

> Zangband uses a more complex "realms of magic" system inspired by the commercial fantasy strategy game Master of Magic (Microprose), which in turn has supposedly borrowed it from

the card game Magic the Gathering (by Wizards of the Coast). The magic system, as implemented in Zangband, consists of seven realms: Life, Arcane, Sorcery, Nature, Trump, Chaos and Death.

The Trump realm, based on a school of magic particular to Zelazny's *Amber* universe, is especially flavorful and unique. There are only six realms of magic in *Master of Magic*, and the seventh Trump realm adds a quirky blend of randomness, teleportation, and summoning whose logic derives from *Amber* (Chapter 8, Section 8.8). In *The Chronicles of Amber*, the Amberites use decks of tarot cards with trumps (the royalty cards) to teleport between dimensions and to summon their regal brethren. The randomness of Trump magic is also inspired by the random element of tarot divination, derived from shuffling cards.

The official *Zangband* documentation effectively explains the relationship between randomness, teleportation, and interdimensional summoning:

Trump

Trump magic seems an independent source of power, although its supposed association with Chaos magic has been mentioned in several places. Although it lacks the unpredictable chaotic side-effects of Chaos magic, it has a few spells whose exact effects seem more or less random. One such spell is Shuffle: the Trump spellbooks actually consist of decks of trumps, and the Shuffle spell allows the caster to shuffle the deck and pick one card at random. The effect depends on the card picked, and is not always pleasant. In the Amber universe, the Trump gateways are also a major method of transportation: Trump magic has, indeed, an admirable selection of teleportation spells. Since the Trump gateways can also be used to summon other creatures, Trump magic has an equally impressive selection of summoning spells. However, not all monsters appreciate being drawn to another place by Trump user. The only summoned creatures whose loyalty is guaranteed are the Phantasmal Servants, who lack a will of their own (but can develop one, if you treat them badly).

Hellband source code for spells is much more organized and easy to read than *Zangband* and, perhaps, the most flavorful magic system of the *Angband* variants. It is dependent on *Zangband*'s seven realms of magic, with a few alterations. The realms of *Hellband* magic are life, sorcery, nature, demonic, death, tarot, charms, somatic, and demonic. Tarot is a heavily modified response to trump magic that simulates a fuller deck of tarot cards, with some minor and major arcana. Demonic magic is a mixture of miscellaneous, unique spell effects named after various demons. In *Hellband*, spells1.c and spells2.c (whose suffixes indicate a source file in the language C), contain the game's magic system. Spells are called through a switch-case statement for each realm.

Each switch-case function offers a message as to what the spell does, and then the case either directly causes the effect or calls a function or functions that will. For example, for the Demonic Realm:

RECIPE 9:   DEMONIC SPELLS (*HELLBAND*, C)

```
case REALM_DEMONIC-1:/* * DEMONIC * */
switch (spell)
      {
                case 0:/* Unholy strength */
         (void)set_timed_effect(TIMED_HERO, p_ptr->hero +
            randint(25) + 25);
         (void)take_hit((p_ptr->lev/10)*5+5, "Strain of
            Unholy Strength");
                break;
            case 1:/* Sense Evil */
                (void)detect_monsters_evil();
            break;
            case 2:/* Scorch */
            if (!get_aim_dir(&dir)) return;
             fire_bolt_or_beam(beam-10, GF_FIRE, dir,
                damroll(3 + ((plev - 1)/5), 4));
            break;
            case 3:/* Perilous Shadows */
                if (!get_aim_dir(&dir)) return;
                fire_bolt_or_beam(beam-10, GF_DARK, dir,
                    damroll(3 + ((plev - 1)/5), 4));
            break;
            case 4:/* Teleport */
                teleport_player(75);
                break;
            case 5:/* Disintegrate */
                if (!get_aim_dir(&dir)) return;
                fire_ball(GF_DISINTEGRATE, dir,
                  damroll(8+((plev-5)/4), 8), 0);
                break;
            case 6:/* Demonic Sigil */
                msg_print("You carefully draw a sigil on
                    the floor...");
                explosive_rune();
                break;
```

```
case 7:/* Hecate's Radiance (weak light
  damage + medium charm/confuse/fear spell) */
     (void)lite_area_hecate(damroll(plev, 2),
        (plev/10) + 1);
     break;
case 8:/* Abaddon's Rage */
     (void)set_timed_effect(TIMED_SHERO,
        p_ptr->shero + randint(25) + 25);
     (void)set_timed_effect(TIMED_BLESSED,
        p_ptr->blessed + randint(25) + 25);
     break;
case 9:/* Mind Leech */
     (void)mind_leech();
     break;
case 10:/* Body Leech*/
     (void)body_leech();
     break;
case 11:/* Glyph of Warding */
     warding_glyph();
     break;
case 12:/* Protection from Evil */
     (void)set_timed_effect(TIMED_PROTEVIL,
        p_ptr->protevil + randint(25) + 3 *
        p_ptr->lev);
     break;
case 13:/* Summon Demons */
     if (!(summon_specific_friendly(py, px,
       plev, FILTER_DEMON, TRUE)))
        if (!(summon_specific_friendly(py,
          px, plev, FILTER_DEVIL, TRUE)))
             none_came = TRUE;
     break;
case 14:/* Summon the Fallen */
     if (!(summon_specific_friendly(py, px,
       plev, FILTER_FALLEN_ANGELS, TRUE)))
     none_came = TRUE;
     break;
case 15:/* Balm of the Cocytus */
     hp_player(300);
     /* Actually set the stat to its new
       value. */
     p_ptr->stat_cur[A_CON] =
       p_ptr->stat_cur[A_CON]-1;
     /* Recalculate bonuses */
     p_ptr->update | = (PU_BONUS);
     break;
case 16:/* Araqiel's Wrath (Earthquake) */
     (void) earthquake(py,px,8);
     break;
```

```
case 17:/*Kokabiel's Call (Summon Spirits,
  lots of them) */
    none_came = summon_specific_friendly(py,
      px, plev, FILTER_SPIRITS, TRUE) +
    summon_specific_friendly(py, px, plev,
      FILTER_SPIRITS, TRUE) +
    summon_specific_friendly(py, px, plev,
      FILTER_SPIRITS, TRUE) +
    summon_specific_friendly(py, px, plev,
      FILTER_SPIRITS, TRUE);
    none_came = !none_came;
    break;
case 18:/* Baraquiel's Guile (detect
  enchantment on entire level of excellents
  and specials) */
    (void)detect_objects_magic(TRUE,TRUE);
    break;
case 19:/* Sariel's Ire */
    dummy = randint(50) + 25;
    (void)set_timed_effect(TIMED_BLESSED,
      p_ptr->blessed + dummy);
    (void)set_timed_effect(TIMED_HERO, p_ptr-
      >hero + dummy);
    (void)set_timed_effect(TIMED_MAGIC_SHELL,
      p_ptr->magic_shell + dummy);
    break;
case 20:/* Azazel's Rule */
    (void)charm_all_goats();
    break;
case 21:/* Danel's Deluge */
    if (!get_aim_dir(&dir)) return;
    fire_ball(GF_LITE, dir,
    (damroll(3, 6) + plev +
    (plev/((p_ptr->pclass = =
    CLASS_HELL_KNIGHT
    || p_ptr->pclass = = CLASS_WARLOCK
    || p_ptr->pclass = = CLASS_BLOOD_MAGE
    || p_ptr->pclass = = CLASS_HIGH_MAGE) ? 1
                          : 3))),
    ((plev < 30) ? 2 : 3));
    break;
case 22:/* Amaros' Grief */
    (void) dispel_demons(plev*4);
    (void) dispel_fallen_angels(plev*4);
    break;
case 23:/* Teachings of Kasyade */
    wiz_lite();
    break;
```

```
case 24:/* Orb of Impending Doom */
    if (!get_aim_dir(&dir)) return;
    fire_ball(GF_HELL_FIRE, dir, (damroll(3, 6)
    + plev + ((plev < 30) ? 2 : 3));
    break;
case 25:/* Temperance */
    dummy = randint(50) + 50;
    (void)set_timed_effect(TIMED_OPPOSE_COLD,
        dummy);
    (void)set_timed_effect(TIMED_OPPOSE_FIRE,
        dummy);
    break;
case 26:/* True Warding */
    warding_glyph();
    glyph_creation();
    break;
case 27:/* Word of Destruction */
    destroy_area(py, px, 15, TRUE);
    break;
case 28:/* Gift of Malphas (Adding weapon
    flags, Malphas being a friend of
    artificers] */
    (void)malphas_gift();
    break;
case 29:/* Lilith's Kiss */
    charm_monsters(p_ptr->lev * 4);
    break;
case 30:/* Behemoth's Call */
    msg_print("You open your mouth while it
        deforms into a gaping hole, spewing
        wind and water!");
    (void)behemoth_call();
    break;
case 31:/* Chaos Rift */
    if (!get_aim_dir(&dir)) return;
    fire_ball(GF_CHAOS,dir,p_ptr->mhp,2);
    break;
default:
    msg_format("You cast an unknown Demonic
        spell:%d.", spell);
    msg_print(NULL);
    }
    break;
```

Hellband also permits the player to be a blood mage, and the mechanics of this class can be represented in a nutshell in the code below. This code represents the inability of non blood mages to cast spells beyond their mana pools, as well as causing fainting and damage to health if they overspend and therefore overexert while casting. The code contrasts these mechanics with blood mages' ability to deliberately overspend, casting spells whose costs exceed their mana pool by spending health.

RECIPE 10:   ROGUELIKE BLOOD MAGIC (*HELLBAND*, C)

```c
if(p_ptr->pclass ! = CLASS_BLOOD_MAGE)
     {
            /* Sufficient mana */
            if (s_ptr->smana < = p_ptr->csp)
            {
                   /* Use some mana */
                   p_ptr->csp - = s_ptr->smana;
            }
            /* Over-exert the player */
            else
            {
                   int oops = s_ptr->smana - p_ptr->csp;

                   /* No mana left */
                   p_ptr->csp = 0;
                   p_ptr->csp_frac = 0;

                   /* Message */
                   msg_print("You faint from the effort!");

                   /* Hack— Bypass free action */
                   (void)set_timed_effect(TIMED_PARALYZED,
                       p_ptr->paralyzed + randint(5 * oops
                       + 1));

                   /* Damage CON (possibly permanently) */
                   if (rand_int(100) < 50)
                   {
                          bool perm = (rand_int(100) < 25);

                          /* Message */
                          msg_print("You have damaged your
                              health!");

                          /* Reduce constitution */
                          (void)dec_stat(A_CON, 15 +
                              randint(10), perm);
                   }
            }
     }
     else
     /*We are dealing with a blood mage*/
     {
```

```
              /* Sufficient hitpoints */
              if (s_ptr->smana < = p_ptr->chp)
              {
                      /* Use some mana */
                      p_ptr->chp - = s_ptr->smana;
              }
              /* Over-exert the player */
              else
              {
                      int oops = s_ptr->smana - p_ptr->chp;

                      /* Leave one hitpoint */
                      p_ptr->chp = 1;
                      p_ptr->chp_frac = 0;

                      /* Message */
                      msg_print("You faint from the effort!");
                      /* Hack— Bypass free action */
                      (void)set_timed_effect(TIMED_PARALYZED,
                          p_ptr->paralyzed + randint(5 * oops
                          + 1));
                      /* Whack that constitution like there is
                          no tomorrow */
                      (void)dec_stat(A_CON, 25, TRUE);

              }
      }

      /* Redraw mana */
      if(p_ptr->pclass ! = CLASS_BLOOD_MAGE)
              p_ptr->redraw | = (PR_MANA);
      else
              p_ptr->redraw | = (PR_HP);

      /* Window stuff */
      p_ptr->window | = (PW_PLAYER);
      p_ptr->window | = (PW_SPELL);

      /* Gain experience, we put this here since leveling
          screws up the spell info pointer,
              that is very bad karma and it is all my fault,
                  big todo!
      */
      if(first_time)
              gain_exp(xp_gain);
}
```

Hellband's spells.c file has almost 6700 lines of initializing various parameters before the all-important function, void do_cmd_cast(void). The casting function begins with a cascading series of checks to make sure that casting requirements are met. A player must have the ability to cast spells, must have light, must not be confused, and must have a spell book. If any of these requirements is not met, the player receives an error message and casting stops.

RECIPE 11:   SPELL MISFIRE EFFECTS (*HELLBAND*, C)

```c
/* Spell failure chance */
    chance = spell_chance(spell,use_realm-1);
    /* Failed spell */
    if (rand_int(100) < chance)
    {
            if (flush_failure) flush();

            msg_format("You failed to get the%s off!",
               prayer);
            if (o_ptr->tval = = TV_CHAOS_BOOK &&
               (randint(100)<spell))
            {
                    msg_print("You produce a chaotic effect!");
                    wild_magic(spell);
            }
            if (o_ptr->tval = = TV_DEMONIC_BOOK &&
               (randint(100)<spell))
            {
               msg_print("You anger your patron!");
               summon_specific(py,px,dun_level,FILTER_DEMON);
            }
            else if (o_ptr->tval = = TV_DEATH_BOOK &&
               (randint(100)<spell))
            {
                    msg_print("It hurts!");
                    take_hit(damroll((o_ptr->sval)+1,6),
                       "a miscast Death spell");
                    if (spell>15 && randint(6) = =1 &&
                       !(p_ptr->hold_life))
                            lose_exp(spell * 250);
            }
    }
```

In this code, failed spells from the chaos realm trigger wild magic spells, failed spells from the demonic realm anger the warlock's infernal patron, and failed spells from the death realm cause random amounts of damage. Many of the life spells trigger constants called timed effects, which last for a specified duration and then abate. For example, the Bless spell triggers the time effect of being blessed (TIMED_BLESSED).

RECIPE 12:   A ROGUELIKE BLESS SPELL (*HELLBAND*)

```
case 2:/* Bless */
(void)set_timed_effect(TIMED_BLESSED, p_ptr->blessed +
    randint(12) + 12);
                        break;
```

Spells that banish or negate often set timed effects to 0, such as "Heal," which negates damage effects.

RECIPE 13:   A ROGUELIKE HEAL SPELL (*HELLBAND*, C)

```
case 14:/* Healing */
                    (void)hp_player(300);
                    (void)set_timed_effect(TIMED_STUN, 0);
                    (void)set_timed_effect(TIMED_CUT, 0);
                     break;
```

Spells often follow the pattern of retrieving a directional value based on player input, then firing an effect in the specified direction. The pattern of the beam (whether beam, cone, square, or other shape) has great strategic impact. As Doull argues in "Designing a Magic System," "One of the greatest games ever made, Chess, depends entirely on the library of attack shapes of the pieces in the game, and your game should as well." For example, here is the code for a lightning bolt, which fires a bolt of lightning in a given direction for ten squares, applies an electric effect to this beam, then calculates damage.

RECIPE 14:   A LIGHTNING BOLT SPELL (*ZANGBAND*, C)**

```
case 9:/* Lightning Bolt */
                    if (!get_aim_dir(&dir)) return;
                    fire_bolt_or_beam(beam-10, GF_ELEC, dir,
                        damroll(3+((plev-5)/4), 8));
                    break;
```

Spells are also frequently scaled up based on the variable plev, which stands for player level. In many cases, the switch-case statement for casting a particular spell simply calls functions that repeat the name of the

---

** Used with permission of Topi Ylinen.

spell, such as the spell "Detect Traps and Secret Doors," which calls the functions detect_traps(), detect_doors(), and detect_stairs().

RECIPE 15: DETECTING SECRET TRAPS AND
DOORS (*ZANGBAND*, C)**

```
case 5:/* Detect Traps + Secret Doors */
                    (void)detect_traps();
                    (void)detect_doors();
                    (void)detect_stairs();
                    break;
```

The file spells2.c contains the actual functions that are called from the switch-case statements associated with spells in spells1.c. Many of these functions alter players' attributes, stored in a pointer variable associated with the player (p_ptr). The ASCII-based intricacy of roguelike magic systems paves the way for graphically-represented magic in the first CRPGs.

3.6 THE RUNES OF *DUNGEON MASTER*

The first-person RPG *Dungeon Master* (1987) transforms a language-based magic system from textually to graphically based by representing the elements of its magical language as runes (see 6.7 below). The *Dungeon Master* manual waxes deeply philosophical on the workings of this magical language when it explains that magicians power magic by shaping magical energy, or mana, through their minds. As the manual explains:

> Know ye that the power of Mana is a power of nature harnessed by the mind. What the mind can conjure, the power of Magick will carry out. Yet, this power is not gained by mere imagining. It requires a knowledge of the true order of things. Our mind must do more than imagine fire to summon it. It must look beyond and see the true nature of fire.

By invoking not just fire but the true nature of fire, the designers of *Dungeon Master* are envisioning a Platonic vision of reality as well as the concept of True Names (see Chapter 8, Section 8.4). The magician must harness the true, essential ideas underlying reality in order to shape it, and he shapes reality by organizing his thoughts about the true ideas into runic sentences. As the manual explains, "a spell is a visualization and recitation that focuses the mind on a specific task and channels Mana to carry it out. A spell is made

---

** Used with permission of Topi Ylinen.

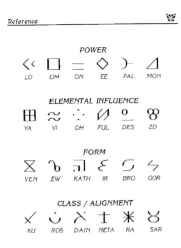

FIGURE 3.1 *Dungeon Master*'s Runic Grammar. (Image by Faster Than Light Games.)

of symbols which have both a form and a name" (18). A fully formed spell in *Dungeon Master* consists of power, element, form, and alignment. Power indicates the intensity of a spell, element governs its substance, form transmits it in a particular direction, and class/alignment connects it to characters and moral influences. These four linguistic categories each include six runes. Figure 3.1 is a chart of the runes in *Dungeon Master* from the game's manual.

Plato was an ancient Greek philosopher who believed that the physical world was only the shadowy reflection of a higher realm of Ideas.

Perhaps most intriguingly, *Dungeon Master* conceives of each rune as representing a type of influence from an alternate plane of existence or combination of planes. As the manual explains, "The six orders can also be visualized as combining the four orders of the material plane with the two orders of the ethereal realm." This relationship between the symbols of magic and the origins of magical energy in planar cosmology is a thread that runs from *Dungeons & Dragons* (especially the *Planescape* campaign setting) to the collectible card game *Magic: The Gathering* (see Chapter 4, Section 4.9) and beyond. The *Dungeon Master* magic system offers one final twist through its representation of the four parameters as vectors in space, specifically points on an icosahedron or eight-sided solid, familiar to gamers as an eight-sided die and to cosmologists as one of the Platonic solids from which the ancient Greeks believed all matter descended. Figure 3.2 shows the cosmological diagram of *Dungeon Master* and its relationship to the game's runic grammar, as depicted in its manual.

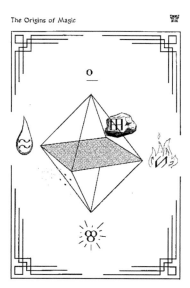

FIGURE 3.2 *Dungeon Master's* Spatial Diagram. (Image by Faster Than Light Games.)

3.7 SORCERIAN

In the same year that *Dungeon Master* was published, an obscure Japanese side-scrolling RPG from 1987 called *Sorcerian* pushes the boundaries of combinatorial and elemental spellcasting in the sheer number of spells available, as well as the resistance to the standard four elements of damage. The primary divisions of magical elements in the game are the Greco-Roman gods of the seven planets known to the ancients: Sun, Moon, Mercury, Mars, Venus, Jupiter, and Saturn. As the *Sorcerian* manual explains, "Since all magic is granted by the seven Gods, magic spells are characterized by those things governed by the Gods whose magic is being called upon" (32). This explanation succinctly expresses the ultimate mythological origin of the schools of magic, in that the gods of various mythologies represent domains over which they have power. In a coherently-designed magic system, the origins of magic in mythological lore are also classifications of spell effects. The combinations of these planetary gods yield 120 possible spells, as well as many potions derived from five herbs (verbena, lavender, sage, hyssop, and savory). Through combinations of the gods and herbs, players can access five categories of spells: offensive, defensive, healing, transformation, and herbal. There is an underlying logic to the combinations of spells in that certain gods work effectively together, while others (such as Venus, the goddess of love) help to ease the combination of otherwise opposed gods.

3.8 THE INCANTATIONS OF *WIZARDRY*

Early CRPGs tended to have in common with the *Enchanter* trilogy the use of text parsers, with an accompanying incantatory method of spell-casting. The *Wizardry* series featured its own invented language of spells, with its own etymology involving root words and prefixes. Certain root words signified common spell effects, like "halito" for fire and "dios" for heal. Other prefixes indicated the target or intensity of the spell, such as "ma" for "big" or "ba" for negation. Thus, the "mahalito" spell is a "big fire" that does massive damage, and the "badios" spell does damage to a group of monsters—the opposite of healing. The magical language of incantations extends throughout *Wizardry I-V,* with some modifications and additions in *Wizardry V: The Heart of the Maelstrom.* Later install-ments of wizardry diverged from a linguistically-based system in favor of a more conventional list of spells, divided into conventional elemental schools by the time of *Wizardry 8.*

For all the evolutions of the game technologically over time, the apex of magic in the *Wizardry* franchise occurs in *Wizardry IV: The Return of Werdna. Wizardry IV* is a striking example of a truly hardcore approach to magic, predicated on the premise that the player takes the role of the vil-lainous wizard who was the end boss destroyed by the party of adventurers in the first *Wizardry* installment, *Proving Grounds of the Mad Overlord.* Rather than playing a party of adventurers who seek to destroy an evil wizard, the player becomes the selfsame evil wizard previously defeated by a party of do-gooders. This role reversal brings with it a corresponding inversion of standard RPG mechanics with a particularly grim vision of magic at its heart. Magic comes to the forefront as the player character's ultimate and only resource for problem-solving. The game transforms a party-based RPG franchise, in which different party members have a diversity of skills, into a single-character RPG in which the player is required to take the role of a once-powerful mage. This mage is initially stripped of his powers, possessing only meager spells and the ability to summon minions by standing on pentagrams scattered throughout levels. These pentagrams save the game but resurrect all the monsters on a level, emphasizing the cost of magic in a particularly devilish way.

The thematic grimness of playing an evil magician resonated naturally with fiendishly difficult gameplay that demanded deep mastery of the magic system developed in the first three *Wizardry* installments. RPG historian Matt Barton states that *Wizardry IV* is "widely considered to be the most difficult CRPG ever created" (75). Like the final installment of the *Enchanter* trilogy but unlike RPG competitors such as *Ultima*, *Wizardry IV* was advertised as an "expert scenario" with the warning "for experienced players only," indicating that it required knowledge of the game's mechanics in order to survive. In particular, players needed to know the magic system and associated magical language of the game intimately. For example, the game begins with the player trapped in a dark room with no visible exits. He can only escape by summoning a group of priests, hoping that they will cast a MILWA spell: a light spell that reveals secret doors. There is no in-game reminder that priests possess MILWA or that it can cause a secret door to become visible, nor any direct control over when or if a group of priests will cast MILWA. These sorts of puzzles, dependent on a deep understanding of the game's magic system, are par for the course in *Wizardry IV*. The game stands as a monument to a vision of magic as the framework for linguistically-based puzzles, a vision which parallels a more accessible but equally rich simulation of magic in the *Ultima* franchise.

3.9 THE MAGICAL SYLLABLES OF THE *ULTIMA* SERIES

Starting in *Ultima V*, the *Ultima* series adopts a similar principle of a set of 24 to 26 magical syllables, one for each letter of the alphabet (with J and O missing in *Ultima V* but assigned in *Ultima VI*). These syllables are listed in the manuals of each *Ultima* game and can be combined in sequences of two or three in order to create a wide variety of effects (Table 3.1).

3.10 SPELL REAGENTS IN THE *ULTIMA* SERIES

Syllables are not the only linguistic tokens in the magic systems of the *Ultima* series. Many games, both digital and non-digital, require players to collect and use objects in order to cast spells. The devil is in the details, since not all objects and ways of using them are equally evocative. Inspired by tabletop role-playing games and the history of alchemy, designer Richard Gariott gave reagents a prominent role in the magic system of the *Ultima* series, especially parts *IV*, *V*, and *VI* (the Avatar Trilogy). Players must combine ingredients in order to prepare spells, which players then trigger through incantations typed into a text parser. Players primarily use the following seven reagents with the associated functions shown in Table 3.2, derived from the official documentation on The Eight Circles of Magic included with *Ultima VI: The False Prophet*.

TABLE 3.1   Magical Syllables in the *Ultima* Series

Syllable	Meaning
An	Negate/Dispel
Bet	Small
Corp	Death
Des	Lower/Down
Ex	Freedom
Flam	Flame
Grav	Energy/Field
Hur	Wind
In	Make/Create/Cause
Jux	Danger/Trap/Harm
Kal	Summon/Invoke
Nox	Poison
Ort	Magic
Port	Move/Movement
Quas	Illusion
Rel	Change
Sanct	Protect/Protection
Tym	Time
Uus	Raise/Up
Vas	Great
Wis	Know/Knowledge
Xen	Creature

TABLE 3.2   Spell Reagents in *Ultima*

Reagent	Function
Black pearl	Propel a spell forward, i.e. "kinetic propellent"
Blood moss	Transportation and speed, i.e. "enhance mobility and movement"
Garlic	Countermagic, i.e. "warding off evil spirits and negating black magic"
Ginseng	Healing, i.e. "curative powers"
Mandrake root	Augmentation, i.e. "increase the power of the desired enchantment"
Nightshade	Illusion and poison
Spider's silk	"binding power"
Sulfurous ash	"adds high levels of energy"

There is an underlying alchemical or pseudo-chemical logic to the functions of particular reagents and how they combine to produce specific spells. Each of these components has its own significance in terms of spell effects, such as a black pearl for projection, blood moss for movement, garlic for warding off malign influences, ginseng for healing, mandrake root for power, nightshade for poison, spider silk for binding, and sulfurous ash for energy. Several of these spell components have a logical, if pseudoscientific, connection to the properties they represent, such as the legendary ability of garlic to ward off vampires, the use of ginseng in herbal medicine, the power of spiderwebs to bind insects, and the actual toxic properties of the herb nightshade. A fireball spell consists of sulfurous ash (to provide fiery energy) and black pearl (to propel the energy forward). Certain spell ingredients require elaborate quests, as in the case of precious mandrake (which can only be harvested in particular swamps during certain phases of the in-game moon). Such quests make particular reagents especially valuable and magical in that even their gathering requires an arcane understanding of the underlying logic of the world of Britannia. The richly cohesive magical logic of the *Ultima* franchise becomes even more enriched by the deep world-building and simulation of *Ultima Underworld*.

3.11 THE MAGICAL LANGUAGE AND WORLD SIMULATION OF *ULTIMA UNDERWORLD*

Ultima Underworld was originally conceived of by its designers as a "3d Dungeon Simulator." In a podcast about Looking Glass games, the lead programmer Dan Schmidt has described *Underworld* as originally more of a simulator than a game, in the sense that the programmers prioritized realistically modeling processes and behaviors of objects and characters in the dungeon, only later incorporating a narrative plot in order to drive the player's actions. As game academic and Harmonix narrative designer Matthew Weise observes in the same podcast, *Ultima Underworld* places a premium on simulating a coherent world. Weise also argues that this simulation can be especially nuanced because the Looking Glass team deliberately chose a highly constrained situation rather than the vast open-world environments that would later characterize *The Elder Scrolls*.

Because of the sophisticated world modeling of *Underworld*, the magic system of *Ultima Underworld* is unusually rich in that the linguistic framework of the magic (its runic grammar) is deeply intertwined with a wide range of objects, variables, and parameters constituting this world simulation. The relationship between the underlying world model of *Ultima: Underworld* and its magic system is expressed in magical terms through a group of runes, which include a set of verbs, a set of nouns, and two adjectives. Some runes, such as change or "rel," can function as both nouns and verbs, but most runes are one or the other.

The nouns describe in broad and abstract terms the domains that can be affected by spells:

- Death
- Time
- Freedom
- Flame
- Energy
- Wind
- Harm
- Light
- Life
- Poison
- Magic
- Movement
- Illusion
- Change
- Protection
- Time
- Knowledge
- Matter

The runes that represent verbs in turn reference ways that these domains can be affected and manipulated, sometimes by flipping a state expressed as a Boolean variable, sometimes by increasing or decreasing a numerical value (effectively pushing a slider in one direction or another).

- Negate
- Cause
- Summon
- Raise

Once the set of objects, attributes, and states has been defined, they can then be expressed as a language. With these verbs, nouns, and adjectives in mind, players can input a variety of simple two and three word sentences, which function as spells (Table 3.3).

3.12 ULTIMA VIII

While the *Ultima Underworld* games move spellcasting to a primarily rune-based, linguistic system, *Ultima VIII: Pagan* offers a strikingly nuanced and rich magic system which might actually be classified as multiple magic systems, including sorcery, tempestry, theurgy, necromancy, and thaumaturgy. As game designer and scholar Matthew Weise explains:

> Although drastically scaled back from its original planned design, one element of Ultima VIII that survives is its crazy magic system—or, I should say, magic system*s*—which (unlike other Ultima games) the entire narrative revolves around. Ultima VIII takes place in a world where four gods have four different competing metaphysical systems. The gods themselves are not that original (they are based on the four elements—yay) but they become somewhat interesting when you realize their separate magic systems actually *work* differently, i.e. they aren't just the same system with different spell-names or reagents. Though perhaps not as fleshed out an idea as it could be, it might be worth investigating all the same. ("Game Prescription: Vagrant Story")

The *Chronicle of Pagan* outlines how reagents and spell foci play a crucial role in several of the game's different magic systems, especially necromancy, theurgy, and sorcery. Necromancy simply requires pouches of reagents scattered during spellcasting to channel the power of the earth Titan, whereas theurgy requires specific metal objects (such as a sextant and a pointing hand) that help to harvest the power of air. Finally, the system of sorcery involves one of the most elaborate game spellcasting systems, which closely resembles actual ceremonial magic. In sorcery, the player prepares spells through a ritual inside of a pentagram. At each of the five points of the pentagram, the player both lights a candle and places one reagent. The player than puts a spell focus (distinct from the reagents) at the center of the pentagram. By intoning the correct incantation (also distinct from reagents and spell focus), the player

TABLE 3.3   The Runes of *Ultima Underworld*

Name	Rune	Meaning
An		Negate
Bet		Small
Corp		Depth
Des		Down
Ex		Freedom
Flam		Flame
Grav		Energy
Hur		Wind
In		Cause
Jux		Harm
Kal		Summon
Lor		Light
Mani		Life
Nox		Poison
Ort		Magic
Por		Movement
Ouas		Illusion

TABLE 3.3 (*Continued*)   The Runes of
Ultima Underworld

Rel		Change
Sanct		Protection
Tym		Time
Uus		Raise
Vas		Great
Wis		Knowledge
Ylem		Matter

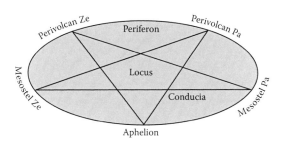

FIGURE 3.3   The Pentagram of Sorcery in *Ultima VIII*. (Image by Origin Systems and Electronic Arts.)

can charge the spell focus, which can then be used to cast the spell at any time. Figure 3.3 shows the pentagram of sorcery in *Ultima VIII*. Figure 3.4 shows how the pentagram can be used to cast particular spells in *Ultima VIII*.

3.13 *LOOM* AND MUSIC AS MAGIC

There is a longstanding connection between music and magic, in which music is regarded as a form of enchantment, capable of moving humans and animals to joy or tears, as well as shaping the cosmos itself. The proverb "Music hath charms to soothe the savage beast" (or breast, depending on one's source) expresses this idea, as does the myth of Orpheus,

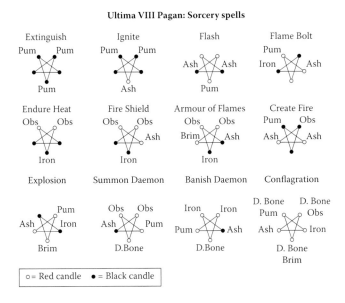

FIGURE 3.4   Sorcery Spells in *Ultima VIII*. (Image by Willem Jan Palenstign. Used with permission.)

the mythical ancient Greek poet and musician who could make the very trees bend to hear his entrancing song. As anyone who has ever performed music knows, there is a powerful connection between spellcasting and music in that both are highly exacting arts, relying on exact timing, the incantation of emotionally charged words, precisely nuanced gestures, and careful ritualistic maintenance of complex instruments.

Recipes for creating music as magic revolve around representing spells as songs. Two classic games that most forcefully simulate music as magic are *Loom* and *The Legend of Zelda: Ocarina of Time*. A more recent example is the upcoming (at time of writing) *Fantasia: Music Evolved*, in which acclaimed music game studio Harmonix (of *Guitar Hero* fame) collaborates with Disney in a motion-controlled, Kinect-driven game about music creation that is narrativized through the fiction of a sorcerer's apprentice learning musical magic.

Spellcasting in the famous LucasArts adventure game *Loom* originates in a pun around the word "staff," which can refer to a musical staff (in written music, a set of parallel lines on which the pitches and durations of musical notes can be represented), a magician's wand through which he channels power, and a weaver's distaff (by which a weaver spins thread). The overriding metaphor of the game, reflected in its mechanics,

OPENING • This fundamental draft is traditionally the first one taught to novice spellweavers. Once mastered, it may be spun into tarpaulins, theater curtains, or any covering that must be whisked aside on command.

FIGURE 3.5   A Draft of Opening in *Loom*. (Image by LucasArts.)

is that wizards create magic through short songs called drafts, which they shape by weaving together colored threads of magical energy. In addition to the pun on distaff, a draft is a weaver's textile pattern by which she records her plans, using a grid. Figure 3.5 shows one of the drafts in *Loom*. Figure 3.6 shows a sample weaver's draft.

Loom revolves around the idea of synesthesia (perceiving one form of sensory input through another sense), since there is a correspondence between notes and colors. In the game's fiction, spellcasters weave the fabric of reality. Player performance and magical fiction are very closely allied in the game if not identical, since players must cast spells by placing colored notes on an interface in the shape of a distaff, through which they receive multimodal feedback. If the player correctly weaves the notes of a draft, then she casts the spell effectively. The effects of drafts can also be inverted by reversing the order of the notes in the song. Because the combination for each draft is randomly chosen from three possibilities at the beginning of each game, the particular combinations of a given draft on a given playthrough are often different, adding replay value and allowing players the pleasure of learning spells each time.

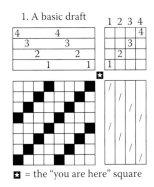

1. A basic draft

▪ = the "you are here" square

FIGURE 3.6   A Textile Weaver's Draft. (Image by WeavingToday.com)

The function of individual drafts in *Loom* tends to be fairly one-off in the sense that individual spells exist primarily to solve particular puzzles. At the same time, the game-world's logic is often sufficiently simulated that spellcasters can try out a draft's effects on objects other than the main puzzle target, allowing for experiment-based learning through trial and error. *Loom* also teaches the player to weave drafts by providing a book containing draft descriptions and blank distaffs, on which players can record draft combinations as each one is learned. *Loom*'s designer, Brian Moriarty, would later go on to create *Perlenspiel*, a highly abstract game engine inspired by Herman Hesse's novel *The Glass Bead Game*, in which a group of musical monks play a synaesthetic, musical game in which glass beads represent harmonious ideas. In some ways, *Perlenspiel* can be thought of as a meta-magic system focused entirely on user-generated content.

Loom paves the way for *The Legend of Zelda: Ocarina of Time*, which allows players to perform magical songs on a small pipe instrument called an ocarina. Players input songs through movements of the Gamecube controller's c-stick up, down, left, and right, as well as alternating the c-stick with presses of the a-button. These movements and button presses mimic the musical structure of the song in terms of ascending and descending runs of notes. As the game's title suggests, many of these songs facilitate time travel, as well as spatial teleportation from one gameplay hub to another. Figure 3.7 shows several of the musical spells from *Ocarina of Time*.

3.14 *STONEKEEP*

Not all immersive magic systems can be fully successful or realized. *Stonekeep* is an example of a highly ambitious and long-delayed game that nevertheless managed to keep a unique magic system as a key feature.

FIGURE 3.7   Song from *The Legend of Zelda: Ocarina of Time*. (Image by Nintendo and Bogan Man at DeviantArt.com)

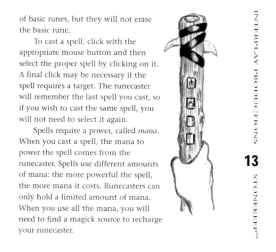

of basic runes, but they will not erase the basic rune.

To cast a spell, click with the appropriate mouse button and then select the proper spell by clicking on it. A final click may be necessary if the spell requires a target. The runecaster will remember the last spell you cast, so if you wish to cast the same spell, you will not need to select it again.

Spells require a power, called *mana*. When you cast a spell, the mana to power the spell comes from the runecaster. Spells use different amounts of mana: the more powerful the spell, the more mana it costs. Runecasters can only hold a limited amount of mana. When you use all the mana, you will need to find a magick source to recharge your runecaster.

FIGURE 3.8   The Spellcasting Staff in *Stonekeep*. (Image by Interplay.)

Stonekeep features a casting staff in the form of a graphical user interface, onto which players inscribe combinations of four types of runes (Mannish, Fae, Throggish, and Meta) in order to cast spells. A magic mirror allows the player character to reflect spells back at himself in order to benefit from their effects. Like *Ultima Underworld* before it and *Arx Fatalis* after, *Stonekeep* overlays its combinatorial approach to magic onto an immersive three-dimensional world. Figure 3.8 shows a casting staff in *Stonekeep*.

3.15 ARX FATALIS

Arx Fatalis builds directly on the model of *Ultima Underworld I* and *II* with runes that stand for verbs, nouns, and adjectives. Figure 3.9 shows the runes in *Arx Fatalis*.

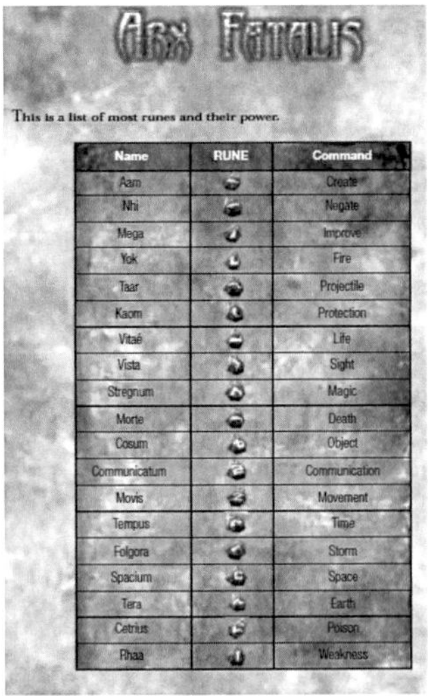

Arx Fatalis

This is a list of most runes and their power.

Name	RUNE	Command
Aam		Create
Nhi		Negate
Mega		Improve
Yok		Fire
Taar		Projectile
Kaom		Protection
Vitae		Life
Vista		Sight
Stregnum		Magic
Morte		Death
Cosum		Object
Communicatum		Communication
Movis		Movement
Tempus		Time
Folgora		Storm
Spacium		Space
Tera		Earth
Cetrius		Poison
Rhaa		Weakness

FIGURE 3.9 *Arx Fatalis* Runes. (Image by Arkane Studios and Zenimax Media. Used with permission.)

As in *Ars Magica*, the rune names are influenced by Latin, though in *Arx Fatalis* they are more often Latinate rather than actual Latin. Vitae (life), vista (vision), tempus (time), communicatum (communication), movis (movement), morte (death), and cosum (thing) are all actual Latin words. Nhi (deny) resembles the Latin nihil or nothing, suggesting the rune's opposition to aam (creation). Mega (improve) is a Greek suffix meaning great, cognate with the Latin magnus. Certius (poison) sounds like Latin but is not. Folgora (storm) resembles the Latin fulgur (lightning). Other runes, such as yok (fire), taar (projectile), and rhaa (weakness) have no obvious relation to Latin.

Because players must trace runes in the air in order to activate spell effects, the designers devise rune shapes that logically reflect the runes' meanings. Conceptually opposite runes have spatially reversed shapes. For example, the rune for create (aam) is a rightward swipe, and the rune for deny (nhi) is a leftward swipe. Similarly, the rune for improve (mega) is an upward swipe, and the rune for weakness (rhaa) is a downward swipe. As in *Eternal Darkness*, a voice chants the name of each rune as the player inscribes it. In the PC version of *Arx Fatalis*, the user interface allows players to keep their Book of Magic open as reference while casting spells, while the simplified interface of the Xbox version allows players to "memorize" a spell by displaying its rune sequence in the upper right-hand corner of the screen as a reference during the casting phase. Both the PC and the

Xbox versions of the game encourage exploration of the system to discover new rune combinations. As the manual for the Xbox version explains, "if you find a rune sequence that has a meaning, it is most likely a new spell. Don't hesitate to experiment and try out new things" (21). This emphasis on experimentation, which allows the player to discover new spells, paves the way for a move toward user-generated content that includes magic.

3.16 USER-GENERATED MAGIC AND *THE ELDER SCROLLS*

Working on the foundations of *Ultima Underworld* and *Arx Fatalis*, several games blur the line between playing as a mage and the creation of magic systems, often in conjunction with a move toward user-generated content, in which players produce playable content for other players using tools provided by the game's designers. Ever since the release of *The Elder Scrolls Construction Set* with *The Elder Scrolls III: Morrowind*, players have been creating mods for the *Elder Scrolls* universe that add new dungeons, quests, and items. Players have also heavily modded the magic of the game, encouraged by invitations to user-generated spells within the game itself, such as the Spellmaker of *The Elder Scrolls: Arena* and the Altar of Spellmaking in *The Elder Scrolls IV: Oblivion*. These in-game artifacts allow players to create new spells by combining a pre-existing set of parameters, such as effect, duration, range, mode of delivery, and cost. (The D.E.M.O.N.S. system of *Two Worlds II*, which stands for Dynamic Enchantment, Magic, Occultism & Necromancy System, is a similar in-game mechanism for creating custom spells, based on combining cards.)

Stepping out of the game and into the construction sets is a great way to understand the underlying scripting logic of magic systems in *The Elder Scrolls Construction Set*, especially since the *Elder Scrolls* games feature a breadth of magical effects well-integrated with a richly simulated world. One good place to start is the "My First Spell" scripting tutorial for *The Elder Scrolls IV: Oblivion* (http://cs.elderscrolls.com/index.php/Scripting_Tutorial:_My_First_Spell). Another relevant tutorial is http://cs.elderscrolls.com/index.php?title=Programmable_Spell_Effects.

Oblivion spells are comprised structurally of three, and only three, blocks of code:

- ScriptEffectStart

- ScriptEffectUpdate

- ScriptEffectFinish

The structure of *The Elder Scrolls* scripting system permits user generated spells and can serve as a guide for designers who want to construct a magic system flexible enough to permit modding. The Creation Kit, the most recent incarnation of the engine and level editor for Elder Scrolls mods, is organized into a hierarchy of objects. This architecture, called object-oriented design, includes a class of objects called spells, which can include another object type called magic effects. Magic effects are in essence the verbs of *The Elder Scrolls'* underlying magical language. There are forty-four total magic effects designed as objects in the game, which are combined in various ways to create the game's spells. Spells themselves are objects which are comprised of magic effects and various associated parameters, such as spell range and duration.

Because *Skyrim* also includes the Dragon Tongue, it is important to distinguish between the high-level language that is part of the game's fiction and the underlying language that is part of the game's scripting. These languages are distinct but related, and the relationship between them is at the heart of what makes a successful magic system. Another object, Word of Power, refers to the words in the Dragon Tongue, which when spoken trigger spell objects comprised of magical effects. The flexibility of this Dragon Tongue has allowed the developers of *Skyrim* to produce a voice recognition mod for the Kinect that lets players input Dragon Shouts using their voices, thereby narrowing the gap between player performance and character action.

3.17 *THE VOID*

Games such as *The Elder Scrolls* and their progenitors, such as *Dungeon Master* and *Ultima Underworld*, open the way for a variety of first-person, immersive magic systems. *The Void*, an independent game by Russian developers Ice-Pick Lodge, features a unique approach to gestural magic based on color understood as a non-renewable biological resource, akin to blood. In *The Void*, color has vanished, leaving behind the gray and empty limbo of the title. Players must scavenge for drops of color, known as Lympha, to store inside multiple hearts, each of which stores a different hue of Lympha inside the player's body. Just as human hearts process oxygenated blood, so the player character's hearts in *The Void* slowly transform Lympha into a resource called Nerva, used to paint magical symbols called glyphs. *The Void* thus features a magic system based simultaneously on color, writing, and intense resource management. In fact, the resource management is so intense that survival is very difficult, prompting both

FIGURE 3.10 (See color insert.)   Hearts and Nerva in *The Void*. (Image by Ice-Pick Lodge.)

Ice-Pick Lodge and fans to produce various patches to create intermediate-level and easy modes. The use of a gestural interface with a mouse proves problematic at times, especially given the game's extreme difficulty, since precise control over drawing is difficult without a touch screen or stylus.

Despite these difficulties, the game's magic system contributes organically to the overall atmosphere of the game, which is eerie and mysterious. Lympha and Nerva form a gorgeous color palette, especially against the murky grays of most background scenes. While many games use standard primary and secondary colors to signify different types of magical effects, *The Void* foregrounds color as the source of all energy and life through seven rich, exotic colors derived and named from precious substances: Silver, Gold, Violet, Azure, Crimson, Amber, and Emerald. Figure 3.10 shows the multi-colored hearts with nerva in *The Void*.

3.18 *THE LEGEND OF GRIMROCK*

The rune-based magic system in *The Legend of Grimrock* (2012), a retro dungeon-crawling RPG, is closely modeled off *Dungeon Master*, as is the game as a whole. There are nine runes, four of them elemental (fire, air, earth, ice), and five of them more abstract (life, death, spirituality, physicality, balance). As designer Antti Tihonen at Almost Human games explains in a blog, the purpose of this system is to make magic feel more immersive, experimental, mysterious, and skill-based: "To us, the systems where you pick a spell from a list have always felt very mundane: invoking magic should feel like you're messing around with mystical forces instead of a spreadsheet!" The rationale for using runes is both aesthetic and magical. As the designers explain:

> Runes are true and tested vessels for arcane power and they certainly make your imagination run wilder than text printed with Arial, size 12, so using them was a pretty obvious choice for us from the get go. And despite them being more abstract than writing, they still have the opportunity of having a logical underlying structure that prevents the spell casting system from turning into a bewildering mess where the player doesn't have a chance to figure out what he's *actually* doing.

The runic system in *Grimrock* allows players to experiment and discover new combinations of spells, but they are unable to use these spells until a given mage character has gained enough spell points in a particular type of magic. Tihonen explains that this dependence on skill points helps to dissuade players from imbalancing the game by looking up all possible spells online or, as he puts it, "to stop the more modern wizards who wield the power of Google from gaining an unreasonable edge."

The rune square is a three-by-three grid reminiscent of the magic squares of medieval magic. Its arrangement has a spatial logic with metaphysical meaning, similar to the radial diagrams and pie charts often used to represent schools of magic. At the center is the rune for balance. Four runes form an equilateral cross whose legs are conceptually opposite pairs of runes: life and death running from top to bottom, and spirituality and physicality running left to right. Similarly, four diagonally placed runes form an *x* of paired elemental oppositions: fire and ice running from top left to bottom right, earth and air running from bottom left to top right. The rune square acts as a graphical user interface of nine buttons, and players cast spells by pressing these buttons in quick succession to form a combination of runes that might constitute a spell. As in the original *Dungeon Master*, gameplay in *Grimrock* is real-time rather than turn-based, so players must learn these combinations well enough to readily cast them under time pressure. Unlike *Dungeon Master*, *Grimrock* has

FIGURE 3.11 *Legend of Grimrock* Runes. (Image by Almost Human Games. Used with permission.)

a vocabulary without a grammar, since its runes consist entirely of nouns. *Grimrock* spells are more like compound words than sentences, resulting in some logical spells and others that are less clear. The Ice Shards spell literally translates to "ice earth" or "earth ice," while the Enchanted Fire Arrow spell is, more inscrutably, "Fire Life Physicality Death." Figure 3.11 shows the runes in *The Legend of Grimrock*.

3.19 DISHONORED

In keeping with first-person immersive magic systems, the magic of *Dishonored* most closely resembles that of *Thief*, a stealth game which exerts a powerful influence on *Dishonored*. Garrett's stealth abilities are contextualized in narrative terms as training from a mystical and monastic order of Keepers, adepts dedicated to preserving balance through stealthy acts of silent intervention in politics, religion, and technology. Garrett's abilities often border on magical, but he has no conventionally defined set of spells. In gameplay terms, *Thief* has no magic system but rather an interesting way of looking at stealth mechanics through the narrative lens of mysticism. In contrast, *Dishonored* has a well-defined magic system, with magical abilities that can be unlocked through runes located in the world and then unleashed at will with the upper left bumper on the gamepad, provided that the player character Corvo has sufficient mana.

While unlockable abilities with mana costs are conventional in magic systems, the magic of *Dishonored* is profoundly fresh, in part because of how well it meshes with the world to which it belongs. The magic of *Dishonored* is a rich, unique, stealth-based magic system. Few of the main abilities are directly offensive combat spells, and those which do exist are quirky and unnerving: summoning a rat swarm to devour enemies, or wielding a wind blast that can break doors as well as damaging opponents. Instead of standard combat attacks, most of the magical abilities in *Dishonored* allow the player character to more gracefully and stealthily explore complex three-dimensional spaces without being detected. For example, one ability, called Blink, allows the player character to teleport instantaneously, often from cover object to cover object, or to high ledges and roofs. Another of the most useful stealth-related abilities is Dark Vision, a power that allows the player character to see through walls, locating enemies and objects (at the second level of upgrades). The Dark Vision ability resembles the various flavors of Detect Life and Clairvoyance from *The Elder Scrolls: Morrowind* and *The Elder Scrolls: Oblivion*, which locate various organic and inorganic objects by changing the rendering properties of solid objects like walls.

The ability to see through a wall is a strategic exploitation of a set of glitches that sometimes occur in three-dimensional engines, in which walls appear as transparent because of clipping issues or one-sided textures. Dark Vision lets players deliberately set walls to be translucent, with relevant objects and enemies becoming color-coded yellow or green to signify their location, as well as displaying the range of vision and level of alertness of enemy guards. As with *Batman: Arkham Asylum*, one danger is that alternate modes of sight become so much more convenient than the default mode that players simply stay in the alternate mode all of the time. This wreaks havoc with a carefully constructed art style, rendering atmospheric lighting and elaborate environmental modeling null and void. Designers who wish to construct a system based on alternate modes of sight should carefully construct their base art style to be aesthetically appealing in both normal and alternate modes, or place limitations on the second sight ability that discourage players from playing only or primarily in this mode.

Despite aesthetic challenges associated with Dark Vision, one of the reasons why sight functions effectively in the magic of *Dishonored* is the game's first-person perspective, a carry-over from *Thief* as well as games by the developer and publisher of *Dishonored*: Arkane Studios and Bethesda. Arkane studios has made effective use of first person in the unique gestural magic system of *Arx Fatalis*, a spiritual successor to *Ultima Underworld*, while Bethesda has consistently explored first-person magic in its RPG series *The Elder Scrolls* (also a descendant of *Ultima Underworld*).

First-person magic systems have the potential to be deeply immersive because they place players firmly within the body of the caster, looking out from his eyes and controlling his arms and hands. Each time the player character uses an ability in *Dishonored*, he activates a tattoo on his left hand, often accompanied by a brief, guttural chant. The player character typically uses magic abilities with the left hand, while cycling between weapons and other artifacts in the left and right hands. Dual wielding allows for quick switches between abilities, many of which can overlap in time, such as scouting an area with Dark Vision while holding a heart to locate runes and simultaneously dispatching guards with a dagger in the right hand. The Possession power takes first-person perspective and ability combination to an even higher plane, allowing the player character to seize control of animals and (after upgrades) other human characters. Because the player character stays in first person, he is able to see through the eyes of rats, wolves, and other humans, giving a powerful sense of shamanic shape-shifting. The Possession ability also makes an appearance in *Risen 2*, another sixth-generation console and PC action-RPG title, where magical mind control is themed as voodoo in keeping with the pirate setting.

The thematic resonance of magic with the narrative framework of *Dishonored* is a major source of its impact. Magic in *Dishonored* is compelling because it fits with the rest of a rich and coherent world comprised equal parts of gameplay, narrative, visuals, and audio. As Matthew Weise argues in "Dishonored: World Building 101," "Coherence and depth is key here—the interconnected-ness of setting, character, mechanics, visual design, and plot—rather than the individual quality of any of these elements alone." In *Dishonored*, magic flows from a mysterious, ambiguous trickster figure named the Outsider, who provides the player character with runes at various shrines. The Outsider ties into many elements of the game world: he is the sworn enemy of the zealot Overseers, who rule the totalitarian government of Dunwall as a repressive theocracy persecuting what it calls "witchcraft" along with any form of political dissidence. The Outsider's runes are carved from whalebone, which relates to an economy driven by whaling and whale-oil, the latter of which fuels the engines of Dunwall's electro-steampunk Victorian technology. The Outsider occupies a space of metaphysical otherness: he is the god of witches in a fundamentalist state, the remnants of magic in a rickety scientific orthodoxy. His moral Otherness in the world of Dunwall—which renders him neither good, evil, or neutral—also allows magic to be an amoral force, the applications of which are left to the player character, who can use his abilities to diminish casualties through non-lethal solutions or to wreak havoc with gusts of wind and swarms of rats. Most likely, the player will end up toggling between these two extremes and all the gray area in between, allowing magic to be something slippery and alien—tied into all the systems and stories of the game world but bound by none of them.

Another strength of the *Dishonored* magic system is the potential for emergent combinations of its powers. The player might use Bend Time to slow time down, then blink behind a guard, stabbing him undetected and triggering the first tier of the Shadow Kill ability, which causes unalerted enemies to disappear into ash when killed. In a talk at the Game Developer's Conference 2013 "Empowering the Player in a Story-Rich World," lead designers Raphael Colantonio and Harvey revealed that there were originally forty abilities, which were later pared down to the ones currently in the game. It is not the number of abilities which make the *Dishonored* magic system interesting, but rather their unexpected combinations based on player ingenuity to progress in the game's non-linear missions.

3.20 *MAGICKA*

The combinatorial strengths of *Dishonored* contrast with a very different, quirkier form of combinatorial logic in *Magicka*. In *Magicka*, players control four diminutive wizards who combine ten elements (two of them hidden), represented by colored runes, in order to cast spells. *Magicka* proves that it is possible to create a linguistic, combinatorial magic system that functions effectively in a fast-paced, multiplayer context. Game designers often remark that a gestural, combinatorial, or otherwise immersive magic system is fine within the context of a puzzle-centric single-player game, but that such a system cannot function in a multi-player environment in which competitive or cooperative response depends on speed. The success of *Magicka* proves the opposite: that a combinatorial magic system can function in such an environment provided certain conditions are met. First, the game must rely on many combinations of a small number of elements.

Magicka allows players to combine five elemental runes at a time and to direct them, resulting in 1123 spell combinations (mapped by Georgia Tech scholar Ben Mulder on an intricate bar graph), as well as several unique spells called Magicks. Second, the controls need to be simple. In *Magicka*, the elemental runes are mapped to the keys QWER and ASDF, chosen because of their adjacency to each other on two parallel rows of a standard QWERTY keyboard. Players direct spell effects through the three buttons on the mouse (right, middle, and left) in order to cast spells on the environment, the self, or the weapon. Area of effect spells and enchantments of weapons require the addition of the shift key, as in shift-left for imbuing weapons or shift-right for area of effect spells. Third, the game's magic system needs to resonate with the themes of its gameplay. In the case of *Magicka*, the magic system resonates with the game's quirky and bizarre sense of humor by allowing for friendly fire, thereby permitting (or encouraging) players to kill their own parties in an ill-timed explosion of flaming death. While such an effect would be frustrating in a different kind of game, in *Magicka* (which includes an expansion which puts its munchkin wizards in Vietnam) it is darkly hilarious. Consequently, the emergent possibilities of unintentional spell combinations performed under time pressure become opportunities for exciting gameplay, in which the worst-case scenario of total party kill may in fact be highly humorous. *Magicka* spells even self-referentially poke fun at the humor of unexpectedly game-breaking combinations, as in the "Crash to Desktop" spell.

3.21 MAGICAL GESTURES

Whether through a wave of the hand or a flick of the wand, gestures are an integral part of magic. Drawing signs in the air is an integral part of the Golden Dawn magic system and Aleister Crowley's work influenced by this system. In particular, Golden Dawn mages draw pentagrams to invoke or banish the five elements, as well as hexagrams to invoke or banish planetary energies. The connection of magic to gesture is heightened by its double connections to religious ritual on the one hand and stage illusionism (a.k.a. conjuring) on the other. Religious ritual is filled with sacred gestures designed to consecrate or protect, such as the cross that Catholics trace over their bodies (a gesture which itself appears in the Lesser Banishing Ritual of the Pentagram as the kabbalistic cross). Figure 3.12 shows the gestures in the Lesser Invoking and Banishing Rituals of the Pentagram. Other sacred religious gestures include the swinging of an incense vessel, or censer, as well as the Elevation of the Host (the communion wafers transfigured as the body of Christ) by Catholic priests.

The Hermetic Order of the Golden Dawn was a mystical society of the late nineteenth and early twentieth centuries. The Golden Dawn systematized many occult theories and practices.

At the other end of the spectrum of seriousness, stage illusionism is often referred to as sleight of hand, prestidigitation (quick fingers),

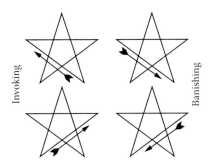

FIGURE 3.12   Lesser Invoking and Banishing Pentagrams.

and legerdemain (French for light of hand). Manual dexterity used to deceive and thereby create a sense of wonder was common to stage illusionists, earning them the name of jugglers even when they did not literally toss spherical balls. The Magician card of the tarot deck is known as Le Jongleur (the juggler) in its original incarnation in the Marseilles deck.

A number of games have attempted gestural magic systems, starting with Peter Molyneux's 2001 god game *Black & White* and extending up to more recent games like *The Void* (2008), *Sorcery* (2012), and *Fable: The Journey* (2012). In the interim, the following games also feature gestural spellcasting interfaces: *The Summoning* (1992), *Black & White* (2001), *Arx Fatalis* (2002), *Castlevania: Dawn of Sorrow* (2005), *Okami* (2006), *Deep Labyrinth* (2006), *Harry Potter and the Order of the Phoenix* (2007), Jonathan Blow's *Galstaff* (2007), *Lego Harry Potter* (2010), *Ni No Kuni* (2011), *Shadow Cities* (2011), and *Paranormal Activity: Sanctuary* (2011).

Recipes for a gestural system would tend to utilize SDK's for gesture recognition, such as the OpenNI gesture library for the Kinect or Microsoft's official Kinect SDK. Gestural technologies will continue to develop and change, so it is important to approach gestural design from a user experience perspective, focusing on designing a smooth and immersive interface for the end user. There are several books on the subject of gestural interface design, including Daniel Wigdor's *Brave NUI World*: *Designing Natural User Interfaces for Touch and Gesture* and Dan Saffer's *Designing Gestural Interfaces*. A more general approach to the creation of user experience through interface design and feedback mechanisms in games is Steve Swink's *Game Feel: A Game Designer's Guide to Virtual Sensation*.

3.21.1 Early Gestural Interfaces: *The Summoning* and *Black & White*

One of the earliest examples of a quasi-gestural interface is *The Summoning*, a top-down isometric CRPG that allows players to memorize spells using hand gestures that vaguely resemble American Sign Language (ASL). Unlike ASL, however, player hand gestures are somewhat arbitrary rather than mimicking the shapes of letters. Due to technological limitations, players do not actually make these gestures with their own hands or through drawing, but rather they line up icons representing the gestures on a tray in the graphical user interface. If a player successfully lines up a sequence of gestures for a spell, then the spell is memorized and ready to be cast. The requirement that spells be memorized on a separate memorization screen that pauses action resembles the Vancian magic system, but without the stringent requirement that all spells be memorized only once a day, after a full night's sleep. Figure 3.13 shows the hand gestures and alphabetic equivalents in *The Summoning*.

One feature common to these games, though by no means necessary, is a technology or set of technologies that makes the process of tracing gestures easier, more natural, or more precise. In many cases, such technologies are optional supplements to already built-in technologies, such as the mouse, which can be made smoother through the addition of extra peripherals. For example, *Black & White* allows players to use the mouse to trace gestures, but it also permits the use of the P5 virtual reality glove, a peripheral that allows the player's hand to map directly onto the in-game godlike hand of the avatar. Figure 3.14 shows a P5 virtual reality glove.

3.21.2 *Galstaff*

In 2007, Jonathan Blow created, prototyped, and presented *Galstaff*, a prototype with a gestural magic system as part of the Experimental Gameplay Workshop that he founded at the Game Developer's Conference. Blow intended *Galstaff* as a response to games like *Black & White* and *Harry Potter and the Order of the Phoenix*, which Blow

FIGURE 3.13 Hand Gestures from *The Summoning*. (Image by Event Horizon.)

FIGURE 3.14 P-5 Virtual Reality Glove. (Courtesy of CyberWorld, Inc. www. cwonline.com)

criticized as having a low degree of responsiveness to player input. In contrast, the detailed shapes of gestures drawn in his prototype were intended to affect various parameters of each spell, such as range, duration, and intensity.

3.21.3 *Castlevania: Dawn of Sorrow*

Both *Castlevania: Dawn of Sorrow* and *Deep Labyrinth* take advantage of the stylus interface of the Nintendo DS in order to allow players to draw magical signs, referred to as magic seals in *Dawn of Sorrow*. In *Dawn of Sorrow*, players must use magic seals to permanently destroy bosses after killing them by normal means. Otherwise, the bosses will resurrect. The seals also function passively as keys to new levels or boss rooms. If the player approaches the doors to these rooms while in possession of the seal, the seal is automatically drawn on the screen, and the door opens. The seals thus function as gating mechanisms in the highly non-linear level design of *Dawn of Sorrow*, pacing player progress by restricting access to certain areas until the player finds the required seal.

There are five seals of increasing complexity, each to be used in a particular area of the castle, as shown below. The interface used to draw the seals consists of a larger circle with small, glowing circular points that players connect with the stylus in order to draw the seals. A practice mode allows players to build up their skills at drawing certain seals in a non-pressured situation. The first seals are not terribly difficult to draw, and the d-pad and stylus can both be successfully used if the player holds the stylus between two fingers of the right hand while also using fingers of the right hand to press buttons. The transition between d pad and stylus would be awkward if the player kept the stylus in the groove under the DS where it is ordinarily stored. A player might also be deeply frustrated by accidentally drawing a seal incorrectly after a boss fight, which would result in the boss being resurrected. In practice, though, the use of dots on the circle as connectors between the lines of the seals is a useful way of guiding players, allowing them to connect the dots rather than forcing them to draw the seals freehand. The connect the dots approach also makes gesture recognition easier, since a matching algorithm can break the seal into discrete line segments rather than attempting to make an overall judgment of how accurately the player traced the seal. The gestural system of *Dawn of Sorrow* is interesting and enjoyable in part because it contributes organically to an overall magic system, which also includes mechanics that allow players to absorb the souls of defeated enemies and either use the souls' powers or fuse them with weapons. Figures 3.15 through 3.19 show sigils from *Castlevania: Dawn of Sorrow*.

FIGURE 3.15   *Castlevania: Dawn of Sorrow* Sigil # 1.

FIGURE 3.16   *Castlevania: Dawn of Sorrow* Sigil # 2.

FIGURE 3.17   *Castlevania: Dawn of Sorrow* Sigil # 3.

FIGURE 3.18   *Castlevania: Dawn of Sorrow* Sigil # 4.

FIGURE 3.19   *Castlevania: Dawn of Sorrow* Sigil # 5.

3.21.4 *Deep Labyrinth*

The gestural spellcasting of *Deep Labyrinth* resembles *Dawn of Sorrow* but is more arbitrary and complex. Players trace runes, called kyrie characters, into a three-by-three grid, either by tapping the points associated with the spell or by actually drawing from the beginning to the end points. For example, the kludon (frost) spell requires a swipe from the bottom right square in the grid to the middle square. The use of the grid allows for easier input and detection of player gestures by allowing for discrete line segments and thus functions much like the connecting points around the circle in *Dawn of Sorrow.*

The contrast between *Dawn of Sorrow* and *Deep Labyrinth* reminds us that constructing a gestural magic system means choosing a carefully limited number of gestures and keeping those gestures relatively simple. This principle is important, since evolving technology can sometimes tempt us as designers to confuse variety and complexity of gestures with elegance. Such a temptation is especially strong given that gesture recognition is becoming increasingly sophisticated with the advent of peripherals like the Nintendo Wiimote and Wiimote Plus, Microsoft Kinect, and the PlayStation Move. In particular, the Kinect can detect full body movements. The touch screens of the iPhone and iPad are also excellent platforms for gestural interfaces. However, gestures are still somewhat imprecise.

A handful of gestures is probably adequate, ranging from five to ten or, at the upward boundaries of a fully developed magical language, twenty. The Nintendo DS game *Deep Labyrinth* features more than fifty individual gestures, resulting in too many spells for most players to remember (and many of these spells serve only a single restrictive purpose, such as opening a particular door). At the other end of the spectrum, *Castlevania: Dawn of Sorrow* features a total of five magical seals, each of which serves only to slay a particular boss on a particular level. Somewhere in the middle is *Arx Fatalis*, a first-person RPG for the Xbox and PC in which players trace runes as part of a larger magical language (see *Arx Fatalis*). As an example of economy and elegance of full-body gestures using the Kinect, *Fable: The Journey* stands out.

3.21.5 *Fable: The Journey*

Fable: The Journey, which allows players to cast spells gesturally using the Kinect, is an installment of Peter Molyneux's *Fable* series. Gabriel, the protagonist, acquires a set of enchanted gauntlets that serve as the narrative rationale for controlling spells through arm movements. The combination of first-person perspective and gestural controls is uniquely and deeply immersive in ways that even *The Elder Scrolls*, with its focus on first-person casting, can manage. Many of the spells themselves, such as bolt and push, operate on the paradigm of magic projectiles that affect enemies or the environment in fairly standard ways. Yet, the method of casting is highly intuitive, since pushing forward with the hands correlates naturally with pushing elements in the environment. The counter spell, which allows players to deflect attacks by brushing one's hand perpendicularly across the body and face, also feels instinctively natural as a reaction to an oncoming projectile in everyday life. These gestures feel non-arbitrary in the sense that they would be naturally connected to performing related tasks in daily life. Hence, the *Fable* interface lives up to the term natural user interface sometimes used to refer to gestural and touch-screen interfaces.

Paradoxically, the most magical aspects of the system are non-combat related, as when the protagonist touches a pool in order to gaze into the future, or places a hand on his beloved horse's wounds in order to heal them. The vision in the pool is a classic example of the actual occultist practice of scrying, specifically water-based divination called hydromancy, as well as a gameplay implementation of the scene in which Frodo consults Galadriel's mirror in a pivotal, magic-defining moment from *Fellowship of the Rings* (see Chapter 4 and Chapter 8).

3.21.6 Guidelines and Recipes for Gestural Magic Systems

In addition to carefully balancing the number of gestures, each gesture needs to be memorable, a quality which can be increased by making any given gesture meaningfully connected to the quality it signifies. For example, in the iPhone game *Crow*, two of the most heavily used gestural spells are for attacking and healing. The attacking gesture is a diagonal swipe across an enemy, which correlates naturally with the gesture of lashing out with talons. Healing the crow avatar involves tracing a circle, suggestive of restoring wholeness and health.

By limiting the number of gestures to a distinct, memorable set, programmers can then create a matching algorithm for a gesture. It is perfectly possible to prototype a gestural magic system within a text-based interactive framework, as I have done in the following recipe using Inform7.

RECIPE 16:   A BASIC GESTURAL SYSTEM IN INFORM7

```
Recipe 2: Gestural Spellcasting Recipe:
Table 3 - Gestures
Topic Appearance      Sephirah     Implement
"pentagram" "You trace a blue pentagram"   "Geburah"    Wand
"hexagram"  "You trace a violet hexagram" "Tiphareth"  Cup

Understand "sigilize [text]" as sigilizing.
Sigilizing is an action applying to one topic.

Carry out sigilizing:
say "You need to trace a particular magical gesture."

Instead of sigilizing a topic listed in the Table of
    Gestures:
say "[appearance entry], the sigil of [sephirah entry]."

Understand "sigilize [text] with [something]" as sigilizing
    it with.
Sigilizing it with is an action applying to one topic and
    one thing.

Carry out sigilizing it with:
say "You need to trace a particular magical gesture."

Instead of sigilizing a topic listed in the Table of
    Gestures with something:
say "[appearance entry], the sigil of [sephirah entry], with
the [second noun][line break]";
if the topic is "pentagram":
                now the Daimon is in the Sanctum;
                say "A dark flame swirls in the summoning
                    triangle. A Daimon is here."
```

In this recipe, the verb "sigilize" takes the place of the more natural "trace," which is a word restricted to Inform7's internal debugging features. The program provides basic feedback to a player's attempt to summon a demon into a triangle by tracing gestures, such as a pentagram or a hexagram (which stand for branches of the tree of life, or sephiroth) with magical implements, such as a wand or a cup. If the player traces a pentagram, a demon is successfully summoned into the ritual triangle. The recipe could be extended to an arbitrary number of gestures, kabbalistic sephiroth, and implements. The core of the recipe is the use of tables to set up a set of symbolic correspondences linked to a particular gesture, which are registered in feedback through text substitution. When a player sigilizes a gesture, they receive feedback of the form, "You traced x sigil with y implement, which corresponds to z sephiroth," as well as feedback about summoning a demon if they trace the correct sigil. By extending the table of correspondences and including a column or table of summoned demons, this basic recipe could be extended into a gesture-based system of ceremonial magic, using traditional Golden Dawn correspondences or others invented from whole cloth.

In addition to this simple text-based recipe, the gestural recognition algorithm by Didier Brun at bytearray.org provides a good example of the principles for constructing a gestural system. Brun's algorithm, written in Flash Actionscript 2.0, is downloadable and runnable from the link http://www.bytearray.org/?p=91. Figure 3.20 illustrates Brun's flash gesture recognition method. Brun succinctly explains his algorithm as follows:

Algorithm

1. Each letter is defined by an 8-direction gesture sequence
2. The mouse moves are saved with the same 8-direction sensibility
3. A Levenshtein distance is calculated from each letter to the user moves
4. The algorithm returns the best candidate (lowest Levenshtein cost)

In this algorithm, Brun breaks down each gesture (such as a letter of the alphabet) into a sequence of small movements in one of eight directions.

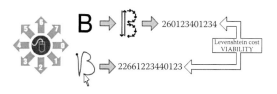

FIGURE 3.20 Flash Gesture Recognition Method. (Image by Didier Brun. Used with permission.)

Since each of these directions is labeled as a number, the gesture can then be encoded as a string of digits, each of which represents one small directional movement in the overall tracing of the gesture. The sequences of digits encode the ideal form of the gesture, against which actual user gestures are measured. When a user attempts to trace a gesture like a letter of the alphabet, the algorithm also encodes the user-traced gesture as a sequence of digits. The algorithm then searches for the closest match of the string, seeking the route of least resistance (calculated through Levenshtein distance, the minimum number of edits required to change one string into another). Using this algorithm, the code matches this sequence of digits against the ideal version in order to make an educated guess as to which gesture the player was trying to trace.

3.22 MAGIC IN MMORPGS

Multimodal, ritualistic magic faces its greatest challenge in one of the genres that most urgently needs it but is least prepared to accommodate it: the online role-playing game. Magic figures heavily in many MMORPGs (massively multiplayer online role-playing games), also known as MMOs. From the beginning of the genre, many MMOs have aspired in part to be adaptations of fantasy role-playing games, including both tabletop role-playing games and single-player computer games. Because magic was a central element of the games that influenced MMO designers, magic also found its way into many MMOs.

Designing magic for MMOs has its own unique challenges that result from the massively online structure of these games. MMOs are networked and community-driven, with their unique appeal stemming almost entirely from opportunities for real-time competition and collaboration with other players. Hence, magic that seeks to emulate ritual in the multimodal, combinatorial way described in this book will tend to put players at a disadvantage in competitive situations if the ritual consumes time during casting. In a PvP (player versus player) duel, a player who can blast a fireball instantaneously has an advantage over one who first has to place candles and reagents at the points of a pentagram. However, if the ritual takes place outside of combat, either before it chronologically or as another part of gameplay (such as solving a puzzle), then elaborate, ritualized magic is possible in MMOs. Moreover, some alternate controllers and peripherals (similar to the motion-sensing Kinect, the virtual reality headset called the Oculus Rift, or the force-feedback driven Novint Falcon) may eventually be well-integrated with

PCs in the same manner as consoles, allowing multimodal dimensions of magic to occur in real-time without interfering with online competition or collaboration.

An MMO is an online role-playing game in which many players can participate simultaneously, acting out an ongoing battle both against computerized enemies and other players.

A massively multiplayer online game in which dueling mages fling gesture-based spells at one another may not be currently feasible in 2012 because of lag, but it could easily be possible in another generation or two of technology. It is also difficult to predict what may occur in the world of online gaming in the near and far future. Big-budget, large-scale MMOs like *World of Warcraft* once dominated online gaming, but attempts to produce a "WoW-Killer" or MMO that would supplant *World of Warcraft* in terms of number of long-term subscribers have been dubiously successful. Online social games in the casual market, such as *Farmville*, have also passed through a period of extreme success that may already be waning in 2012. The best we can do as designers is to learn from the history of magic in MMOs, with the knowledge that whatever lessons we gain will need to be carefully adapted to the present moment and the changes that it brings.

In the history of MMOs the most relevant classifications of spells have to do with combat effects. MMO spells are overwhelmingly combat-driven, and they tend to be most easily classified according to what kind of damage they deal. Classifications include DPS (damage per second) and DoT (damage over time). The classification AoE (area of effect) refers to the range of damage dealt (i.e. spreading over an area, like a fire or an explosive blast). Other common spell types include buffs, which increase the strengths of the caster or other players, and debuffs, which weaken enemies. Terms like DPS and DoT can refer to many aspects of MMOs besides spells, including the roles played by various party members (such as a melee DPS character who functions as a party's "tank," dealing massive damage to a boss and shielding other players from attacks). That spells share these names indicates that magic systems in MMOs are rarely separate from combat. Indeed, MMO spells are often glorified artillery, unleashed through the simple and repetitive click of a button. MMO magic is in some ways the least magical of all game magic, and the most in need of re-enchantment.

3.22.1 *Ultima Online*

To learn lessons from the past, it is best to start at the beginning. The roots of MMOs stretch back as far as early MUDs (Multi User Dungeons/ Domains): text-based virtual worlds that were often direct adaptations of *Dungeons & Dragons*. One of the first MMOs, if not the first, was *Ultima Online* (1997), a direct adaptation of Richard Garriott's fantastic and innovative *Ultima* series of single-player computer role-playing games. While the *Ultima* series has long featured a complex magic system that evolved from game to game, *Ultima: Online* simplified this system. While the game still features spells named after the runic invocations from the earlier games (such as "In Mani Ylem" for "create food"), players activate these spells by double-clicking on icons in a spellbook or by binding the spells to macros. Players no longer input the spells through the keyboard, as in *Ultima IV-VI*, or by configuring runes, as in *Ultima Underworld I and II*. Spells do still require the classic eight reagents, such as sulfurous ash and black pearl. As the *Ultima Online* Guide explains, players learn spells by collecting scrolls and placing them inside spellbooks, with eight available spellbooks for particular character classes (mage, mystic, necromancer, ninja, paladin, samurai, spellweaver, and bard). Figure 3.21 shows the spellbook interface from *Ultima Online*.

3.22.2 *Everquest*

After *Ultima Online*, one of the first massively popular MMOs was *Everquest* (1999), developed by Brad McQuaid, Steve Clover, and Bill Trost. As Almar's Guide to *Everquest* explains, the game features five schools of magic, with names derived from *Advanced Dungeons & Dragons*: Alteration, Abjuration, Conjuration, Evocation, and Divination. Alteration and abjuration encompass different types of buffs, whereas conjuration involves summoning pets and weapons into existence. The school of evocation includes damage spells, and divination classifies any other kind of spell. As Almar's Guide succinctly observes, "All the 'Weird' spells go here." While this comment is meant dismissively in context,

FIGURE 3.21   *Ultima Online* Spellbook. (Image by Origin Systems and Electronic Arts.)

it nevertheless indicates a space for innovation. True magic is weird in the sense of running counter to the status quo; otherwise, magic would not be magical. Divination spells often entail extensions of perception, such as the spell "Assiduous Sight," which allows the caster to transfer her vision into a target, allowing her to see through the eyes of another character. Stealth spells, including invisibility and camouflage, also qualify as divination. Much like *Ultima Online*, *Everquest* includes a user interface based on a spellbook, in which spells can be learned and then memorized by being dragged to gemstone slots at the side. Figure 3.22 shows a spellbook interface from *Everquest*.

In terms of lore, the magic of *Everquest* originates from the energy of alternate planes of existence. Figure 3.23 depicts Bill Trost's conceptual diagram of the *Everquest* cosmology.

FIGURE 3.22   *Everquest* Spellbook. (Image by Sony.)

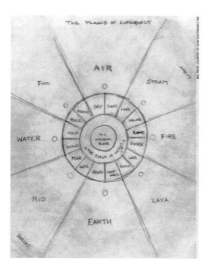

FIGURE 3.23   *Everquest* Cosmology. (Image by Sony.)

3.22.3 *World of Warcraft*

After *Everquest*, the next groundbreaking MMO is *World of Warcraft* (a.k.a. *WoW*), a massively popular and successful game that at one time claimed fifteen million subscribers. *World of Warcraft* suffers from many of the common problems with MMO magic, including a simplified interface that involves clicking spell icons repeatedly and waiting for them to cool down. *World of Warcraft* spells are also predominantly combat-based, falling into the trap of mage as glorified artillery. Mages and warlocks are two primary casting classes in *World of Warcraft*, in addition to hybrid classes like druid, shaman, and death knight that can fill multiple roles. As the WoW wiki explains, mages perform powerful AoE damage attacks, while warlocks perform DoT attacks and summon demons as pets. Skill trees allow for multiple routes of specialization, so that a warlock could choose to specialize in DoT or demonology. Druid spells involve shapeshifting for a variety of purposes, and the death class involves a unique enchantment skill called runeforging that allows them to inscribe a particular rune on a given weapon in order to imbue it with magical powers.

3.22.4 *Age of Conan*

After *World of Warcraft*, various MMO designers have attempted to fill a similar fantasy niche while breaking new ground that would distinguish them from competition, resulting in differing approaches to magic. In particular, Funcom's *Age of Conan* offers a distinctly dark, visceral approach to magic inspired by the gritty low fantasy of Robert E. Howard (the author of the original Conan stories, discussed in the chapter on magic in fantasy). The designers of *Age of Conan* state their goal of an innovative magic system clearly on their official wiki:

> There is a fully functional magic system that closely relates to the Conan lore and the original books of Robert E. Howard. Just as we're making huge advancements in the field of combat in massive online games, we're also handling magic and spellcasting quite differently than other games in the genre. Spellcasting will not only require certain skills and feats of your character, but there is also a very interactive system to it that will take human skill to master.

This developer commentary emphasizes a few key characteristics of *Age of Conan*. Magic is not just a sprawling list of spells invented off the cuff, but a coherent system intended to reflect a larger fictional lore through mechanics. The system requires skillful *player* interaction rather than relying only on skills possessed by *characters*, which could be acquired by grinding and then forgotten about. Moreover, the developers explain that the magic of *Age of Conan* is intended to look and feel differently than the average MMO:

> The traditional fireball-tossing magic users in pointy hats, with puffs and multicolored robes, are not part of the Hyborian universe. In Conan's age, magic is dangerous, hidden, and dark. Men who meddle with dark magic may fall to its temptation and powers, so magic uses you as much as you use it! Naturally, the ultimate power comes when you are able to walk the fine line—the one between destruction and creation.

This quotation vividly dismisses the clichés of many magic systems, highlighting the reasons why game magic needs to be re-enchanted. "Fireball-tossing magic users in pointy hats" accurately describes mages in many games, highlighting both the mechanical repetitiveness of elemental damage spells and the cartoonish art style of a Tolkien-influenced fantasy wizard. Instead, the *Age of Conan* developers express the heart of their game's magic in three words: "dangerous, hidden, and dark." Hidden implies potential secrets at work in the game's magic, such as spells and spell combinations that are not officially described in the documentation. Dangerous implies the potential for unintended recoil of a Faustian bargain or demonic pact, requiring sorcerers to "walk a fine line" or face the consequences.

The mechanic at the heart of these potential dangerous consequences is called spellweaving, which allows the player to combine spells to create a more powerful spell. Spellweaving simulates an elaborate ritual in that the mage's avatar is rooted in place, caught in a trance and unable to perform other actions as they weave spells. If the player combines too many spells of too great power, the spellweaving could recoil as a curse. In addition, players accumulate "magic burden" as they weave spells, and this burden can produce further negative consequences if magic resources are not carefully shepherded. The uniqueness of *Age of Conan*'s magic system is also seen in the demonologist, one of the game's three casting classes. The demonologist is a powerful DPS class that can also summon fearsome demons. In the ability to summon demons, the demonologist resembles

World of Warcraft's warlock class, but the demonologist's destructive abilities focus more on DPS rather than the DoT most commonly associated with the warlock. Whereas the dark lore associated with the *World of Warcraft* warlock is intriguing but somewhat cartoonish, the lore of the demonologist is unmitigated darkness. The official developer description of the demonologist class is poetic and dark, capturing both the danger and the beauty of the magic system as refracted through a particular class:

> The demonologist is the mightiest of sorcerers, wielding the power of hell and earth and capable of conjuring pillars of flame or titanic storms of electricity.
>
> So great is their occult knowledge they can bargain a servant of hell into doing their bidding; a guardian daemon of warped beauty and terrible might.
>
> Demonologists concentrate solely on sorcery and the potency of their spells is unmatched, as capable of eliminating a single enemy in a hellish inferno as destroying enemy lines with forks of lightning. They can sacrifice their own life-force in return for more occult power and they are most potent when they can devote their spell energies solely to attack.

This description has the aesthetic quality that might be called the sublime, distinguished from the beautiful by a sense of danger seen in natural phenomena like "titanic storms of electricity" and "pillars of flame." Even though these are fire-based spells, they are pushed to their infernal, mythic extreme (a quality they have in common with pyromancy in *Dark Souls*, in which fire ties together the game's entire mythology). Moreover, the description overtly embraces the occult, referencing "occult knowledge" and the concept of a "guardian daemon of warped beauty and terrible might." The spelling "guardian daemon," while charmingly archaic, also echoes the "daimon" or guardian spirit whose knowledge and conversation are sought by many ceremonial magicians. The designers of *Age of Conan* take a remarkably insightful approach to the magic system of their game by considering all aspects as part of the magic system: mechanics, themes, lore, and visual appearance.

3.22.5 *The Secret World*

Age of Conan paves the way for the innovations of another, later Funcom MMO: *The Secret World*. Conceived by Ragnar Tornquist, the designer of the famously elaborate adventure game *The Longest Journey*, *The Secret World* revolves around the theme of secrets in its every aspect, including its magic. Magic in *The Secret World* falls into three schools: blood, chaos, and elemental. Blood magic involves DoT attacks and healing, chaos magic entails summoning magical weapons and incapacitating enemies, and elemental magic offers blasts of DPS damage. Blood magic is the only school of magic that allows the player to overspend magic energy through an ability called blood offering, sacrificing health in order to cast spells without otherwise having sufficient energy to do so (see Chapter 4, Section 4.10.1). The chaos magic skills are directly from actual chaos magic practices (e.g. "gnosis," an early spell that refers to the altered states of consciousness key to chaos magic, as well as "paradigm shift," the deliberate exploitation of changes in frameworks of belief practiced by chaos magicians, as derived from a reading of science historian Thomas Kuhn). Chaos magic spells also contain references to the lore of the Discordians, occultists who base their ideas on a sect from the *Illuminatus!* trilogy (e.g. "Call for Eris"—a reference to the Greek goddess of chaos).

The magic of *The Secret World* is heavily tied in with the game's complex combat system, in which various spells interact with each other synergistically. Some spells put enemies into states (such as afflicted, penetrated, and hindered) which can then amplify the damage and probabilities of hits associated with other spells. Some spells build resources, whereas others consume them—allowing for complex loops of resource management and synergy. A player can equip only two weapons at once, including two spell foci if the player so chooses, and a player can equip a maximum of seven active skills and seven passive skills at a time. The vast number of possible combinations of weapons and skills results in many builds that can be switched out at any time, creating a deep flexibility that stems in part from the game's absence of character classes or levels. Players unlock magic spells as part of an ability wheel, in which abilities are nested within each other and uncovered recursively by spending ability wheels. While the ability wheel resembles a skill tree in some respects, players are able to fill in various slices of the pie at will, allowing them to continually customize a character rather than closing off some branches of a tree and choosing others. The magic of *The Secret World* partakes of this deep flexibility: because all characters are magically gifted, magic is simply another set of skills in a complex wheel of unlockable, interrelated abilities.

Yet, the real magic of *The Secret World* is the lore: the way that occultist thought pervades the entire world. The game takes place in a version of the real-life, modern world, in which all branches of myth and magic turn out to be true. The brilliance of the secret world is its willingness to integrate magic with its mission and puzzle structure. Many of the quests are ultimately acts of magic, in the manner of the fourth edition *Dungeons & Dragons* rituals, which were based on the quest spell from *The Tome of Magic*. The real magic in *The Secret World* often takes the form of puzzles, which often take the form of rituals (see Chapter 2, Section 2.7). For example, the player performs a magical ritual of evocation (spirit-summoning) by placing five raven feathers around a fountain to form a pentagram configuration, in order to summon a malefic scarecrow spirit. The player undertakes necromancy by deliberately dying in order to enter ghost form, then confronting the spirit of a murderer and re-enacting an incantatory children's rhyme by touching a certain set of white ravens. The player opens an Illuminati gate by ritualistically placing objects of power (including a yin-yang, a skull, a phoenix, and a pyramid).

A quest involving fictional diabolist Theodore Wicker exemplifies *The Secret World's* puzzle-driven magic. Before his disappearance, Wicker was a brilliant occultist driven by the theory that demons and humans once lived side by side. In order to communicate with Wicker's shade, the player must activate several séance circles comprised of a secret alphabet of runes, each of which has both a symbol and a name. In order to activate each circle, the player must spell out one of several phrases in Latin, each of which is relevant to Wicker's quest. While Wicker's journal provides a partial key phrase, the player must methodically decipher the runic alphabet, using careful pattern recognition skills and the process of elimination in order to determine which runes correspond to which letters. While performing these complex acts of decoding, the player inevitably learns the alphabet both by sight and name, resulting in almost involuntary chanting as one talks oneself through each puzzle. Players learn this alphabet of runes in much the same way that they learn the magical language of *Eternal Darkness*, through multiple channels of reinforcement.

3.23 THE MAGIC OF ALTERNATIVE CONTROLLERS

3.23.1 The Emotiv Epoc Headset: Mind Magic

The Emotiv Epoc headset is one of several peripherals that allows users to control a computer using brainwaves, thereby opening the way for the fulfillment of one of the central fantasies about magic: altering reality directly through the will. The designers and marketers and Emotiv have recognized this potential application of their hardware, proclaiming on their site that "for the first time, the fantasy of magic and supernatural power can be experienced." In particular, the Emotiv Epoc headset seems well-suited to the simulation of Force powers from the *Star Wars* universe and other telekinetic or psionic abilities that involve concentrating in order to alter the physical world by moving objects. One of the demo apps for the Emotiv Epoc offers a rudimentary version of this mystical scenario, in which the player takes the role of a kung fu monk on an island, learning to perform supernatural feats such as rebuilding a bridge with his mind.

Son of Nor, a game crowdfunded through Kickstarter at time of writing, offers a more complex version of a similar idea.

3.23.2 Tablet Magic

The popularity of mobile devices, especially tablets with touch-screen capabilities, holds great potential for designers of magic systems. In size, format, and interface, a tablet resembles a book, but a book augmented with multimedia and interactive functions that resemble those of a fabled magician's grimoire. Grimoires have always been multimedia compilations, densely illustrated with plates, charts, and diagrams. They have also always been interactive in the sense that they are intended as guides to practice, to be consulted as recipe books rather than perused passively.

Tablets are magic books, and some game designers have used this resemblance to create unique magical experiences on tablet and mobile platforms. The PS3 Wonderbook is a prime example of a peripheral created specifically for the Harry Potter game *Miranda Goshawk's Book of Spells*. Similarly, the independent game *Year Walk* uses the tablet as a device for a game about summoning spirits. *Year Walk* also features a companion app in the form of a *Year Walk Guide*, a grimoire complete with electronically rendered woodcuts and cryptic instructions for peering beyond the veil. *Spirit Camera*, a spiritual successor to the *Fatal Frame* series, includes a diary that functions as a set of augmented reality cards, allowing players to enter into the book and solve a set of arcane riddles. These games could all be thought of as augmented books in the sense of augmented reality, functioning as an informational overlay on the mundane world.

In addition to augmenting the book through multimedia and interactive elements, *Superbrothers Sword & Sworcery EP*, *Year Walk*, and *The Room* are all examples of independent games on tablets that push the boundaries of tablet magic, taking advantage of the unique capabilities of these devices to create touch and time-sensitive visions of sorcery that break with the past of conventional magic systems while preserving the all-important feeling of enchantment. *Superbrothers Sword & Sworcery EP* simulates the idea of magical timing by using the tablet's clock to coordinate in-game events, such as opening gates, with the real-world phases of the moon. The in-game tutorial guide, a psychiatrist non-player character (NPC) conducting an experiment into the psychological effects of mythology, advises that the third section of the game will take a lunar month to complete. This real-time element requires players to be aware of the cycles of nature, as well as committing to gameplay in a ritualistic manner at regular intervals during specified times. (Michael Brough's indie Roguelike VESPER.5, part of a ritual-themed game competition called Superfriends Ritual Pageant, takes the *Sword and Sworcery* premise one step further by allowing players only one turn per real-world day, thereby encouraging them to make playing the game a ritualistic aspect of their own daily routine.) Most if not all modern computers feature some form of onboard clock, yet the portability of tablets makes real-world time more directly relevant to gameplay, since the player might well be playing the game under the light of the moon. In keeping with its overall rock and roll aesthetics, the magic system of *Superbrothers Sword & Sworcery EP* is also musically driven and puzzle-centric through a unique touch-screen interface. The player summons forest spirits, called Sylvan Sprites, by drawing energy out of natural objects and entities, including water, sheep, and rainbows. By repeatedly touching the summoned sprites, the player invokes musical enchantments that consist of rising tones.

Each of these enchantments takes on a meditative, ritualistic mood, requiring the player to hold, press, and pause in particular combinations in order to make the player character focus energy. *Sword & Sworcery* also features its own variety of dream magic (see Chapter 4, Section 4.10.4), in which the player character must go dream walking inside the slumbering minds of NPCs. The outcome of these surreal dream sequences, which feature verbs such as "believe" that allow the player character to walk on water, depend upon the phases of the moon. The game thus ties together dream magic, moon magic, musical magic, and gestural magic into one highly unique and innovative game. Reinforcing the idea that true originality comes from creative adaptation of rich source material, the Superbrothers credit both mythic and literary sources for their game, which they acknowledge "has been built with the mythopoeic psychocosmology of Robert E. Howard's sword and sorcery stories in mind" (see Chapter 8, Section 8.3).

The Room makes equally creative use of historical source material in that it is a classic, first-person puzzle game in the style of *Myst* that allows players to manipulate a complex contraption of nested boxes, which are gradually revealed to have occult significance. The process of opening the box is reminiscent of the ritualistically charged manipulations of the Lament Configuration (see Chapter 2, Section 2.7). Like *Year Walk*, *The Room* requires abstract pattern recognition, which begins with highly local patterns (like a hexagon on the side of a wooden panel) and then extends them to cosmic designs (such as the configuration of stars that open the door to another dimension). Success in both games entails recognition of larger patterns that extend from small to big—what ancient magicians would have called the correspondence between the microcosm (little universe) and the macrocosm (large universe). The intricate, embedded, and interlinked puzzles of *The Room* are chilling and eerie, evoking a sense of mysterious wonder that feels deeply magical in a way that few conventional magic systems do. The game uses puzzles to simulate an elaborate magical device that blurs the lines between sorcery and technology, requiring all of the player's wits to unlock its secrets.

As with tablets, the unique affordance of mobile devices such as the PlayStation Vita and the Nintendo 3ds have both enabled unique magic systems in games such as *Soul Sacrifice* and *Crimson Shroud*.

3.24 AUGMENTED REALITY AND LOCATION-BASED MAGIC

Tablet and mobile computing often intersect with the concept of augmented reality (displaying digital information as an overlay over the real world), and location-based gaming (using real-world locations as virtual game environments, often through augmented reality). These technologies mirror aspects of magical practice, which frequently entails the projection of a symbolic overlay—such as the Tree of Life or a pantheon of spirits—over physical reality. Like augmented reality, magic enables the enchantment of place by transforming seemingly mundane sites into shrines and temples. The "thin places" of Celtic lore—spots where the veil between the physical and the spirit world have grown thin—are realized through augmented reality technologies, in which the barrier between digital and physical becomes permeable. *Shadow Cities* and *Paranormal Activity: Sanctuary* both draw upon the resources of augmented and location-based gaming in order to simulate aspects of magic. *Shadow Cities* is a location-based MMO about battling mages, in which the GPS technologies of mobile phones allow players to compete for magical territory within maps based on their actual locations. Mobile touch interfaces also enable gestural spellcasting.

Paranormal Activity: Sanctuary, a tie-in with the *Paranormal Activity* horror movie about a demonic haunting, starts from the same GPS-driven, location-based premise as *Shadow Cities*, but shifts into first person to allow players to capture and exorcise demons using a built-in phone camera. Players close hell-mouths and other nexuses of demonic energy using gesture-based spells.

Having examined the many ways that players can control a simulated reality through magic, it is time to think about what aspects of reality can be controlled.

CHAPTER 4

Schools of Game Magic

4.1 CHAPTER SUMMARY

The definition of a magic system from the introduction could be sharpened from "any set of rules designed to simulate supernatural powers and abilities" to "any set of rules and symbols designed to simulate the alteration of reality through the will." This definition echoes Crowley's first axiom from *Magick in Theory and Practice* ("magic is the science and art of causing change to occur in conformity with will"), though it can apply to games without requiring designers to buy into any particular philosophical scheme. Rather, an appreciation of magic requires only a little reflection on the profound mystery of the will: by deciding to do something, we can make it happen. For example, we focus our will to pick up a glass of water at lunch, and we do pick it up. Magic is an extension of similar taken-for-granted acts of will into a more profound longing: to control not just our immediate surroundings through the direct use of our body, but to shape nature, technology, other human beings, and the spirit world through the force of the will.

Perhaps most specifically, the fascination with magic stems from a desire to guide and shape the forces that govern the course of our individual human lives. The exercise of will to create change in life is murky and difficult, thwarted as it often is by forces both internal and external beyond our control. But in games, there is the potential of mastery, of understanding rules and then manipulating them through strategy in order to achieve a desired outcome. "Here I rule" is a marketing slogan of *Magic: The Gathering*, a declaration sometimes accompanied by depictions of a skinny adolescent smirking confidently while surrounded by fearsome monsters. As gamers, many of us identify with that sentiment.

As magic systems in games evolve, various forms of alteration of reality become formalized into types or "schools" of magic to categorize the ways in which players can alter a simulated reality. As early as 1976, Gary Gygax reflected on the varied possible effects of spells in his article "The D & D Magic System":

> Spells do various things, and just what they do is an important consideration, for some order of effect in regard to the game would have to be determined. Magic purports to have these sorts of effects: 1) the alteration of existing substance (including its transposition or dissolution); 2) the creation of new substance; 3) the changing of normal functions of mind and/or body; 4) the addition of new functions to mind and/or body; 5) summon and/or command existing entities; and 6) create new entities. In considering these functions, comparatively weak and strong spells could be devised from any one of the six. Knowing the parameters within which the work was to be done then enabled the creation of the system.

Schools of magic evolve through the history of first-generation CRPGs such as *The Bard's Tale* and *Wizardry* until they solidify into a fairly uniform set of spell effects, with variations in individual spell possibilities from game to game. For example, the classic *Bard's Tale* (1985) divides magic into four schools: conjuring (damage and production of magical items), sorcery (illusion), magic (lingering spell effects), and wizardry (summoning creatures).

As a relatively recent culmination of basic RPG magic schools (and of the single-player Western RPG generally), *The Elder Scrolls IV: Oblivion* (2006) offers a strong contemporary baseline for the possibilities of spell effects. Like *Oblivion* as a whole, the magic system is smoothly implemented and richly complex, if firmly grounded in the history of RPGs and not particularly original. *Oblivion* features six schools: Destruction (damage), Alteration (buffing), Illusion (sensory deceptions like invisibility and silence), Conjuration (summoning creatures, especially daedra), Restoration (healing), and Mysticism (harnessing unusual telekinetic effects and the ability to detect life by lighting up all living creatures on the map). The fascination of the school of mysticism in *Oblivion* suggests that magic systems can be most interesting from a gameplay perspective when they incorporate as many of the game's mechanics and systems as possible, rather than restricting themselves to combat or character statistics. This extension of magic beyond combat and healing (or its enmeshment with more sophisticated combat systems) requires clever programming to implement.

Based on a historical consideration of magic systems, common schools of magic, present in almost any RPG, include:

- Damage

- Healing

- Buffing (raising stats of character or item)

- Summoning

Less common schools include:

- Telekinesis

- Architecture (opening, closing, moving, building)

- Sight (or insight)

- Teleportation (especially interdimensional)

- Mapping and navigation

- Illusion and dispelling illusion

One problem with magic systems, especially those focused on damage and healing, is a tendency to rely on a simplistic cosmology based on the four classical elements of the ancient Greeks (earth, air, water, and fire). MMOs abound in fire and ice mages, as well as an endless parade of wizards, druids, and shamans who manipulate the powers of the four elements. Even obscure cult classics lauded by their devotees for innovative customizable spell systems (such as *Magic and Mayhem: The Art of Magic* [2001] and *The Dawn of Magic* [2005]) end up falling back on combinations of the four elements, sometimes with light and darkness or chaos and order thrown in for good measure. While this cosmology can result in many flashy damage spells with stunning particle effects and explosions, it is a reduction of human experience that soon seems routine rather than enchanted. The experiences of fire and water are certainly primal and compelling, as anyone who has witnessed a forest blaze or an ocean tempest can attest. Yet, both in day to day life and the furthest flights of our imaginations, we do more than admire campfires and swim; consequently, in simulated magic we should do more than throw fireballs and iceblasts.

In contrast to this simplification of reality down to four physical elements, schools of magic eventually evolve into or intersect with a larger cosmological ambition of mapping out reality. Pragmatic considerations of how to simulate alterations of reality leads to philosophical reflection on what aspects of reality can be altered, resulting in a kind of metaphysical taxonomy.

To display these abstract concepts in ways that are easily graspable for use in gameplay, designers often assign symbolic colors to schools of magic. Examples include:

- The color pie in *Magic: The Gathering* (1993)

- The eight winds of magic in *Warhammer* (both tabletop [1987] and online [2008])

- In *Eternal Darkness* (2002), the colors associated with the runic magick of the three Ancients (as well as a hidden purple rune, and an implied yellow school of magick discussed by Denis Dyack in *The Escapist*)

- The colors of magic corresponding to the spheres of magic in *Mage: The Ascension* (1993) 1. Correspondence: Purple 2. Life: Red 3. Prime: White 4. Entropy: Indigo 5. Matter: Brown 6. Spirit: Gold 7. Forces: Orange 8. Mind: Blue 9. Time: Green

- The nine colored pillars of Nosgoth in *Blood Omen: The Legacy of Kain* (1996) and their associated spheres of "Death, Conflict, States, Energy, Time, Dimension, Nature, Mind, and Balance"

In all of these examples, the cosmology simulated or implied by the schools of magic is substantially richer and more complex than the four elements or the opposition of law and chaos. Symbolic color also resonates with a deep-seated human association between mood and color (which results in entire design classes on color theory), as well as occultist tendency to assign esoteric meaning to color (as in the King and Queen scales of the Golden Dawn and their display in tarot as well as the Rosicrucian-inspired Vault of the Adepti). Figure 4.1 represents seven color-coded schools of magic that are particularly archetypal and resonant, and Figure 4.2 is

FIGURE 4.1 (See color insert.) Seven Schools of Magic. (Original image by Giles Timms.)

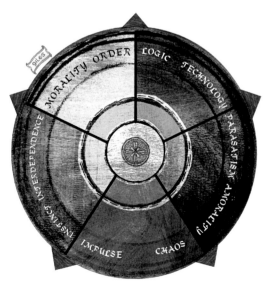

FIGURE 4.2 (See color insert.) An Abstract Representation of Five Influential Schools of Magic. (Original image by Giles Timms.)

FIGURE 4.3 (See color insert.) The Schools of Magic in This Chapter. (Original image by Giles Timms.)

an abstract representation of an influential division of schools of magic. Figure 4.3 is a color-coded representation of the schools of magic in this chapter.

The metaphysical taxonomy of reality in magic systems occurs to varying degrees of depth, ranging from flavor text in small or large amounts (the backs of *Magic: The Gathering* cards exemplify short flavor text, while the codexes/codices in *Dragon Age* contain more elaborate philosophical ruminations) to deep integration with gameplay. As such, these metaphysical mappings of reality tend to resemble both tarot and kabbalistic mappings of the universe in the tree of life, which in the Golden Dawn system has many associated attributions of colors, tarot cards, and other elements.

At this point, magic begins to intersect with planar lore: specifically, the idea of a multiverse with many different dimensions or planes, a notion derived from many realms of mysticism, including the theosophic lore of Madam Blavatsky (in which the particular term "plane" gains popularity). (As for multiverse, the word shows up in the philosophical writings of Henry James and is later popularized in the *Eternal Champion* saga of Michael Moorcock). The first meeting of the planes and magic appear in *Dungeons & Dragons* supplements, such as *The Manual of the Planes* (1987) and the *Planescape* campaign. The principle of planar magic is that "belief and imagination rule the multiverse," so that one's philosophical outlook can directly shape physical reality if those beliefs are held with sufficient strength. The planar cosmology results in a radial diagram called the Great Wheel, whose dimensions do correlate with the various alignment possibilities of the *D & D* moral universe. While the permutations of "lawful," "chaotic," "good," "evil," and "neutral" are in their own way as limited as the four elements, the factions of *Planescape* are philosophically nuanced and sophisticated, representing the dense concepts of solipsism (the Sign of One) and anarchism (the Xaosects). Figure 4.4 is the Great Wheel of the Planes in the *Dungeons & Dragons* universe.

Similarly, in *Magic: The Gathering*, dueling magicians called Planeswalkers gain their different colors of mana from multiple planes of existence in the multiverse. *Magic*'s colors bear a superficial relation to three out of the four elements (red = fire, green = earth, blue = water). Yet the five colors of mana represent a more abstract and nuanced set of

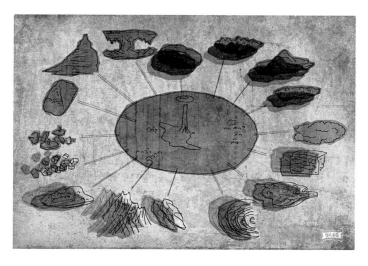

FIGURE 4.4   The Great Wheel of the Planes. (Original image by Giles Timms.)

human experiences. According to the official released color pie and the official site of *Magic*, the following color correspondences apply:

- Red = chaos and impulse

- Green = life and growth

- Blue = deception, calculation, and illusion

- Black = ambition and power

- White = order and justice

Magic: The Gathering is relatively unique in that its multi-colored schools of magic manifest primarily through gameplay and are only reinforced through flavor text and images. For example, as the school of ambition and control, black magic entails seeking mastery of the game at any cost, resulting in a mechanic of sacrifice in which black strategically gives up any resource (creatures, mana, life points, graveyard cards) in order to gain an advantage. As the school of freedom and impulse, red magic involves a mechanic of quickly doing damage that either gains a decisive advantage early or loses within a few rounds.

Passing beyond the colored schools of magic is the dark, often forbidden school of blood magic, which appears in many games as one example of how to push outside the constraints of elemental damage and law versus chaos cosmology. Blood Magic often shows up in horror-themed games, sometimes vampiric and at other times simply Gothic. All of the magic in *Vampire the Masquerade: Redemption* (2000) involves ghoulish varieties of blood magic, as does the similarly themed Gothic vampire game *Blood Omen: The Legacy of Kain* (1996). In *Blood Omen*, the developers connect the antihero protagonist's blood magic to actual occultism by way of an unattributed quotation from Aleister Crowley that opens the game: "There is a Magical operation of maximum importance: the Initiation of a New Aeon. When it becomes necessary to utter a Word, the whole Planet must be bathed in blood," which comes from the chapter in *Magick in Theory and Practice* called "On the Blood Sacrifice and Matters Cognate" (208). Blood Magic also shows up as a hidden school in *Dragon Age*. In each case, blood magic involves especially gory and disturbing varieties of RPG gameplay, ranging from gory damage and restoration spells to mental manipulation powered by human sacrifice.

The two most striking implementations of blood magic appear in the cult *Killer7* and the horror-themed squad-based shooter, *Jericho* (2007).

In *Killer7*, Kaede Smith, a svelte and ferocious beauty with a Gothic pallor, slits her own arms to release a spray of blood, which is then channeled by a phantom bondage queen in order to dissolve barriers. Kaede Smith's blood magic opens barriers, both literal and metaphorical, by using her trauma to see beyond the apparently solid limitations of the physical world as experienced by the other six assassin personalities. The metaphorical element of breaking through barriers is more strongly highlighted in a game that foregrounds its own preoccupation with transcendent insight through imagery of a third eye, including a health meter on the HUD which is itself a gradually opening and closing eye. (In *Killer7*, blood magic is part of a larger [and highly taboo] thematic preoccupation with disability and sadomasochism. Harman Smith, an assassin whose participation in a game of cosmic chess borders on godlike, is also a wheelchair-bound masochist who alternates dispensation of Zen-like wisdom with dominatrix sessions at the hands of a young woman doubling as his maid.) Figure 4.5 is an illustration of a magician performing a blood magic ritual.

A similar character appears in Clive Barker's *Jericho* in the form of Billie Church, a Blood Mage. *Jericho* is an enjoyably horrific game whose squad-based AI is somewhat broken, but this one element of magic in its paranormal squad-based arsenal is powerfully successful. Billie is a lapsed Southern Baptist, abused by her father and institutionalized in an insane asylum, where demons carved biblical verses into her flesh. In gameplay, she uses her katana to carve glyphs in her arms, which then explode into tendrils and bulbs of blood, enwrapping and immobilizing enemies, who can be sliced to ribbons or blown to bits. Like Kaede Smith, Billie makes

FIGURE 4.5   Blood Magic. (Original image by Giles Timms.)

FIGURE 4.6   Death Magic Ritual. (Original image by Giles Timms.)

a sacrifice of her most precious life fluid for insight, in a maneuver that Barker calls (in other contexts) "using the wound"—a deliberate exploitation of debilitation and trauma as a paradoxical means of shamanic enlightenment. Figure 4.6 is an illustration of a necromancer performing a death magic ritual.

Barker's use of blood magic parallels his own attempts as a designer to expand and deepen the variety of spell effects, seen perhaps more effectively in the cult horror classic FPS *Undying* (2001). *Undying* features a scry spell that allows players to see beyond the veil into hidden sights, such as apparitions and messages scrawled in blood. As Barker memorably and humorously explains:

> *Undying* is about being smarter, faster, cleverer, and a better magician than a gunslinger. It's about magic. The idea of scrying—seeing things you normally can't see—is very interesting. Much more interesting than a f_g big gun. We've seen that stuff before. I think that's had its day. I think as the new millennium has dawned, we are in a different kind of space. We think more spiritually, we think more about magic and transformation. We think more about the self rather than how many guns we can muster. I'm not saying that *Undying* is a metaphysical treatise, but its heart is not in the big gun territory (Twelker).

The presence of innovative spells in games like *Undying* and *Killer7* suggests that in order to expand the diversity of useful spell effects and schools of magic, we need to look outside of the RPG genre into other genres that sometimes simulate magic, like survival horror, first-person shooters, strategy games, and action-adventure games. Game genre shapes game world, which dictates the affordances and limitations of spellcasting, i.e. what is possible in magic and what is useful.

4.2 THE SCHOOLS OF MAGIC

Magic is traditionally divided up into schools of magic, which represent various aspects of reality over which the magician has control. For example, *Dungeons & Dragons* featured a classic set of eight schools: alteration, illusion, enchantment, divination, conjuration, invocation, necromancy, and abjuration. The term "school" is typically used in the same sense as a school of thought, referring to a particular perspective on the universe, as in the Platonic school of philosophy or the Many Worlds school of quantum mechanics. The phrase "spell domain" would be equally accurate, especially if domain is defined in the software development sense as a particular subject area to which a language refers. Agile Development in particular refers to domain experts who have mastered whatever area of existence the software is intended to model or work with, such as finances, robotics, music, or weather.

School does not necessarily refer to an academic institution for learning and teaching, although the natural correlation between academic study and magical training has led to game narratives in which various approaches to magic are formally championed by particular academic colleges or sub-colleges. The academic structure of Hogwarts or the mages guilds in *Oblivion* are both examples; the members of each guild in *Oblivion* specialize in a particular school of magic, such as destruction or conjuration.

Schools of magic constitute a taxonomy of reality, in the sense of a methodical and ordered classification of the chaos of existence and experience into a structured and ordered whole. The domains are aspects of existence over which various spells operate, which typically represent deep, fundamental forces at work in the universe and the human psyche. Hence the schools of magic tend to be represented as geometrical figures (especially circles), representing the totality of magic and (indirectly) the totality of the powers at work in a simulated universe. Because the schools of magic represent the full range of forces in a given universe, the diagrams representing schools of magic often strongly resemble mythological diagrams that map out the relationships between the various gods. As explained in Chapter 6, Section 6.6, magic was referred to as theurgy, which means working with the gods.

In mythological and religious tradition, magic involves direct contact with deep spiritual forces, which myths serve to organize and explain. Sociologist of religion Peter Berger has defined mythologies and religions as symbol systems, which provide a particular culture with a totalizing vision of the world, also known as a worldview. In mythologies, these symbol systems often take the form of a pantheon, a word meaning "all the gods" that refers to the totality of all deities in a given culture. These deities tend to incarnate all of the forces, both external and psychological, that are important to a given culture. For example, the twelve major heavenly gods of the ancient Greeks (known as the twelve Olympians), each represent a different aspect of the cosmos, along with their counterparts (the underworld or chthonic gods). Taken together, the gods represent a map of all the forces in the cosmos in the form of a symbol system. Peter Carroll's collection of "psychocosms" or "mental maps" from *Liber Null* provides an excellent vision of the organized and balanced total visions provided by various symbol systems (40). Of particular relevance are the diagrams involving planetary symbols, since the names of planets are derived from the Greek and Roman gods. Many Renaissance images of the human body portrayed man as a microcosm, or little universe, comprised of the totality of the planets, gods, and elements. Figure 4.7 is a painting of the Twelve Olympians arranged in a circle that encompasses the whole of the universe. Figure 4.8 represents the human body as a microcosm, with symbols of the planetary gods.

The *Advanced Dungeons & Dragons* spell schools represent nine such fundamental categories or domains, which exert a heavy influence on many subsequent game magic systems. These nine schools resemble in many ways actual sub-systems of occult magic, though the *Advanced Dungeons & Dragons* system is much less subtle and more physical than actual historical occultism. The following schools of magic are mentioned by name in the first edition *Advanced Dungeons & Dragons Player's Handbook*, though they are not described as schools of magic until the

FIGURE 4.7 The Twelve Olympians.

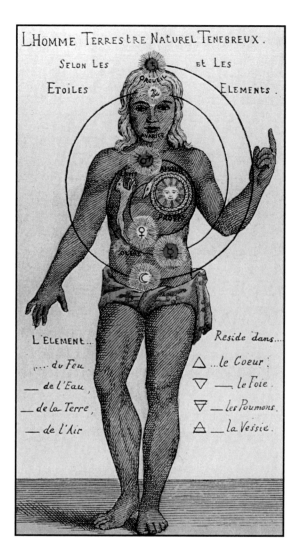

FIGURE 4.8   Man as Microcosm. (Image from Dover Pictura *Esoteric and Occult Art* [*Royalty-Free CD-ROM/Book Image Archive*]. Used with permission.)

second edition: Alteration, illusion, enchantment/charm, divination, conjuration/summoning, necromantic, invocation/evocation, and abjuration. The schools are slightly adjusted and formalized in the second edition Player's Handbook, which declares that "The nine schools of magic are Abjuration, Alteration, Conjuration/Summoning, Enchantment/Charm, Greater Divination, Illusion, Invocation/Evocation, Necromancy, and Lesser Divination." After multiple editions of *Dungeons & Dragons* left the concept of schools of magic vague, the second edition at last succinctly

FIGURE 4.9 *Dungeons & Dragons* Schools of Magic Diagram.

defines a school of magic as "an approach to magic and spellcasting that emphasizes a particular sort of spell," adding that each spell type draws upon a different form of energy (67). The second edition of *Advanced Dungeons & Dragons* also features a diagram which represents the totality of the schools in the form of a nine-pointed star like a compass rose with mystical sigils at each point. Figure 4.9 represents the nine schools of magic in *Advanced Dungeons & Dragons*.

Although the diagram appears to serve primarily a cosmetic function, decorating the book by depicting the schools with a mystical emblem, this type of diagram will later become pervasive and revealing in everything from the *Magic: The Gathering* color pie to the *Warhammer: Online* winds of magic diagram. The *Advanced Dungeons & Dragons Complete Wizard's Handbook* also diagrams the schools of magic as oppositional to one another, as reflected in their distribution around the spokes of a wheel or star. The *Complete Wizard's Handbook*, however, does not provide much rationale for why one school opposes another, but instead only mentions that in creating new schools of magic the dungeon master should consider allies and opposers of the new school (Swan 30).

By examining the similarities and differences surrounding *Advanced Dungeon & Dragons* schools and real occult magic, we can locate spaces for innovation and improvement by which game systems can be re-connected with real magic.

- *Invocation/evocation* is the school of magic with the strongest relationship to occultism, such that these names are probably derived directly from occultist texts, even though the concepts in *Advanced Dungeons & Dragons* are both simpler and less interesting. In *Advanced Dungeons & Dragons*, invocation and evocation pertain to creating matter and energy, called up out of nothing (in direct violation of the first law of thermodynamics, which states that matter and energy cannot be created or destroyed, only transformed). The classic spells magic missile and burning hands, both of which call up destructive energy with which to attack enemies, are both examples of evocation.

In contrast, though perhaps with a hidden relationship that could be exploited in interesting ways, the invocation and evocation of occultism pertain to calling up gods and spirits, representative of ideas and states of being. As Crowley explains in *Magick*, "to *invoke* is to *call in*, just as to *evoke* is to *call forth* or out" (147). Crowley means that invocation is a method of achieving oneness with a deity by identifying with it devotionally, dramatically, or through meditation—thereby calling it into the magician such that he becomes one with it. Evocation means to summon a being in the magician's immediate environment so that the spirit manifests in a way accessible to the senses.

- *Alteration* involves the ability to change matter, such as transforming the magician into the form of an animal or monster, or changing water into ice.

  - Shapeshifting is a large part of shamanic tradition, and transmutation of objects is certainly promised by many occultist traditions, especially alchemy.

- *Illusion* involves the ability to change the appearance of something, by creating a phantasm. (In first edition *Dungeons & Dragons*, there was a separate sub-class of magic user called an illusionist, with a completely different set of spells whose distinguishing characteristic was that they entailed changing appearances.)

  - Illusion has a complex relationship to Western occultism, since an illusion is by definition a deceptive appearance rather than a genuine miracle. For an occultist to describe his own craft as an illusion would be to blur the line between stage tricks (which the British refer to as "conjuring") and miracle-working. Nevertheless, grimoires such as *Three Books of Occult Philosophy* do promise the ability to create phantasms to frighten enemies. The tarot card often called The Magician is Le Bateleur in the Marseilles deck, which translates from French to the Juggler or Mountebank, with juggler being a term for a stage performer who

FIGURE 4.10   The Juggler Tarot Card.

performs all manner of tricks, including illusions. Figure 4.10 is
the Juggler/Magician card from the Marseilles tarot deck. The
Juggler is playing with cups and balls, a toy-like form of stage illusion akin to a shell game. Moreover, the contemporary graphic
novelist and occultist Alan Moore has gone so far as to embrace
illusion as the heart of magic because of its connection to imagination; Moore views his precursor, Alexander, as a magician precisely because his patron snake-god Glycon was actually a sock
puppet (Babcock). The line between occultist and stage magician
often blurs in exciting ways that could be useful to game designers. For example, the Jane Jensen adventure game *Gray Matter*
allows players to perform magic tricks, which entail a sleight of
hand interface that allows them to set up illusions.

- *Enchantment/charm* involves the ability to imbue objects with
  magical effects, often by improving weapons or armor.

  - In Western occultism, especially the grimoire tradition, there
    are elaborate ceremonies for consecrating magical tools, though
    generally these consecration rituals serve the purpose of preparing
    the tools for further ceremonial use rather than everyday combat.

- *Divination* entails the acquisition of information, often by foretelling
  the future, by seeking out a location, or by granting extrasensory
  access to hidden objects or facts.

  In historical occultism, there is a vast storehouse of divination
  methods, including Tarot, I Ching, and various forms of augury. Many
  actual schools of divination end in the suffix "-mancy," which means

"speaking with," implying that magicians converse with various aspects of the universe in order to gain secret information about the future or the present. There are many actual historical forms of divination, some of which have worked their way into videogame systems, including:

- Necromancy (literally "speaking with the dead")

- Cartomancy: (reading cards), the divinatory reading of cards, which includes Tarot-based fortune-telling

- Geomancy: (speaking with the earth), casting stones or marking the earth. As feng shui expert and scholar of magic Stephen Skinner explains in *The Complete Magician's Tables* (p. 328), geomancy is a Western practice distinct from feng shui, a Taoist art of directing energy through living spaces.

- Chiromancy: palm-reading, as practiced by fortune tellers who read signs of a person's future in her hand

- Pyromancy: ("speaking with the fire"), referring to gazing into the patterns of fire to tell the future. This school of magic differs from the usage of the word "pyromancer" in games like *Dark Souls*, where magicians conjure fire as a weapon. (*Dark Souls* does have the distinction of a richly contextualized mythology for fire magic, which explores the mystical beauty and dark heresies of a fire religion.)

- In *Advanced Dungeons & Dragons*, *conjuration* is the summoning of creatures, often monsters, as familiars or for assistance in battle.

  The equivalent technical term in Western ceremonial magic is evocation, which is the summoning of spirits, often in order to ask questions or gain information about more advanced magical techniques. Evocation thus overlaps historically with divination, and in this respect the historical practice of evocation is subtler than conjuration because it is used for intellectual and spiritual purposes rather than immediate combat advantages. That said, there is certainly an extensive tradition of evoking demons for the purpose of harming enemies or rival magicians.

- *Abjuration* is counter-magic, used to overcome or dispel the effects of other magicians' spells. The equivalent of this school in historical voodoo is called uncrossing, a method of deflecting a hex cast on someone.

4.3 BEYOND THE FOUR ELEMENTS

The four elements have been overused to the point of cliché and exhaustion as schools of magic or ways of classifying magic. The idea of the four elements has its roots in classical philosophy and, later, occultism. The ancient Greek shaman Empedocles was the first philosopher to assert that all physical objects were constituted of fire, water, air, and earth. Other Greek philosophers known as Platonists and Neo-Platonists later adopted and expanded on this classification scheme, passing it on to Renaissance Hermeticists and many subsequent occult groups.

The four elements appear very early in game magic, showing up as the four elemental planes in *Dungeons & Dragons*. They then proliferate through many videogames as ways of classifying spells, including:

- *Dungeon Master* (as four runes governing elemental energies)

- *Wizardry VI*

- *Final Fantasy I-XIII*

- *King's Field I-IV, Shadow Tower, Shadow Tower: Abyss, Eternal Ring*

- *Soulbringer* (in a rock-paper-scissors arrangement built around the pentagram)

- *Grim Grimoire* (as the basis of the spells acquired in the magical school)

- *World of Warcraft* (as various elemental skill trees for magic specializations, such as fire magic)

- *Guild Wars I, Guild Wars II*

- *Knights in the Knightmare* (as forms of damage)

- *Two Worlds II* (as the underlying scheme of the Demons spell management system)

- *The Legend of Grimrock* (as four runes governing elemental energies, much like *Dungeonmaster*)

Disturbingly, many magic systems that are advertised as "innovative" or "interesting" adopt the arrangement of the four elements, including *Soulbringer, Grim Grimoire,* and *Two Worlds II.* Games often add an extra school or two, such as life and death, or light and darkness, but the underlying restrictions of the four elements remain the same. The attraction of the four elements is that the qualities surrounding the properties of fire, earth, air, and water are diverse and susceptible to metaphorical application. For example, it is easy to associate fire with aggression, earth with protection, air with alteration, and water with healing on the basis of the destructiveness of flame, the solidity of earth, the elusiveness and mutability of air, and the purity of water.

However, there are many problems with making the four elements the primary basis of spell schools.

- The first problem is that such a system is too familiar because of the massive number of game magic systems that already use the four elements. Any magic system based on these elements must struggle against the sheer weight of tradition. Magic, almost by definition, pertains to the otherworldly, the unfamiliar, the uncanny, and the strange. It is very difficult for even an interesting or well-constructed elemental system to be any of these things because of the historical burden of magic based on the four elements.

- The second problem is the sheer physicality of the four elements. It is very tempting to simply create a set of projectiles or area of effect spells that are skinned elementally, such as fireballs, earthquakes, tornadoes, and icebolts. The magic systems that go this route end up being glorified elemental artillery, often devoid of metaphysical, emotional, or intellectual significance.

- The third problem is the restrictiveness of only four categories. Even if one interprets the four elements metaphorically, one is still stuck with a square configuration of elements that must be kept in balance. Systems tend to become more interesting when they are diverse, showing a fuller range of aspects of the universe. More than four schools leaves room for subtleties and ambiguities, instead of four clear-cut categories. For example, the seven planets of antiquity (Earth, Moon, Mercury, Venus, Mars, Sun, Saturn) can be expressive of a broader range of human energies by way of these planets' association with the Greek and Roman gods. In such a system, earth might be associated with physicality, the moon with change, Mercury with logic and language, Venus with love and beauty, Mars with aggression, the Sun with enlightenment, and Saturn with time.

- The fourth problem with the four elements is their failure to take advantage of the richness of a worldview inspired by modern science. It is perfectly acceptable for a magic system to be non-scientific, since most magic would be classified by rationalists as pseudoscience. On the other hand, magic often has its basis in mythology, and mythologies tend to draw their symbols from current scientific knowledge, from which the creators of these mythologies then make speculative leaps and metaphorical inter-pretations. As weird fiction author H.P. Lovecraft (whose fictions have inspired countless games) defines supernatural horror, it is comprised of "*supplements* rather than *contradictions* of the vis-ible & measurable universe." Ancient Greek magic was based on ancient Greek science and philosophy, and other game worlds would demand other elements. The current periodic table contains 118 elements rather than four. Moreover, the four elements of the Greeks were never actually elements in the chemical sense. Modern chemistry shows us that fire is the effect of other chemicals turn-ing into oxygen, while water is a compound molecule composed of one hydrogen and two oxygen atoms (H_2O). Earth is comprised of carbon and many minerals, and air is a mixture of oxygen, hydrogen, nitrogen, and other gases. Because the four elements have no chemical basis, they are useful only to game designers only as metaphors for game mechanics. When they cease to spark original ideas for game magic, designers should look elsewhere, starting often with more current science. If the current scientific worldview teaches us anything, it is that there are far more than four elements, far more than seven planets, and infinitely more than twelve signs.

4.4 *MAGE* AND *VAMPIRE'S* ALTERNATIVE SPHERES AND DISCIPLINES

Perhaps no game magic system has responded so well to this shift in sci-entific worldview than White Wolf's *Mage: The Ascension*, whose psyche-delic abstractions and subtleties have yet to be translated into videogame form. The nine spheres of magick (spelled with the k as a nod to Crowley) in *Mage: The Ascension* are correspondences, entropy, forces, life, matter, mind, prime, spirit, and time—as well as a potential tenth sphere that might operate as a kind of unified field, synthesizing the other nine. These nine spheres are refreshingly abstract, shaped by a mixture of ancient philosophy and new physics. Instead of falling back on the heavenly spheres of the ancients (which only made sense in the context of an earth-centered cosmos based on naked-eye astronomy), the mage designers invent their own spheres. These spheres are broadly conceptual and abstract, but each in some way is shaped by a contemporary branch of science. Entropy as a concept comes directly from the second law of thermodynamics as well as information theory, both of which are combined in the summary of "the forces of probability, disorder, and destruction." The sphere of forces comes primarily from physics and, while it includes the "forces of the elements," these forces are not limited to four and instead include "electricity, magnetism, fire, wind, gravity, kinetic energy, and even nuclear energy." Five out of seven of these forces come directly from modern physics, post-Newtonian and (in the case of nuclear energy) sub-atomic. The next sphere, Life, draws from the science of biology in its study of "organic life patterns." The sphere of Matter comes from modern chemistry in its emphasis on "physical, inorganic patterns," alluding to the specific distinction between organic and inorganic molecules. The sphere of Mind in one sense references many schools of mysticism, in which creation often begins with a primal mind, with the modern twist of the "mysteries of the human brain," referencing neuroscientific views of cognition. The sphere of Prime returns the *Mage* system to mysticism, referencing "reality in its rawest forms," a description that falls midway between Platonism and atomic physics.

Like so many games with representations of schools of magic, *Mage: The Ascension* also contains a geometrical diagram of the spheres of magick displayed around a polygon, with each sphere coded as a sigil. Yet, unlike so many of these diagrams, there is a logic to the position of each school that goes beyond the relative power of the spheres in a rock-paper-scissors arrangement. Instead, the spheres are arranged in a cycle of creation and dissolution, in which pure ideas pass from the raw energy of prime into the world of matter, subsequently to be dissolved into entropy and recreated in prime. The stages of the cycle are conception, focus, form, perception, decay, and return. The sigils themselves are beautiful and fresh from a design perspective, with heavy black-seriffed alchemical signs that eschew the clichéd elemental or planetary symbols. The spheres of magick, like so much else in White Wolf's *World of Darkness*, manage to draw on the power of authentic occult tradition without losing a sense of individuality and newness.

While it would be difficult to translate the spheres of magic into video-game form, the magic systems of the *World of Darkness* actually have been successfully adapted in multiple videogames. *Vampire: The Masquerade Redemption* is a CRPG from 2000 that was deep, dark, thematically mature, and expressed these qualities in part through its magic system. This game's unique schools of magic, called disciplines, affect a multitude of different spell domains and, in turn, diverse game mechanics tied into many varied aspects of the simulated world. These disciplines include:

- *Animalism*, which entails control over animals, both inner and outer

- *Auspex*, which encompasses telepathy and extrasensory perception. In *Redemption*, this discipline includes spells that allow players to project themselves astrally in ghost objects, as well as gaining information about objects both visible and hidden. The spells in Auspex resemble the scrying of Clive Barker's *Undying* as well as the astral projection mechanic of Clive Barker's *Jericho*, both games which attempted to push the boundaries of magic toward subtlety and metaphysics. Astral projection is a major component of many real-world schools of magic.

- *Celerity*, which increases speed

- *Dementation*, which primarily drives enemies mad but can also heighten the perception of the caster and his allies. As the *Redemption* manual describes the spell called the Eye of Chaos, "This peculiar power allows the user to take advantage of the fractured wisdom hidden in insanity. With it, the character can detect the aura of another." The idea of madness as a source of enlightenment is a classic element of shamanism as well as a concept of genius popular among nineteenth century romantic poets and the Gothic culture they inspired, which pervades the *World of Darkness*. It is a testament to the subtlety of White Wolf's designers that they include a school of madness magic in the first place, and even more so that they represent the school as having positive aspects.

- *Dominate*, or mind control. While *Dungeons & Dragons* has long included charm spells and other spells that affect the minds of other characters during combat, *Redemption* contains spells to avoid combat altogether, as well as to possess characters in order to control them as a remote avatar. The notion of possession will return more than a decade later in the voodoo magic of *Risen 2*.

- *Fortitude*: increases strength

- *Mortis*: necromancy and immediate death spells

- *Obfuscate*: stealth and invisibility spells

- *Potence*: buffing spells that increase resistance to damage

- *Presence*: charisma spells, at least one of which is tied into the game's vampiric feeding mechanic because the Awe spell allows the caster to seduce mortals in order to drink their blood

- *Protean*: Transformation spells, including one that allows the player to assume the form of a wolf and another that allows him to tunnel into the earth

- Thaumaturgy

The discipline specifically designated thaumaturgy has its own sub-schools of magic, which are somewhat dull and clichéd (fire, destruction, and—perhaps less clichéd—blood). If blood magic is the secret school of magic of *Dragon Age*, all of *Vampire* is like this secret school—and the game promises hidden disciplines and mysteries, saying "Rare vampires and stranger creatures may have powers not on this list, as there are mysteries that remain hidden within the *World of Darkness*."

Magic systems are strongest when they track and take into account as many different states as possible, and *Vampire* does this in spades, allowing for astral projection, possession of animals, resurrection, and manipulation of frenzy. The roots of White Wolf's magical subtlety are in a tabletop role-playing game called *Ars Magica*, which blurs the lines between schools of magic and a magical grammar (see Chapter 7, Section 7.3).

4.5 *ETERNAL DARKNESS*

There is perhaps no better magic system exemplifying nearly all of the principles put forth in this book than the magic system in Silicon Knight's cult classic horror game *Eternal Darkness: Sanity's Requiem*. The magic system of *Eternal Darkness* is the closest thing to a ceremonial magic simulator, meant to approximate the experience of an occult magic ritual, in all of its complexity and depth. As Silicon Knights and Precursor Games lead designer Denis Dyack explains in an interview with Shannon Drake in *The Escapist*, "We did a lot of research into the occult [and] magic systems, and we really tried to pull it into something that would really make sense and be fun for people to play" (Drake 1). The authentic occultism of *Eternal Darkness* begins with a set of four Elder Gods (and a fifth implied one), each associated with a particular force, color, and rune. Figure 4.11 is a rune chart for *Eternal Darkness*, including the spells in the game.

Elder God	Mantorok	Chattur'gha	Ulyaoth	Xel'lotath
Force	All forces	Body	Mind	Sanity
Color	Purple	Red	Blue	Green

The forces represented by each Elder God are both fundamental and subtler than the typical four elements: they represent the constituent parts of the human soul (body, mind, and sanity), and each of these faculties is key to gameplay as a resource that must be managed (health, mana, and sanity points). Figure 4.12 shows the menu of *Eternal Darkness* inside the in-game Tome of Eternal Darkness, including the meters for health, mana, and sanity. The colors of three of the runes (red, blue, and green) are health, mana, and sanity bars in the heads up display (HUD) of the game. Each rune trumps one rune and is also trumped by another rune, in a classic rock-paper-scissors arrangement.

FIGURE 4.11 The *Eternal Darkness* Rune Chart.

FIGURE 4.12 *Eternal Darkness* Journal.

Moreover, the runes representing the gods are part of a larger magical grammar of runes that forms the basis of spellcasting. Silicon Knights shows conscious or subconscious awareness of the connection between grammar and grimoires, since a magical grimoire called the Tome of Eternal Darkness serves as the entire basis for the game's spellcasting interface, journal, map, and cutscene frame. Inside the spellcasting interface portion of *Eternal Darkness* is a set of disks with slots in various geometrical configurations, in which runes can be placed. These disks can have three, five, or seven slots, indicating how many times the spell can be powered up through the placement of additional pargon (power) runes. Like the magic system of *Ultima Underworld*, the runes of *Eternal Darkness* constitute a full grammar with a basic syntax and a limited but gameplay-relevant vocabulary, illustrated in the following chart.

Elder God Runes	Verb/Effect Runes	Noun/Target Runes	Empowering Rune
Chattur'gha	Bankarok: protect	Magormor: item	Pargon: power
Ulyaoth	Tier: summon	Redgormor: area	
Xel'lotath	Narokath: absorb	Aretak: creature	
Mantorok	Nekleth: dispel	Santak: self	
	Antorbok: project		

Selective combination of these fourteen runes results in twelve recognized spells, shown in the following chart:

Runes	Meaning	Spell
Antorbok Magormor	Project Item	Enchant Item
Narokath Santak	Absorb Self	Recover
Narokath Redgormor	Absorb Area	Reveal Invisible
Bankorok Redgormor	Protect Area	Damage Field
Nethlek Redgormor	Dispel Area	Dispel Magick
Tier Aretak (in disk with 3 slots)	Summon Creature	Summon Trapper
Tier Aretak (in disk with 5 slots)	Summon Creature	Summon Zombie
Tier Aretak (in disk with 7 slots)	Summon Creature	Summon Horror
Bankorok Santak	Protect Self	Shield
Antorbok Redgormor	Project Area	Magical Attack
Tier Redgormor	Summon Area	Magick Pool
Bankorok Aretak	Protect Creature	Bind Creature

Many possible combinations do nothing in order to keep the player from having to memorize too many spells. At the same time, fourteen runes is a reasonable amount of density, providing enough rewards to keep players experimenting as they learn the system. Players slowly acquire runes one by one, curtailing their initial ability to experiment and nudging them in the direction of productive combinations by limiting the number of possibilities.

In addition to a syntactical logic, there is also a logic by which individual words are constructed in terms of prefixes, suffixes, and similar sounds. Because "project" and "protect" are analogous concepts (and perhaps because they are only one letter apart in English), they are expressed through phonetically similar words: bankorok and antorbok. Because "self" and "creature" both refer to living, breathing individuals, the two words both end in the suffix of "-tak": santak and aretak. Because "object" and "area" both refer to inanimate entities, they both have the suffix of "gormor," as in magormor and redgormor. On every level (syllable, word, sentence), the runic language of *Eternal Darkness* makes sense and is cohesive, qualities that Dyack attributes more broadly to the game as a whole and all games made by Silicon Knights. As he explains, "whenever you create any kind of fiction, you have to set up your own ruleset, and if you break those rules, you're going to upset the audience" (Drake 2).

The method of casting spells by placing symbolic objects at particular points of a sacred geometrical figure resembles actual occultist magicians' arrangements of objects within their temples, such as the distribution of lamps at the points of pentagrams, hexagrams, heptagrams, and octagrams inscribed within a magician's circle. Players prepare spells by placing their runes, then casting the spell and hearing its syllables recited in the voice of the particular god. Figure 4.13 shows a spell circle in *Eternal Darkness*. In the grammar of *Eternal Darkness*, the first rune is always the

FIGURE 4.13   *Eternal Darkness* Spell Circle.

chosen Elder God, whose power inflects the spell toward a particular realm of influence or against a particular enemy. For example, if the player wishes to dispel a green magic force field placed by the energy of Xel'latoth, then one needs to begin the spell by invoking Chattur'gah, the Elder god of the body whose red rune trumps the green rune of Xel'latoth. Subsequent runes establish the verb of a spell, indicating what function the spell should have, and direct objects of the spell, designating the intended target.

The spells of *Eternal Darkness* are deeply multimodal, engaging multiple forms of input and various senses in order to create an atmosphere of dark magic and eldritch mysticism. The colored runes glow and shimmer with mystic energy as they are placed, appealing to the emotional power of color, and the voices of the Elder Gods chant the names of the runes, appealing to the power of sound associated with the "barbarous names of evocation." Moreover, the GameCube controller vibrates with sorcerous energy as the player casts a spell, addressing the sense of touch without requiring direct gestural input. *Eternal Darkness* does a fantastic job of making the player feel like an initiate, gradually acquiring occult knowledge on his way to adepthood, since features like the intoning of the runes actually teach the player the language. While spells in *Eternal Darkness* can effectively be mapped to hotkeys once they have been assembled, the caster still watches each time as the runes glow into life around his third-person avatar while the names of the runes are intoned through an otherworldly voice. Even players who attempt to bypass the more work-intensive aspects of the magic system will still learn the system almost subconsciously or subliminally, reinforcing the game's goal of creating an uncanny atmosphere through eerie breakages of the fourth wall that usually separates the simulated and real worlds.

Shadow of the Eternals, the proposed crowdfunded spiritual successor to *Eternal Darkness* led by Silicon Knights alumni at a new company called Precursor Games, promises to extend and enrich the already deep magic system of *Eternal Darkness*. As creative director Denis Dyack explains in a message, "I am glad you like the magick system in ED:SR. We hope to take it much further in SotE." The Kickstarter project update #15 confirms the ambition to extend the rich complexity of the *Eternal Darkness* magic system in *Shadow of the Eternals*. Posted as a journal entry written by a character in the game called Whateley, the update contains an elaborate magical diagram called the Ae'lanoic Rosette, most closely resembling the Enochian magician John Dee's sigil of Ameth. Whateley then unpacks the elaborate symbolism of this sign, which comprises a nine-pointed star of interlaced line segments, as well as multiple layers of sigils on an inner ring, an intermediate triangle, inside the line segments of the star, and at the points of each intersecting line segment. Whateley speculates that three of these sigils represent the powers of body, magic, and mind (in keeping with the three main gods' runes in *Eternal Darkness*), and further suggests that other glyphs may represent "sigils of control and influence," as well as the "philosophies posed by connection" to a cult's god. Whateley's remarks are deliberately tentative and speculative, reflective both of a mysterious undeciphered language in the game's fiction as well as the in-progress status of the game in the real world. Yet, this journal entry suggests that *Shadow of the Eternals* is building on what made the magic of *Eternal Darkness* so excellent: a rich combinatorial magic grammar, intertwined inextricably with a well-developed metaphysical lore. Figure 4.14 is the Ae'lanoic Rosette.

In a further Kickstarter Update video, Dyack and another designer elaborate on the function of the rosette within the game's magic system.

FIGURE 4.14   Ae'lanoic Rosette.

The designers define the rosette as depicting the "cosmology of the universe" in the game, and further explain that it "defines the universe of *Shadow of the Eternals*." In terms that echo this book's section on schools of magic, Dyack explains that the spells represent "a map of the cosmology and magic system" of *Eternal Darkness*. Clarifying Whateley's vague and speculative in-game voice, the designers explain that each point represents a power, one of the Eternals. The structure also defines a hierarchy of power, with the center being most powerful. The center, most powerful circle can in Dyack's terms represent a singularity, thereby blurring the line between magic and science in a way that the two designers attribute to Lovecraft and Clarke's famous Third Law of Prediction that "sufficiently advanced technology is indistinguishable from magic," as formulated in "Hazards of Prophecy: The Failure of Imagination." The designers argue that the purpose of magic is to focus the will through words, sounds, and precise geometry.

Dyack also reveals an aspect of the *Eternal Darkness* magic system that deepens the system's linguistic origins and points toward opportunities for their future development. Dyack explains that the original *Eternal Darkness* magic system was inspired by his master's thesis on computer speech voice recognition and patterns, which stressed the importance of context in shaping the human pronunciation of phones. The two designers explain that while neither the context of utterance nor the order of runes mattered in *Eternal Darkness*, order and context will matter in *Shadows of the Eternal*. The emphasis on order and context, as well as the overall complexity of the rosette, allows room for mastery of the system, as players become more and more skilled at choosing and expressing an utterance in a given situation. Figure 4.15 shows an in-game rendition of the Tome of Eternal Darkness. Figure 4.16 is a chart of the runes in *Eternal Darkness*. Figure 4.17 shows the rune interface in *Eternal Darkness*. Figure 4.18 is an expanded version of a chart of the runes in *Eternal Darkness*.

FIGURE 4.15   Cutscene graphic of *The Tome of Eternal Darkness*.

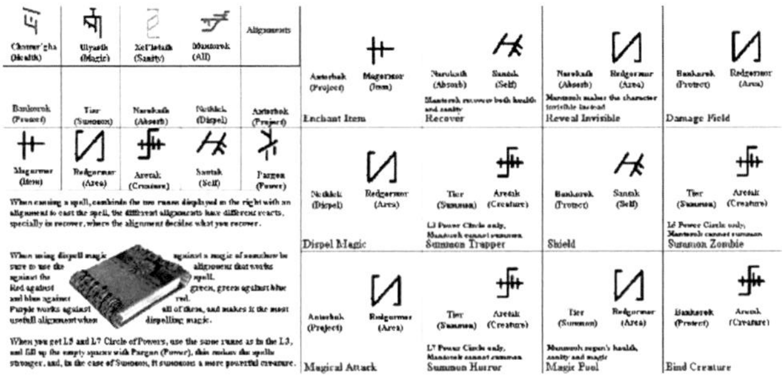

FIGURE 4.16 *Eternal Darkness* Spell Chart #2.

FIGURE 4.17 *Eternal Darkness* Rune Interface.

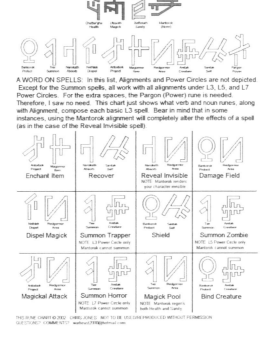

FIGURE 4.18 Large *Eternal Darkness* Rune Chart.

4.6 THE COLORS OF MAGIC

There is a strong correlation between schools of magic and divisions of the visible spectrum into discrete sections of color, such as color wheels and rainbows. Color is one way of classifying the totality of visual experience, which human beings ordinarily tend to perceive as a chaotic blur of hues and shades. Early students of light and color, such as Isaac Newton, noticed that white light could be separated into bands of color, which he referred to collectively as the visible spectrum. Newton's work with the spectrum was fueled in part by his work as an alchemist, the branch of knowledge dedicated to investigating the secrets of chemical transformation, in which various colors had symbolic significance as representing the various stages of transmutation. Figure 4.19 shows Newton's original color wheel from his book *Opticks*, with planetary and musical correspondences. Wolfgang von Goethe followed Newton by asserting a direct emotional, almost mystical impact for each color on the human soul.

By dividing up and classifying color into discrete bands or sections of a pie graph, game designers appeal to the human desire to separate the chaotic totality of existence into ordered, manageable domains. The color pie from *Magic: The Gathering* represents schools of magic as wedges of color that stand for types of spell energy or mana, derived from different planes and representing different philosophies, which are in turn expressed as rule systems. The five colors of *Magic: The Gathering* are black, white, blue, red, and green. Each color is associated with multiple philosophical traits, which can often be expressed as a single sentence or thesis. Red represents chaos and impulse, often represented through fiery burn spells that directly damage an opponent. Green represents nature and growth, typically incarnated in large creatures with the ability to trample enemies, as well as heavy sources of land gain and energy from mana. Blue represents reason and manipulation. Its cards tend to involve counterspells and ways to draw extra cards,

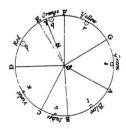

FIGURE 4.19 Isaac Newton's Color Wheel with Musical and Planetary Correspondences. (Image from *Opticks*. In public domain due to age.)

as well as ways to see into other players' hands, simulating telepathy. White represents balance and order, typically in the form of flying creatures, life gain, and spells that grant all players equal benefits. White's version of justice is almost socialist in its drive to level the playing field.

The greatest strength of the color pie is how relentlessly *Magic: The Gathering* has made the rules of each card express the philosophies of the colors. Even if a card were unnamed and visually uncolored, an experienced *Magic* player could know what section of the color pie it belonged to based on the mechanics described in its rules text. Black is an especially dramatic example of this rule-based expressiveness.

Black represents death and hunger for power, often associated with paranoia and selfishness. In classic *Magic: The Gathering*, black's philosophy is that "I can have anything I want, as long as I am willing to pay the price." In terms of rules, black's cards tend to be slightly overcosted, and they often entail sacrifices, such as sacrificing a creature or dealing damage to the caster, in order to achieve greater gains. The tendency of black to quickly gain power at the risk of harming or destroying itself resulted in the phrase "suicide black," a deck archetype built around quick gains and difficult sacrifices. Perhaps no card represents black's philosophy quite so well as the infamous Necropotence, which allows players to deliberately skip their own draw step (effectively cutting off their ordinary source of resource renewal). Players then exchange life for cards, whittling away at their own life total in exchange for quickened access to spells and mana. Formulated rigorously as a rule, the card reads: "Skip your draw phase. If you discard a card from your hand, remove that card from the game. 0: Pay 1 life to set aside the top card of your library. At the beginning of your next discard phase, put that card into your hand. Effects that prevent or redirect damage cannot be used to counter this loss of life." The mechanics associated with the Necropotence card are the perfect expression of the experience of being a necromancer, hell-bent on power at any cost, including the Faustian cost of playing with one's own death. Figure 4.20 shows Faust, the archetypal representation of self-destructive magical bargains. Playing a deck built around Necropotence gives the player the thrill of being drunk on power and risk, conveying the feeling of black magic almost entirely through abstract, numerically based rules. Each of the colors provides a similar experience. Each also has a set of strengths and weaknesses, as well as a set of enemy and ally colors. Much like the color pie, magic in the *Warhammer* universe is divided according to a diagram of the winds of

FIGURE 4.20 *Faust in His Study*. (Rembrandt. In public domain due to age.)

magic, which is influenced by Michael Moorcock's star of chaos and Peter Carroll's chaos magic. The winds are represented in the following table.

Hysh	White	Lore of Light
Ghamon	Yellow	Lore of Metal
Ghyran	Green	Lore of Life
Azyr	Blue	Lore of Heavens
Ulgu	Gray	Lore of Shadows
Shyish	Purple	Lore of Death
Aqshy	Red	Lore of Fire
Ghur	Brown	Lore of Beasts

4.7 MYTHOLOGY AND SCHOOLS OF MAGIC

The construction of schools of magic is ultimately historically related back to the intersection between magic and mythology, in which the seven planets of the ancients and the twelve Olympian gods are often correlated with fundamental forces underlying the universe. These planets are important because they do not represent only physical forces, but also emotional, psychological, social, and ultimately metaphysical forces. (The ancients would have regarded all the above forces as metaphysical, since they all ultimately derived from gods and spirits, though some forces would have been more or less subtle.) Each of the planets traditionally has a color, as codified by the Golden Dawn and earlier magical texts and embraced in Peter Carroll's version of chaos magic.

Planet	Quality	Color
Moon	Airiness, changeability	Violet
Mercury	Eloquence, rationality, thievery	Orange
Venus	Love and beauty	Green
Mars	War and aggression	Red
Jupiter	Joy, benevolence, kingliness	Blue
Saturn	Death, time, sadness	Black

The planets ultimately derive their associations from the gods of the Greek and Romans, from which they acquire their names. The planetary correspondences are a subset of the Olympian correspondences, chosen based on the planets visible by the ancients with the naked eye. There are twelve Olympian gods, so named because they live on Mount Olympus. Their attributes are as follows:

Greek God	Equivalent Roman God	Attributes and Domain
Aphrodite	Venus	Love, beauty
Apollo	Apollo	Art, order, archery
Ares	Mars	War, aggression
Artemis	Diana	The hunt, virginity, the moon
Athena	Minerva	Wisdom, strategic war
Demeter	Ceres	The harvest, grain
Dionysus	Bacchus	Drunkenness, frenzy
Hephaestus	Vulcan	Craftsmanship
Hera	Juno	Fertility, motherhood
Hermes	Mercury	Eloquence, rationality, thievery
Poseidon	Neptune	The sea
Zeus	Jupiter	Kingliness

The gods constitute a map of the universe. The division of a whole into colors is also often accompanied geometrically through the use of polygonal figures that represent the totality of existence or, as magicians would call it, the macrocosm. The circle in particular tends to denote wholeness, and it can be divided into sectors through lineal figures such as the pentagram, hexagram, heptagram (seven-pointed star), and octagram.

4.8 COLORS OF THE TREE OF LIFE

One of the first and most complex sources of color symbolism in magic are the color scales of the Golden Dawn, a magical society of the late nineteenth century. The color scales are four ways of coloring the branches and paths of the kabbalistic tree of life. These colors are not arbitrarily chosen, but rather correspond to particular planets, astrological signs, and elements. For example, the fourth (or fourteenth) path of the Hebrew letter daleth is emerald green because it corresponds to Venus, a planet and goddess traditionally associated with fertility, nature, and the metal copper (which acquires a greenish patina, or verdigris, as it weathers).

The Flash-based demo downloadable from the book's website shows a Tree of Life interface whose paths will light up according to the Queen and King scales of color when the corresponding tarot cards and gems are dragged onto the paths and sephiroth. Figure 4.21 shows the kabbalistic tree of life colored according to the Queen and King scales.

Another real magical philosophy that places great emphasis on color is Chaos magic, especially in the work of Peter Carroll. Many schools of game magic have been influenced by Chaos magic, including *Warhammer* and its many digital and non-digital incarnations, as well as *Mage: The Ascension*. White Wolf's spheres of magic are contextualized within a framework called paradigm, which derives from chaos magic. A paradigm is a system of beliefs, a way of looking at the world, a worldview. The term derives from Thomas Kuhn's *Structure of Scientific Revolutions*, in which Kuhn argues that the development of scientific knowledge is marked by periodic paradigm shifts. An example of paradigm shift would be the movement from a geocentric view of the universe, in which earth is at the center, to a heliocentric view, in which the sun is at the center. Whereas scientific paradigms shift slowly and gradually based often on centuries of experimentation, some chaos magicians attempt to instantaneously create the equivalent of paradigm shifts in their own minds, based on the idea that "belief is a tool."

In *Liber Chaos*, Peter Carroll associates various paradigms of magic with eight colors arrayed around the eight-pointed star of chaos, a symbol derived from fantasy writer Michael Moorcock (Carroll 109) (see Chapter 8, Section 8.9).

4.9 PLANAR MAGIC

The ultimate root of the schools of magic is cosmological, in that the schools of magic provide an ordered map of the universe, split up into its domains. A common idea in game magic is that the magic energies

FIGURE 4.21 (See color insert.)   Tree of Life with Color Scales.

that fuel spellcasting come from another world—often, multiple other worlds. Many contemporary RPGs allude to alternate planes as the source of all magic, such as the Aetherium in *Skyrim* and the Fade in *Dragon Age: Origin*. The cosmological images that show up in conjunction with schools of magic—trees of life, stars of chaos, winds of magic—are often ultimately pictures of an entire universe or, more frequently, multiverse.

Planar magic is one of the most interesting and neglected schools of magic because it involves a voyage into other realities. The planes are pure, abstract manifestations of particular facets of reality. Such a voyage is shamanic in its content but ceremonial in its approach, which is to say methodical and symbolic. In *Secrets of the Magical Grimoires*, Aaron Leitch makes a distinction between shamanic magic, including tribal magic and (counter-intuitively) the magic of the grimoires, and "lodge-based" magic, including Masonic-influenced Rosicrucian orders like the Golden Dawn. Game magic can benefit most directly from lodge-based magic because this view of magic is overtly systemic and hence readily adaptable into a set of rules. Leitch observes that shamanic magic has no need of gating spells like the rituals of the hexagram and pentagram because the shaman alters his consciousness directly through fasting, meditation, and psychotropics. Yet as game designers we have no direct access to the consciousness of our players, whose behavior we can primarily shape through the rules of gameplay.

Dungeons & Dragons takes its first steps out of restrictive and clichéd elemental magic with spells like "gate" and "planar contact." This view of magic reaches its apex in the view of magic in *The Manual of the Planes* and *Planescape*. The connection between magic and the planes is evident as early as first edition *Advanced Dungeons & Dragons*. Several spells, such as Planar Shift, allow players to travel between planes. While these spells reference the relationship between magic and the planes, the *Manual of the Planes* and *Planescape* expands this idea into a full-fledged mythology.

The entire system of *Magic: The Gathering* is also based upon planar lore, in which magicians are planeswalkers who draw energy from the planes they have visited in their travels. Each block of cards represents a plane, and each color of basic land depicts a particular place within a given plane from which a color of mana can be drawn. When a player taps a swamp for one black mana, in terms of the game's fiction he is drawing energy from a swamp he has encountered on a plane. Consequently, the color pie of *Magic: The Gathering* doubles as a diagram of the multiverse. The color pie is not coincidentally similar in appearance to the Great Wheel of the Planes.

The double nature of schools of magic as maps of alternate realities or planes is crucial because it highlights the relationship between magic systems and world-building. Different types of spells represent varieties of energy that modify simulated realities, which in turn are governed by particular philosophies, which are in turn expressed through rules systems.

4.10 ALTERNATIVE SCHOOLS OF MAGIC AND WORLD SIMULATION

Schools of magic can be thought of in terms of programming as spell domains: particular aspects of a simulated world that can be altered and affected through spells. In general, a magic system is at its deepest and richest when its spells have "hooks" into as many different aspects of a simulated world as possible by way of a diverse set of game systems. When spells can only operate in one domain, such as combat, then the differences between schools of magic are between trivial and cosmetic. An ice blast, a fireball, a lightning bolt, and a poison puff may supposedly belong to different schools of elemental magic, but if they only operate within the domain of combat by causing damage to enemies or protecting and healing players from damage, then functionally they all belong to the same school of magic. This dull uniformity of spell effects within supposedly diverse schools of magic is one of the main flaws of magic systems in MMOs, in which AoE, DPS, buffs, and healing spells serve primarily combat-related functions as ways of reducing enemies' health or preserving and improving the player's health.

In contrast, a game like *Ultima: Underworld* exhibits a true diversity of spell effects because of the robustness of its world simulation, which incorporates many interlocking game systems to track the following objects, attributes, and states (see Chapter 3, Section 3.11).

- Rooms and tunnels, which can be in varying states of *light and darkness*
- Player *hunger*, which is a numerical value from *x* to *y*
- *Time*, which can be slowed or stopped
- Player *speed*, a numerical value from *x* to *y*, which can be slowed or increased
- *Noise*, a value which correlates with enemies' awareness of the player and can be dampened by spells like *stealth*
- *Gravity*, the effects of which can be reduced or negated for the player by spells like *slow fall* and *fly* and for objects by *telekinesis*
- *Visibility* of objects and enemies
- Strength of doors
- The quality of being *locked* and *unlocked*, which can apply to doors and chests
- *Wards*, which can be disturbed or undisturbed
- Player perspective and mapping

As is the case with many early computer role-playing games, some of the most unique spell effects would become incorporated as common, default features in later role-playing games. For example, a divination spell in *Wizardry VI: Crusaders of the Dark Savant* that reveals the location of a quest item would be a powerful godsend in an old-school CRPG in which players mapped dungeons with graph paper but would be rendered superfluous by automapping with quest targets, as in *The Elder Scrolls IV: Oblivion*. In some ways, the hardcore difficulty of early RPGs and their absence of handholding made unique spells more powerful and intriguing. Yet, the evolution of game systems for player convenience does not mean that magic must be relegated to clichéd effects or confined to combat only. Instead, we as designers should think about ways to create varied and interesting spell effects within contemporary game systems, as well as ways to build game systems that will facilitate the creation of unique spells.

4.10.1 Blood Magic (Sangromancy)

Blood magic is one of the most primal and compelling schools of sorcery, drawing as it does on the power of one of living beings' most precious and charged bodily fluids. Dracula's servant Renfield's feverish declaration that "the blood is the life" plunges to the essence of the magical fascination with blood: even prior to scientific understandings of oxygenated blood, blood seems to carry the essence of vitality (Stoker 130). This association of blood and life can be traced in part to the Biblical Old Testament, in which Leviticus 17:11 declares that "the life of the flesh *is* in the blood: and I have given it to you upon the altar to make an atonement for your souls: for it *is* the blood *that* maketh an atonement for the soul." The Leviticus verse also suggests that blood is closely connected to sacrifice in the classical sense of giving up something precious in order to attain a desired power or other spiritual effect, such as atonement.

This idea of blood as sacrifice directly translates into two recipes for magic. The required words in the magical language are health, blood, and sacrifice.

RECIPE 17: BLOOD MAGIC (ORIGINAL PSEUDOCODE)

```
//Recipe # 2a: Blood sacrifice
//In the first recipe, health powers spells instead of mana.
//The amount of energy required to cast the spell is
//decremented from the player's total health.

CastBloodSpell()
```

```
{
     GetPlayerHealth() = GetPlayerHealth()- SpellCost;
          if GetPlayerHealth() < = 0
               {
               Print ("You have spent too much blood!
You faint!);
               Killplayer();
               }
          Otherwise
          {
          CastSpell();
          }
}
```

RECIPE 18:   BLOOD MAGIC (ORIGINAL PSEUDOCODE)

```
//Recipe # 2b:Vampirism
//A second recipe revolves around the idea of vampirism. One
//player leeches energy from another player or NPC, thereby
//increasing the player's own health proportionally.

CastVampiricSpell()
{
GetEnemyHealth() = GetEnemyHealth() - Damage;
GetPlayerHealth() = GetPlayerHealth() + Damage;
Print("You do [Damage] points of damage to the enemy, and
   you gain [Damage] points of health.");

}
```

For blood magic to be a genuine school of magic, its mechanics must reinforce its flavor, to the point that they are one and the same. Blogger Bill Coberly of Nightmaremode.net emphasizes the importance of integrated magical mechanics and themes when he critiques the absence of mysterious or dangerous mechanics for blood magic in *Dragon Age*, which he contrasts with the actual danger and mystery of casting spells in the Sierra RPG *Betrayal in Antara*. Coberly writes:

> In the lore of Antara (much like Dragon Age), magic is a volatile, dangerous force which is not completely understood even by the greatest mages. Unlike Dragon Age, however, the game's mechanics actually support this conception. Spellcasting is dangerous because it causes physical damage to the caster and places him in direct harm. It's mysterious because you never know exactly how many spells are available or what certain combinations of elements will give you.

Coberly's point is that *Dragon Age*'s fiction of blood magic as a forbidden and dangerous practice does not resonate with its mechanics, in which blood magic carries no more risk of danger than any other form of magic.

4.10.2 Death Magic (Necromancy)

Necromancy is a longstanding practice among magicians, who seek to summon the spirits of the dead in order to gain wisdom or to carry out commands. The word "necromancy" means "speaking with the dead," resulting in a variety of similarly-patterned words for schools of magic historical and fictional, such as pyromancy (fire magic), chiromancy (palm-reading), and cartomancy (fortune-telling with cards) (see Chapter 4, Section 4.2).

Necromancy can entail many recipes for spells, including resurrection of party members and allies, as well as zombie creation to swell the ranks of one's army with walking dead servants. In order for necromancy to function within a simulated game world, the game must be capable of tracking life and death as states attributed to objects. There may also need to be various intermediate states, such as undead and permanently dead. Bones, skulls, and corpses will tend to be spell foci, and graveyards, tombs, and mausoleums will serve as temples. Some magic systems that incorporate necromancy keep track of whether a spellcaster is standing on earth, only allowing for the summoning of zombies or skulls if bones could be interred in the ground below. Examples include the spell Skullstorm in *Undying*, which allows the player to pull flaming skull projectiles from the ground only if the caster is standing on earth, as well as the Summon Undead spell of *Arx Fatalis* which has a similar condition. A conditional in the form of an "if" statement can keep track of this requirement for the spell, or the requirement can be part of a larger state machine.

Spells that relate to death will often involve toggling or sliding between states related to mortality, such as turning a live entity into a dead one, a dead entity into a live one, a live entity into a zombie, or a zombie into an immobile corpse. This aspect of necromancy is a form of transmutation or transformation. At the same time, because the "-mancy" suffix of necromancy implies speaking, necromancers will often summon the dead in order to communicate with them in order to acquire information, frequently related to the underworld, such as the location of buried treasure.

Necromantic recipes involve reclaiming data from the game that has been discarded as no longer relevant to the game state. In many games, corpses are no longer part of active gameplay because they are not alive and cannot act. First-person shooters often have algorithms for removing corpses from the screen in puffs of smoke or explosions in order to avoid clogging up precious processing power by rendering unnecessary polygons. Similarly, *Magic: The Gathering* features a graveyard: a pile of cards that can normally no longer be played because they are dead, both in the fictional sense of deprived of life and in the gameplay sense of inert and irrelevant. However, there are several spells in *Magic: The Gathering* that resurrect cards by removing them from the graveyard and returning them to a player's hand or directly into play. The phenomenon of cycling cards in and out of the graveyard is known as graveyard recursion.

RECIPE 19:   NECROMANCY (ORIGINAL PSEUDOCODE)

```
//Required Ingredients:
//In order to express necromantic spells, a linguistic magic
//system requires words for death, life, speak, summon.

//World state: live and dead

//To resurrect:
//Toggle states between live and dead;

ResurrectCorpse ()
{
if (GetIsObjectDead = = true)
{
SetIsObjectDead = = false;
Print("Covered with flies and shambling, the corpse rises
   from the dead.");
}
}
```

While Roguelike *Dwarf Fortress* does not yet have a fully implemented magic system, work has begun on such a system, starting with necromancer NPCs (symbolized by a purple 'I') who can raise corpses. It is possible to become a necromancer in the game's adventure mode by either touching the slab in one of their towers or by reading one of their books, such as *The Secrets of Life and Death*. Some of the raw data files for *Dwarf Fortress* necromancy are available on the Github repository from which the game's files can be downloaded, at https://github.com/ minorred/Dwarf-fortress/blob/master/raw/interaction%20examples/ interaction_secret.txt.

The raw object data for necromancy is contained in a file called inter-action_secret.txt, in which necromancers are defined as objects with attributes, such as immunity to normal human needs, coded through a set of tags ([CE _ ADD _ TAG:NOEXERT:NO _ AGING:NO _ EAT:NO _ DRINK:NO _ SLEEP:NO _ PHYS _ ATT _ GAIN:NO _ PHYS _ ATT _ RUST:START:0]). In keeping with the overall procedural structure of *Dwarf Fortress*, the actions of necromancers are not pre-scripted, but rather coded through a central goal ("IS _ SECRET _ GOAL: IMMORTALITY") that the necromancers pursue, using the defined action of raising corpses. The code below encapsulates the necromancers' ability to raise the dead:

```
[CE_CAN_DO_INTERACTION:START:0]
                        [CDI:ADV_NAME:Animate corpse]
                        [CDI:INTERACTION:EXAMPLE RAISE]
                        [CDI:TARGET:A:LINE_OF_SIGHT]
                        [CDI:TARGET_RANGE:A:10]
                        [CDI:VERB:gesture:gestures:NA]
                        [CDI:TARGET_VERB:shudder and
begin to move:shudders and begins to move]
                        [CDI:WAIT_PERIOD:10]
```

We will not know the secrets of magic in *Dwarf Fortress* until its lead designers, brothers Tarn and Zach Adams, have fully implemented their magic system. Until then, a glimpse into the code behind their necromancy can provide inspiration for a system of magic that is deeply procedural, driven by actors with their own unique, individual goals and abilities. Necromancy is a fitting start for magical innovation because of its dark, flavorful atmosphere, and the raising of the dead occupies a niche within the broader sphere of the black arts, which often focus on the related task of summoning demons.

4.10.3 Demon Magic

Black magic will tend to exact a heavy cost in terms of energy, health, and—potentially—sanity. Magic systems that emphasize demonic sorcery tend to represent magic as a transaction, a pact, a deal with the devil or his minions. *Warhammer 40k* or the Pact Magic of *Dungeons & Dragons* are examples, as is the staggeringly gory cost of spells in *Soul Sacrifice*, in which players might be required to sever their own limbs or rip out their own spines in order to cast a spell. Such magic systems tend to emphasize the possibility of backlash, especially toward the caster's sanity, either as the result of misfire or as an inevitable consequence of magic.

The penalty for eldritch spellcasting can be exacted at various points in the process, depending on whether magic itself or only an aspect of magic is regarded as dangerous to the caster. In the *Call of Cthulhu* tabletop RPG, even learning about a spell is perilous to a player character's sanity, so that reading a grimoire has a chance of increasing a player character's mythos rating (her understanding of the Cthulhu mythos) and a proportional chance of lowering her sanity rating. In *Warhammer 40k*, the ritualistic summoning of demons from the Lovecraftian interdimensional abyss called the Warp has a strong chance of going disastrously awry, resulting in an outcome chosen from exotic tables of macabre penalties and punishments. *The Radical's Handbook* explains:

> Such rituals are phenomenally dangerous and little comprehended even by those depraved savants who have spent several human lifespans attempting to uncover and master their secrets, and even when successful, these rituals threaten both body and soul in the baleful backwash of their effect (162).

Table 5-2m, The Contempt of the Warp, from the same handbook expresses the peril of chaos rituals through mechanics, as it lists off the chance of a destructive effect as determined by rolling a d100 (hundred-side die). The 50% chance of being ignored is nearly the best possible outcome, followed by a chance of being "mocked," "struck down," "assailed," "possessed," or "devoured" (Watson 165). Almost equally disturbing is the Table of Basic Ritual Modifiers, in which a favorable modifier of +10 is the providing of a sacrifice for a daemon, while unfavorable modifier of −30 is an incomplete understanding of the ritual, dubbed a "meddling amateur penalty" to suggest the way that the fictional trope of an overeager apprentice has been translated into mechanics (164). The *Bronze Grimoire* supplement from the *Elric* role-playing game also contains tables for the relative difficulty of controlling a demon based on his power relative to that of the caster.

A coded example of Demonic Magic from *Hellband* shows another example of summoning a demon along with a random penalty for making a mistake in casting.

RECIPE 20:   SUMMONING A DEMON (*HELLBAND*, C)

```
case 23:/* Summon monster, demon */
if (randint(3) = = 1)
{

if (summon_specific(py, px, (plev*3)/2, FILTER_DEMON))
        {
msg_print("The area fills with a stench of sulphur and
  brimstone.");
msg_print("'NON SERVIAM! Wretch! I shall feast on thy mortal
  soul!'");
        }
}
else
{
if (summon_specific_friendly((int)py,(int) px, (plev*3)/2,
  FILTER_DEMON, (bool)(plev = = 50 ? TRUE : FALSE)))
        {
msg_print("The area fills with a stench of sulphur and
  brimstone.");
msg_print("'What is thy bidding... Master?'");
        }
}
break;
```

Despite the appeal of darkness and horror in game design, not all dealings with the supernatural must involve the dead or the demonic. Necromancy and diabolism can be viewed as part of a much larger dream world in which anything is possible.

4.10.4 Dream Magic (Oneiromancy)

A powerful relationship between dreams and magic runs throughout the literature of the fantastic and its extensions into game worlds, from the sublimity of Neil Gaiman's incarnation of Dream in *The Sandman* (see Chapter 8, Section 8.15.4) to the slasher gore of *A Nightmare on Elm Street*. Dreams and magic are connected because dreams are unconstrained by the limitations of everyday waking reality, just as magic allows its practitioners to break free from the shackles of mundane law and experience the freedom of the supernatural and transcendent.

Dreams and magic are, in a word, weird. Indeed, one might argue that for magic to be magic, it must be weird, not in the sense of gratuitously or nonsensically bizarre, but in the sense of otherworldly and uncanny. The most powerful fantastic literature often aspires to the condition of the weird, to the point that fantasist Jeff Van Der Meer has dubbed a group of writers "the New Weird," gesturing back at the original Weird Fiction that included Lovecraft's Cthulhu mythos and Robert E. Howard's Conan (both of which have also exerted a powerful influence on game magic). Gaiman, Patricia McKillip, China Miéville, and the new Weird all owe a debt of influence to Lovecraft's Dream Cycle, a series of interconnected stories about protagonist Randolph Carter's nocturnal visits to the Dream Lands, where he encounters an eerie and surreal world. The earliest literature of the fantastic conjoins magic, dreams, and the weird, in much the same way that famed adventure game *The Longest Journey* contrasts the science of the world called Stark (as in "stark reality") with the magic of Arcadia, the world of dreams.

To be magical, a mechanic must run counter to the baseline simulation of the world. If ordinarily players are constrained by gravity, then magic lets them float. If dungeons are typically shrouded in darkness, then magic lets players fill dungeons with light. In this way, all magic is dream magic, which is not necessarily a school of magic as much as a meta-reflective perspective on magic as a whole.

It is also possible to create a dedicated school of dream magic. Dream magic allows players to travel into dream worlds or to warp waking reality by merging it with dream states. Dream magic is characterized by seemingly random effects and strange transformations, yet these effects are always governed by an underlying logic which psychologist Sigmund Freud labeled dream logic.

Dream magic is about an alternate state of existence or consciousness. From the standpoint of mechanics, designers must figure out how long a player stays in the dream state, what powers or penalties are granted while in this state, and what are the conditions for awakening. The NES *Nightmare on Elm Street* is an intriguing example of dream logic, in which players whose sleep meter grows too high due to wandering at night without finding coffee power-ups fall asleep into a dream state, in which they are granted special powers loosely based on the abilities of the Dream Warriors in *Nightmare on Elm Street,* part III. The player's abilities in this world are so overpowered that there is little reason to return to mundane reality, except that the longer one stays asleep the greater the risk of an attack by Freddy Krueger. Loud stereos in the world can wake the player, who then loses his powers and returns to normal. While the implementation of this waking-sleep-dream-waking cycle is imbalanced, there is an inspiring overall idea of a dream state that grants rewarding powers at the expense of gradually building risk of a nightmare attack.

More avant-garde examples of simulating dream logic through game mechanics are *LSD: Dream Emulator*, a rare PS1 title, and *Yume Nikki*, a freeware cult classic adventure game developed in RPG Maker. The gaming history site Hardcoregaming101.net contains excellent articles on both *LSD* and *Yume Nikki*. Both games model the dream state as a set of open, surreal spaces in which exploration is the primary goal. Both games also tantalize players with possibilities of deciphering a network of obscure symbolism. In *Yume Nikki,* the player's goal is to navigate multiple dream worlds via a connecting nexus while searching for 24 effects or magical abilities. In *LSD*, players have little goal other than exploration, but bumping into objects allows players to link between worlds. As adaptations of the shamanic quest to explore other planes of existence, these avant-garde games point the way to something dream-like, outside the boundaries of most commercial gaming. (It is worth noting, though, that exploring dream dimensions by way of a central nexus of doors is a mechanic and trope that appears in commercially successful games from *Ultima Underworld II: Labyrinth of Worlds* to *Demon's Souls*, so the possibility of relatively mainstream dream magic remains.) How far a game designer chooses to plunge his players into the nightmare logic of dream magic will depend greatly on a given game's intended audience.

4.10.5 Space Magic

One of the persistent fantasies associated with magic is the ability to move quickly through space, sometimes through flight and at other times instantaneously through teleportation.

The great literary inspiration for magical planar travel is Roger Zelazny's *Chronicles of Amber*, in which a group of powerful godlike beings travel between shadowy dimensional reflections of their own sacred realm (see Chapter 8, Section 8.8). The tabletop supplement the *GURPS Grimoire* introduces a school of magic called "gate magic," which (like all teleportation magic) ultimately owes a debt to the early *Dungeons & Dragons* spell Dimension Door. Dimension Door was burned onto the consciousness of many early gamers through the 1982 *Dungeons & Dragons* minicomic advertisement that depicts a wizard using a scroll of Dimension Door to open a portal, which transports his fellow adventurers through a tunnel of light into a mysterious castle.

In keeping with the legacy of Dimension Door, there are multiple ways to set up a system of spatial magic, many of which are centered around the idea of portals. In the *Ultima* series, each of the Moongates is a nexus to which the player can return through the use of a spell during a particular phase of the moon. The Moongates are an early version of the role-playing convention of fast travel, which allows players to move rapidly from one location on the overworld map of a game to another without having to tediously and manually walk through the intervening spaces. In a way, all fast travel systems are systems of spatial magic, but their fictive status can resonate with their gameplay systems to greater and lesser degrees.

Gating magic feels more like an exercise of magical skill if passing through a portal has conditions, which can be expressed as a series of checks. The simplest is the need for a portal key. Be creative! If passing through a portal is a lock and key puzzle, then the nature of the key must be highly unique in order for the puzzle to feel like magic. The planar gates in *Planescape: Torment* often require quirky items, even intangibles or abstractions, such as a memory or a song, to pass through.

RECIPE 21: A PORTAL WITH A KEY (ORIGINAL PSEUDOCODE)

```
if (!playerhasportalkey)
     {
     print"The portal buzzes listlessly, as if you are
missing some key item";
     }
otherwise
     {
     print "The portal springs to life with electrical
energy, beckoning you onward into another dimension!";
moveplayerto(dimension);
     }
```

More interesting teleportation systems depend on more complex preconditions to either open the portals or specify the caster's destination, such as randomizers or the phases of the moon. The Moongates in the *Ultima* series were inspired by the map of timegates in Terry Gilliam's film

Time Bandits, in which portals open only rarely and at particular times and places.

RECIPE 22:   A PORTAL WITH PHASES (ORIGINAL PSEUDOCODE)

```
enterportal()
{
if (!playerhasportalkey)
{print"The portal buzzes listlessly, as if you are missing
   some key item";}
otherwise {print "The portal springs to life with electrical
   energy, beckoning you onward into another dimension!";}

if (getrandommoonphase ! = openportal)
{
Print "The new moon is only a sliver in the sky, and the
   portal remains shut.";
}
otherwise
{
print "The portal springs to life with electrical energy,
   beckoning you onward into another dimension!";
moveplayerto(dimension);
}
```

One of the ways to distinguish your teleportation system from those in other games is through unique destinations and ways of traveling there. Do players teleport to another level of a dungeon, to another town, or to another plane of existence altogether? Rather than simply allowing a player to blink from one location to another, try representing the labyrinth through which he travels. In *The Chronicles of Amber,* the nobles of Amber move through dimensions by navigating the Pattern, a twisting labyrinth two-dimensional floor labyrinth in the classical sense, while the Lords of Chaos travel through a morphing three-dimensional maze called the Logrus. Such a scheme of teleportation might most appropriately be represented through a mini-game in which players are teleported to another level. The *Nine Princes in Amber* adventure game simulates negotiating the Patterns as a mini-game in which the player places pieces to form a multi-colored line that forks and twists. Similarly, *Torment: Tides of Numenera,* the crowdfunded spiritual successor to *Planescape: Torment,* will require players to navigate a lore-filled labyrinth every time they die in order to return to the mortal plane.

Arranging a portal-based transportation system would be an exercise in graphing, setting up the nodes across a world and the connecting line segments representing a player's ability to move between them. An entire discipline of mathematics known as graphic theory represents ways of mapping the connections between nodes, resulting in navigational and connect-the-dot puzzles that often underlie traveling within a role-playing game. Nodes could be arranged as hubs with spokes emanating from them (a common trope in games that involve planar travel such as *Gauntlet: Dark Legacy* or *Ultima Underworld II*). Some connecting paths could be two-way, while others could be one-way or active only under certain conditions, such as the possession of a talisman or a moon phase. The use of moon phases as spell conditions requires a system for tracking time.

RECIPE 23:   TELEPORTATION MAGIC (ORIGINAL PSEUDOCODE)

```
Required ingredients
Word required: space, movement,

Teleportation points A, B, and C
Move between them

Or

Move wherever your cursor is
```

4.10.6 Time Magic

RECIPE 24:   TIME MAGIC (ORIGINAL PSEUDOCODE)

```
Arx Fatalis: Slow time: Rhaa Tempum (Weakness Time)
Ultima Underworld: Speed: Rel Tym Por (Change Time Movement)
Recipe # 1:
Variable time T
Slow down
Speed up
Rewind
```

4.10.7 Vision Magic (Scrying)

One of the great promises of magic is to reveal that which is hidden, to see into other dimensions or into the future. In historical occultism, this practice is called scrying: gazing into a crystal ball, mirror, or pool of ink in order to catch glimpses of the future or the spirit world. The stereotyped gypsy telling fortunes in a crystal ball or the teenager looking into the bathroom mirror to see Bloody Mary or Candyman are both examples of scrying.

For scrying to work as a gameplay mechanic, certain elements of the environment must be designated as hidden, once again reinforcing the connection between level design and magic systems (see Chapter 6, Section 6.11). These hidden elements could be secret doors, hidden buttons, or messages scrawled in blood or invisible ink. By hiding certain elements, level designers and systems designers set up the possibility of spells that reveal these secrets. Scrying spells can simply toggle the state of hidden objects to the revealed state, possibly for a limited duration specified either by a fixed interval, until the mana pool runs out, or until a counterspell or other in-game event interrupts the scrying.

Alternatively, vision spells can be tied into the lighting mechanics of the game, resulting in a more analog approach in which spells can brighten or dim the environment much in the same way that torches, candles, or other natural light sources do. Brightness settings in modern games are often on a sliding scale that can be manipulated by players to some degree when setting up the game. Such a value is likely to be stored in a floating-point variable (i.e. a variable with a decimal point that can occupy intermediate values between 0 and 1), or multiple variables to represent diverse kinds of light. Various spells that enhance vision (such as Night Vision, Night Eye, Enhance Vision, and Enhance Eye) can manipulate the light variable or variables to allow players to see objects that are otherwise hidden.

A third type of vision magic involves remote viewing, which refers to the ability to see things from a distance, as if through a disembodied, roving eye. Remote viewing and astral projection both involve the separation of the soul or the sight from the body. Such a spell allows the player to explore unknown environments without risk of detection or attack, enabling scouting and planning. From a programming perspective, this is simply the manipulation of a camera, detaching the camera from the avatar so that it can move through a level or world and provide a view that the player could otherwise not see. Both *Ultima Underworld* and *Arx Fatalis* feature this spell, in the form of Roaming Sight: Ort Por Wis (Magic Movement Knowledge) and Flying Eye: Vista Movis (Vision Movement). In *Arx Fatalis*, this spell allows the player to shift to see his own avatar from a first-person perspective, resulting in an eerie and emergent experience of astral projection.

For such a spell of revealing to operate, the language of the magic system must contain words that refer to vision, improvement, illusion, and negation. Three of the most overtly linguistic magic systems (*Ultima Underworld*, *Arx Fatalis,* and *Eternal Darkness*) all accommodate spells for scrying because their vocabularies can express ideas related to vision.

In *Ultima Underworld*, the spells are Quas Lor (Illusion Light) and Ort An Quas (Magic Negate Illusion). In *Arx Fatalis*, these spells are Night Vision: Mega Vista (Improve Vision) and Reveal: Nhi Stregum Vista (Negate Magic Vision). In both games, there is a spell to enhance vision on a sliding, analog scale related to light (Quas Lor and Mega Vista) as well as a spell to reveal hidden objects on a binary scale by toggling a state from hidden to revealed. The concept of revelation can be expressed linguistically either positively or negatively, as dispelling an illusion or revealing something hidden. Generally, the binary approach tends to work well in puzzle-based situations, where a hidden object, such as a message, is either visible or invisible. In *Eternal Darkness*, which emphasizes puzzles of detection, the spell is Narokath Redgormor (Absorb Area).

RECIPE 25:   SCRYING MAGIC (ORIGINAL PSEUDOCODE)

```
//Reveal hidden things
//Binary toggle (hidden/revealed) of certain objects
//(messages, switches, buttons, secret doors);

RevealHiddenDoors()
{
      for(i = 1; i < = CurrentlyVisibleScreenSizeX; i++;)
            for (j = 1; j < = CurrentlyVisibleScreenSizeY; j++)
                  if(ObjectIsHiddenDoor())
                        {
                            SetObjectIsHiddenDoor() = false;
                        }

}
```

4.10.8 Invisibility Magic

From Frodo's ring to H.G. Wells' invisible man, human beings have longed to be invisible. Stealth games such as *Thief* and *Dishonored* often integrate magic with the core mechanic of remaining hidden. Despite the title of the game *Thief*, Garrett is more a magician than a rogue, or rather his thievery is a form of magic when successfully enacted by the player. Garrett's training in the monastic order of the Keepers involves abilities to become invisible that border on the supernatural, as well as the acquisition of arcane knowledge, including glyphs of power. The classification of Thief and the associated image of a diminutive, cowled figure hiding in the shadows derives in part from the thief character class that originates in *Dungeons & Dragons* as well as the fantasy characters that inspired it, including rogues like Fritz Leiber's Grey Mouser (who was by training a magician's apprentice). Yet, Garrett's abilities and actions are not constrained to hiding in shadows or backstabbing; he is a quintessential opportunist who does whatever he needs to get the job done. An extra objective available at a higher difficulty level in the prison level of Dark Project involves retrieving Garrett's favorite "Hand of Glory." The Hand is an infamous black magical artifact described in the *Petit Albert* grimoire as the severed hand of a hanged corpse taken from the gallows and used by cat burglars to evade detection by otherworldly means. As the *Petit Albert* explains, "The hand of glory [...] is used by villains thieves to enter houses at night without hindrance." Figure 4.22 depicts the Hand of Glory.

In addition to this talismanic magic, Garrett plunders magical artifacts and even engages in complex acts of counter-magic as he disrupts the extra-dimensional ritual of the Trickster in the Maw of Chaos or activates the glyphs in *Deadly Shadows*. It is not surprising that Garrett's cowl and long flowing robes are equal parts monastic garb and magician's robe. He is a Master of hiding and the hidden: literally, the occult.

When skillfully guided by a player, Garrett's magic consists in his ability to "keep silent," one of the four powers of the sphinx extolled by French occultist Eliphas Lévi in *The Dogma and Ritual of High Magic*. Lévi argued that magicians must learn "to know, to dare, to will, and to keep silent," powers that he attributed to the four elements of classical antiquity (air, water, fire, and earth). To keep silent means literally to maintain the secrecy of the mysteries of initiation, but it can be extended as a metaphorical principle of efficiency and noiseless grace: in other words,

FIGURE 4.22   The Hand of Glory.

stealth. As British occultist Aleister Crowley explains in his *Confessions*, "to dare must be backed by to will and to know, all three being ruled by to keep silence. Which last means many things, but most of all so to control oneself that every act is done noiselessly; all disturbance means clumsiness or blundering." A stance of self-controlled noiselessness is the strategic condition of success in *Thief* and a style of gameplay that activates Garrett's full abilities as an avatar. "Disturbance," "clumsiness," and "blundering" are the fail conditions of the *Thief* series which assure detection and death.

Garrett's apparent physical weakness, signified by hit points sufficient only for a few sword blows from a guard, is counterbalanced by preternatural abilities of stealth. Ordinary mortals risk detection when they hide in shadows, because only the deepest darkness can reliably block out peering eyes. But when a player guides Garrett into shadow and reduces his light gem to pure black, Garrett can vanish, even as a guard walks a few inches beside him. These abilities are built into the game systems of *Thief*, which rewards ritualistic behaviors of stealth: always tread in the shadows, walk rather than run when possible, extinguish light strategically, and close doors behind you. While we never learn the ultimate essence of Keeper training (which is itself shrouded within the game systems of *Thief*), our success in *Thief* depends on our identification with Garrett and his training, which forces us to ask "What Would Garrett Do?"

The merging of stealth and mysticism gives rise to the arcane discipline of the Ḥashshāshīn in *Assassin's Creed*, whose credo "nothing is true, everything is permitted" conceals a mystical insight under the veil of anarchic nihilism: a Neo-Platonic belief in the irreality of the sensible world. Altair, like Garrett, "works in shadows to serve the light," or rather to unwittingly maintain the balance of the Keepers against which he rebelled. *Thief* teaches the gamers and game designers inspired by it that direct confrontation is often counter-productive, and that the ability to judiciously "keep silent" and move quietly is a higher magic than a carelessly tossed fireball or a poorly chosen word.

Invisibility is the inverse and mirror image of vision magic. As such, the problems of designing a system of magical invisibility are similar. Invisibility can be on a binary scale of detected or undetected, as in *Mark of the Ninja*, or on a sliding scale such as degrees of exposure to light, as in *Thief*. Linguistically, invisibility spells of the binary sort could also be inversions of vision-enhancing spells, as in *Ultima Underworld*, where the invisibility spells based on Sanct Lor (Protection Light) are the semantic reversals of the Light spells based on In Lor (Create Light).

RECIPE 26:   INVISIBILITY (ORIGINAL PSEUDOCODE)

```
//Recipe # 1: Binary (An object is either totally visible or
  totally invisible)

MakeInvisible();
{
     target = GetTargetedObject();//select an object to
make invisible
     if (GetTargetedObject.Visible = true)
            {
                  SetTargetedObject.Visible = false;
            }
}
//Recipe # 2:
//Spectrum of visibility

//A slider between totally concealed and totally visible

MakeLessVisible();
{
     int target = GetTargetedObject();//select an object to
//make invisible
     float visibilitylevel = GetTargetObject.
VisibilityLevel();
     GetTargetedObject.LowerVisibilityLevel(-10);
}
int amounttolower
LowerVisibilityLevel(amounttolower)
{
NewObjectVisibilityLevel =
   GetTargetedObjectVisibilityLevel() -amounttolower;

}
```

4.10.9 Flight Magic

One of the most primal fantasies associated with sorcery is the dream of flight, whether through a magic carpet, a broomstick, or through the sheer power of will. Levitation has been a spell since early CRPGs, where it referred primarily to the ability to teleport upward or downward in a dungeon by increments of floors, as in *The Bard's Tale* or *Ultima.*

This crude form of levitation derives from the way that space is represented in the game as dungeons with discrete floors represented as layouts on orthogonal graph paper. Levitation in terms of relative distance from the floor or intermediate position is irrelevant in this type of game. Of course, this way of representing space is neither the most common nor the most conducive to gripping flight magic.

Flight is potentially much more powerful when simulated through physics, negating gravity enough to allow players to soar but still permitting nuanced gliding with and against the wind. In keeping with a desire for analog, simulated flight, *Ultima Underworld* featured a variety of flight spells, ranging from Feather Fall (a slowing of downward movement) to levitation, to full flight. The levitation spell of *Arx Fatalis* is severely limited by the inability to change vertical height (i.e. movement on the Y or Z axis, depending on one's coordinate system). The levitation spell in *The Elder Scrolls III: Morrowind*, allows for movement along all three axes, greatly aiding in exploration and navigation of vast labyrinthine spaces.

RECIPE 27:   FLIGHT MAGIC (ORIGINAL PSEUDOCODE)

```
//Required Ingredients:
//In order to allow for flight, the language of a given
//magic system must include words that reference space and
//movement. Words that refer to up would make the language
//even clearer, though in practice neither Arx Fatalis or
//Ultima Underworld specifies upward movement. In Ultima
//Underworld, the three spells pertaining to flight are:
//Rel Des Por (Change Down Movement)
//Hur Por (Wind Movement)
//Vas Hur Por (Great Wind Movement)
//In Arx Fatalis, the Levitate spell is Mega Spacium Movis
   (Improve Space//Movement)
//Digital flight
//0 = on ground
//1 = flying

//Analog flight
//Variable z = vertical height
```

The *Elder Scrolls* games, often regarded as spiritual successors to the *Ultima Underworld* series, feature multiple levitation and flight spells. Forum contributor Cid88 also released his own lifting script. This levitation spell from *The Elder Scrolls Construction* set relies on moving a player up along the z-axis (the axis perpendicular to the ground plane that measures vertical motion), using the function "setzpos." The script resets an object's z-position.

RECIPE 28:   A LEVITATION SPELL (CID88, ELDER SCROLLS SCRIPT)

```
CODE
scn Liftother

ref self
short done
float zpos
float zpos2
float inc2
float fat

Begin ScriptEffectStart
set self to GetSelf
if (self.IsActor ! = 1)
return
endif
set fat to self.GetAV fatigue
if (self.IsInInterior ! = 1)
set inc2 to 400
else
set inc2 to 100
endif
if (done = = 0)
self.SetAV fatigue 0
set zpos to self.GetPos z
set zpos2 to zpos + inc2
self.SetPos z zpos2
set done to 1
else
return
endif
End

Begin ScriptEffectFinish
self.SetAV fatigue fat
if (done = = 1)
set done to 0
return
else
return
endif
End
```

4.10.10 Dragon Magic

In fiction and occultism, there has been a longstanding association between dragons and magic. Dragons are primal and primordial, masters of both ice and fire in the language of George R.R. Martin. A common trope is that dragons speak the language of magic. Their language may be part of the magic of True Names, as in *A Wizard of Earthsea* (see Chapter 8, Section 8.4). The return of dragons in a disenchanted world may herald the return of enchantment, as in *A Song of Ice and Fire*, in which Daenerys uses the magical language High Valyrian to train her new dragons. In occultism, there is also a longstanding connection between magic and dragons, sometimes through the Typhonian magic of the Egyptian god Seth, who occultist Kenneth Grant associated with serpentine or ophidian magic, and later through the rare *Dragon Book of Essex* of Andrew Chumbley (see Chapter 6, Section 6.15.1).

The connection between dragons and magic comes to the forefront in *The Elder Scrolls V: Skyrim*, in which the player-character takes the role of the Dragonborn, a descendant of the dragons who can cast powerful spells called Dragon Shouts by mastering the vocabulary of the dragons' language. These shouts have varied effects, including controlling the weather (Clear Skies) and Divination (Aura) and Telekinesis (the infamous Fus Ro Dah, which means "Force Balance Push"). The conventional magic of *Skyrim* taught in the last remaining college of Winterhold seems oddly underpowered and shallow, in large part because the true depth of the game's magic system is in the Dragon Shouts.

The best way to construct dragon magic is to consider the mythological powers of dragons, which vary greatly between mythologies. The Western, European dragon is a fearsome and malevolent creature who flies, breathes fire, and hordes gold in burrows deep beneath the earth. The Eastern dragon of China and Japan is a more jovial creature, bearing tidings of good luck and joy to those he encounters.

4.10.11 Star Magic

Astrology, the belief that the stars and other heavenly bodies influence human affairs, has been one of the major branches of the occult since ancient times. Astrology is closely connected to the principle of magical timing: the idea that magical operations are best performed during certain phases and alignments of celestial bodies, such as the conjunctions of planets.

4.10.12 Music Magic

Many ancient cultures correlate music and magic (see Chapter 3, Section 3.13). Music requires skillful performance in much the way that magic is fabled to, and the abstract mathematical patterns of music directly affect the emotions in ways that seem sorcerous. The ancient Greeks believed that each of the seven planets emitted a single tone, and these tones were collectively known as the music of the spheres. The Pythagoreans and the Platonists, two groups of ancient Greek philosophers, both made the music of the spheres central elements of their cosmologies. Pythagorean and Platonic thought in turn influenced the Renaissance philosophers of magic known as hermeticists.

In keeping with the overall occult theory of correspondences, many occultists correlate particular notes with shades of color. Isaac Newton's color wheel in *Opticks* included seven shades of the visible spectrum, to correspond with seven notes of a scale and the seven known planets. As Becky Koenig explains in *Color Workbook*, some artists still refer to "color chords" comprised of hues at regular intervals on the color wheel that work harmoniously together (32).

Music magic is traditionally the power of bards, who cast spells in the form of songs. Such songs could be exempt from typical spellcasting, such as allowing for unlimited casts per day without recourse to Vancian slots or mana pools required of other mage classes. Bardic songs might also have another requirement, such as the requirement in the original *Bard's Tale* to drink alcohol before singing in order to avoid a dry throat or lack of inspiration. Musical magic need not be jolly—the Arcanoi of Keening in *Wraith: The Oblivion* is wielded by musically inclined spectres to evoke melancholy, thereby feeding the precious resource of Pathos that can fuel further spells and abilities.

The genre of musical games, such as *Guitar Hero, Rock Band,* and *Rocksmith*, opens up possibilities for bridging the gap between player performance and character action. Using specialized controllers and interfaces, players can perform an approximation of music in which gameplay takes into account rhythms, pitches, and gestures associated with actual musical performance. The same fidelity of musical performance can be applied to musical magic as core mechanics that goes beyond the effective but simple pattern recognition of *Loom* and *The Legnd of Zelda: Ocarina of Time.*

An understanding of music theory and musical mysticism can help to create more sophisticated recipes for game magic. The auditory equivalent of Newton's color wheel is the Circle of Fifths. Figure 4.23 shows the Circle of Fifths. Proceeding clockwise, this wheel shows notes distributed at intervals of five whole steps: C, G, D, A, E, B. These notes sound harmonious when used together, and the chords based on the notes are common sequences known as progressions. The circle of fifths, and the process of chord building more generally, would be a powerful basis for a musical magic system in which spells consist of chords or songs based on chords.

Certain intervals have occult associations, such as the flatted fifth, known as the Devil's interval. Now a staple of blues, rock and roll, and heavy metal, this interval was once regarded as the work of Satan because of its dissonant and jarring tone, thought to be both infernal and sexually arousing. In game terms, a run or chord with the devil's interval could trigger an infernal spell, possibly summoning a demon. A major chord might heal, while a minor chord might harm. In addition, one could easily imagine the equivalent of a Robert Johnson expansion pack for *Guitar Hero* in which the player can sell his soul for infinite star power, gaining access to a wealth of blues-based spells that might be themed through the voodoo crossroads lore popularized by the television show *Supernatural.* The possibilities of chord construction and the resultant spells are as nuanced and varied as the emotions evoked by music. It is no coincidence that a popular guitar instruction

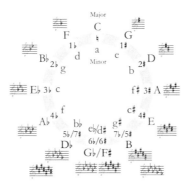

FIGURE 4.23   Circle of Fifths. (Image by Just plain bill, under Creative Commons Attribution-Share Alike 3.0 Unported License.)

book called *The Guitar Grimoire* teaches pages of chord formations and music theory (or that the Gothically lettered, red-and-black cover of this book displays the circle of fifths, as well as an authorship credit to the kabbalistic divine-man, Adam Kadmon). The vocabulary and structure of music are intuitively close to magic and to games, and musically driven game magic completes the circle of these related systems.

4.10.13 Summoning (Invocation/Evocation)

This school of magic bears the most resemblance to classical Western occultism, including grimoire magic, the Enochian system, and Golden Dawn magic. These systems consist primarily of mechanisms and protocol for summoning and conversing with spirits, including angels and demons, in order to acquire information and command the spirits to accomplish tasks. The heart of classic occultism is conversation, so that the languages in these systems are primarily intended to communicate in a call and response fashion with spirits: to ask them queries and to command them to accomplish things.

4.10.14 Chaos Magic

Chaos magic thrives on randomness and probability: the perspective dependence and multiple worlds of quantum physics rather than the predictable certainty of Newtonian determinism. If other forms of magic involve wielding powers, then Chaos unleashes them. The chaos magician does not so much control magic as he is controlled by it. However, like all random and unpredictable elements in games, chaos magic must be carefully chosen and balanced.

The primary fictional inspirations for chaos magic are Roger Zelazny, Michael Moorcock, and offshoots in the *Warhammer* universe, in which Chaos patrons fickly grant dubiously valuable boons that may turn out to be mutations or outright hindrances. For example, most of the sixteen chaos patrons in the roguelike *Zangband* come directly from Michael Moorcock's multiverse, especially the Elric saga, with the addition of four *Warhammer* deities (the standard Slaanesh, Khorne, and Tzeentch, as well as the more ambiguous Khaine). There is an actual modern variety of occultism called chaos magic which can sometimes intersect productively with these fictions (see Chapter 8, Section 8.5).

Roguelikes *Zangband* and *Hellband* simulate chaos magic through Chaos Warriors and Chaos Knights, who serve a patron who grants boons when they level up. These boons derive from tables, each of them unique to a particular chaos patron, from which abilities and events are randomly selected. Chaos doesn't feel like chaos if there are only a few effects, or if they are predictable. Chaos instead glories in variety and unpredictability. A particular chaos patron may grant a vast experience point multiplier or a powerful chaos blade. He might summon a crowd of difficult enemies out of nothingness or destroy the enemies who beleaguer the player. (A particular fickle chaos patron could first summon enemies and then vaporize them; the beauty of randomness is that anything is possible, including irony.)

The recipes for chaos magic and demon magic are similar because both involve risky pacts with otherworldly forces that may rebound on the caster. The three schools of chaos magic, demonic magic, and necromancy are all related as black arts requiring sacrifice and heavy costs. Chaos magic in the popular imagination tends to be more directly aggressive, involving explosive force that does not merely burn the world, but unmakes it altogether.

But it would be worthwhile to consider less direct alternatives that are actually more chaotic, such as polymorphing, mutations, and the three-dimensional chaos labyrinth called the Logrus in Zelazny. All of these are well within the grasp of programmers: they are already present in nascent form within roguelikes. The *Hellband* spells Alter Reality, Earthquake, and Behemoth's Call could all be viewed as aspects of chaos magic, which tends to lead into the meta-formula of reality warping. These spells all change the level layout of already procedurally generated levels in unpredictable ways. This meta-referential aspect of chaos magic makes sense, because the occultist practice of chaos magic is eclectic, treating all other systems as perspective or paradigms that can be adopted or discarded at will. Mutually influenced by role-playing games, theorists of chaos magic often divide the paradigms of magic into color-coded radial diagrams, sometimes distributed around the eight-pointed star of chaos (see Chapter 4, Section 4.6 and Chapter 8, Section 8.5).

4.10.15 Divination Magic

Divination magic is one of the most natural formulae for digital games. Because a virtual world is a digital collection of information about that world, retrieving that information and relaying it to the player comes readily from a programming perspective. Any time a function takes the form of Get X, the function is retrieving information in the form of a stored variable, such as player health, number of zombies in a given radius, or the dungeon level that the player is currently exploring.

The challenge from a design perspective becomes how much information to divulge and in what form. In a tabletop game, divination magic can be used with great flexibility, since it entails a conversation with the dungeon master, who possesses all information about the game world and can dole it out in amounts that are useful for dramatic and gameplay purposes. A role-player playing a well-prepared divination mage once completed the entire infamously difficult *Dungeons & Dragons* module *Tomb of Horrors* by predicting the possible results of each action before doing anything. Without complex artificial intelligence schemes, it is difficult for a computer to judge which information will be most dramatically useful from a narrative point of view. On the other hand, computers are notoriously efficient at making predictions based on patterns of data, so it is quite plausible to incorporate divination sub-systems that make predictions on the order of "there is a strong chance that you will die on this level." Even without such systems, a random set of relevant and cryptic hints can at least create the illusion of divination. The quirky mystery game *Deadly Premonition* allows the detective player character to divine by looking at the patterns of swirling cream in a hot cup of coffee, and at least one set of initials revealed through this process has massive bearing on the game's plot.

Many real-world systems of divination already exist, and some of them take the form of games. Some of the earliest games of chance and their associated randomizers, such as dice and tarot cards, were originally forms of divination (see Chapter 7, Section 7.1). Other games, like the Ouija board eventually made by Parker Brothers and later Hasbro, were marketed specifically as party games in which participants would pretend to be consulting with spirits. (Automatic writing using planchettes did exist prior to the Ouija board in China and elsewhere.)

Given the game-like nature of many divinatory systems, it is no surprise that videogame versions of these games did show up eventually, both in the early and modern era. *Taboo: The Sixth Sense* is an NES game that offers tarot readings, horoscopes, and lucky lottery numbers. The more recent iOS application *SpiritPad: The Oracle* is an implementation of the

Ouija board. As Stephen Toltilo's *Kotaku* article explains, the application's creators plan to implement artificial intelligence to simulate a spirit on the other side. The progressive rock band The Mars Volta's concept album *Bedlam in Goliath* purports to tell a murder mystery inspired by malevolent spirits communicating through a Ouija board. The album was developed as a supernatural adventure game called *Goliath: The Soothsayer*, in which the player must unravel a mystery surrounding his vanished brother.

A simple version of divination involves granting the player extended or amplified senses in the virtual world. Many of the Mysticism spells in The Elder Scrolls series follow this pattern, such as Nighteye (which grants players vision in the dark) and Detect Life (which shows players nearby enemies, either on a mini-map or by rendering walls translucent). Many roguelikes feature multiple such detection spells, which in terms of code consist of scanning the map for a given entity and then revealing all instances of the ASCII character that stands for that entity.

Yet while detection spells may simulate the experience of ESP, they do not fully represent the experience of divination, which involves communing with spirits to gain information. Divination magic would be more engaging and effective if it were connected to more gameplay systems. A game with an advanced weather system could track weather several turns in advance, and the computer's AI could therefore answer queries about the future weather before players embarked on a sea voyage. A game that tracked who killed whom (such as *Dwarf Fortress*) could answer questions about a murderer's identity, perhaps as part of a murder mystery quest. Any aspect of the world that the game's code tracks could be the object of a divinatory query. Therefore, if game designers want better divination magic, they need more robust world simulation. One of the divination methods most amenable to game magic is the tarot, which was a card game before it acquired mystical associations as a mode of fortune-telling.

4.10.16 Tarot Magic

Tarot magic recipes would draw on some variation of the Tarot pack, which consists traditionally of 78 cards (22 trumps or Major Arcana, 10 numbered cards of four suits [cups, wands, swords, pentacles], and 16 court cards [Knight, Queen, King, Ace for each suit]). Seventy-eight is a high number of spells for one school of magic, so it might be advisable to concentrate on the Major Arcana or a selection of other cards.

FIGURE 1.1　A Symbolic Key of Intended Audiences. (Pentagram image from Clickr.com)

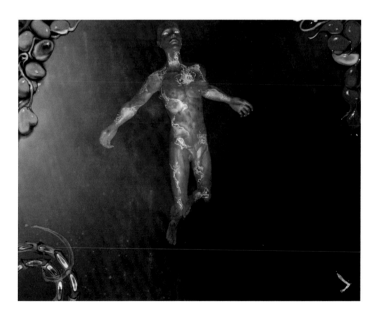

FIGURE 3.10　Hearts and Nerva in *The Void*. (Image by Ice-Pick Lodge.)

FIGURE 4.1   Seven Schools of Magic. (Original image by Giles Timms.)

FIGURE 4.2   An Abstract Representation of Five Influential Schools of Magic. (Original image by Giles Timms.)

FIGURE 4.3   The Schools of Magic in This Chapter. (Original image by Giles Timms.)

FIGURE 4.21   Tree of Life with Color Scales.

FIGURE 5.2   Demon Profiles in *Arcana*.

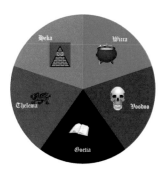

FIGURE 6.2   Schools of Occult Magic. (Original image by Giles Timms.)

FIGURE 6.3   Pie Chart of Voodoo Loa. (Original image by Giles Timms.)

FIGURE 6.7   Rose Cross. (By the Order of the Golden Dawn. Public domain due to age.)

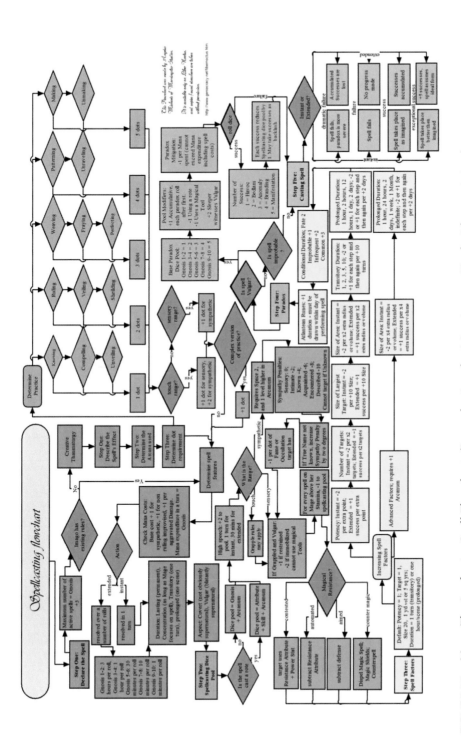

FIGURE 7.2 *Mage: The Awakening* Spell Flowchart. (Image by Angelus Morningstar. Used with permission.)

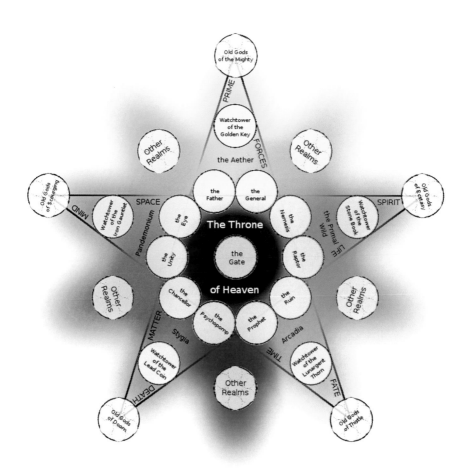

FIGURE 7.3 The Ten Arcana of *Mage: The Awakening*. (Image by Dataweaver. Used with permission.)

The heart of Tarot magic is a correlation between the image on the card and a unique magical effect, usually one powerful enough to merit its own major Arcana card. Tarot spells also depend on random number generators, which are the digital equivalent of shuffling. In C, a relevant function is "rand," which generates a random integer.

Tabletop role-playing games have used dice-derived random integers to simulate drawing cards ever since the Deck of Many Things appeared in the first *Greyhawk* module. The Deck of Many Things is a powerful magical item in the *Dungeons & Dragons* universe which a player activates by drawing a card. This artifact has evolved through several editions of *Dungeons & Dragons*, starting with the first edition of *Greyhawk*. As Bart Caroll and Steve Winter observe in their "Alumni: Deck of Many Things" article for *Dragon Magazine,* the randomizing element of the Deck is exactly what makes it fascinating and engaging. Whereas other artifacts offer predictable effects, using the Deck involves drawing from a standard deck of playing cards in order to receive a magic effect at random.

The *Greyhawk* version of the Deck of Many Things includes a limited number of suit and court cards without major arcana, but by first edition the deck evolves into its own set of twenty-two emblematic Major Arcana, including the Balance, the Comet, the Donjon, Euryale (one of the ancient Greek vengeful spirits called furies), the Fates, Flames, the Fool, the Gem, the Idiot, the Jester, the Key, the Knight, the Moon, the Rogue, the Ruin, the Skull, the Star, the Sun, the Talons, the Throne, the Vizier, and the Void. The fascination of this deck consists in its status as Tarot through the looking glass: it refracts the Tarot deck into a modified version of emblematic images that are reminiscent of the standard Major Arcana but original to the *Dungeons & Dragons* universe. Of the cards, only a few belong directly to the Tarot, including the Fool, the Moon, and the Sun. The cards have been modified to images whose associated magical effects make sense in *Dungeons & Dragons*. Rather than foretelling the future, the Deck of Many Things creates the future, so that a player who draws the Balance card experiences a shift in alignment (versus a Tarot reader who draws the Justice card, suggesting that a morally righteous judgment may occur in the future).

Like the Deck of Many Things, a key example of Tarot-inspired magic is Trump magic in *Zangband*. Trump magic in *Zangband* is exemplary, thematically resonant with the *Chronicles of Amber* (see Chapter 8, Section 8.8), and productively inspired by the actual occult tradition of the

Tarot (see Chapter 7, Section 7.1). There are 32 Trump spells with a variety of effects, most of them pertaining to either teleportation or summoning. *Zangband* includes a function of the form `randintx(y)`, which effectively rolls a die with a number of faces equal to *y*. The trump spells draw some of their unpredictability by recursively embedding random integers: a recipe that could be emulated in other contexts. Shuffle, a spell-within-a-spell, simulates the shuffling of a Tarot deck with (strangely) 24 cards. If the player draws the Wheel of Fortune card, they trigger another `randint` function that selects a wild magic effect randomly from among 32 possibilities. Wild magic could itself fall through into a function that summons a random creature.

These recursive random functions have the effect of extreme unpredictability that also retains some degree of order so that lower cards in a shuffle have less beneficial effects than higher ones, allowing players to benefit from luck bonuses. The most powerful trump spells tend to be major summonings (such as Trump Greater Undead, Trump Ancient Dragon, and Trump Demon) or intensified divination spells, such as Trump Divination (which invokes the omniscient function `detectall()`) and Trump Lore (which calls the `identifyfully()` function).

Another example of Tarot magic is the *Persona* series of role-playing games, itself part of the larger universe of *Shin Megami Tensei* (Japanese for True Goddess Reincarnation).

Divination and Tarot magic offer alternative ways to think about fire magic, moving it out of the form of magical projectiles and into the realm of mystic revelation.

4.10.17 Fire Magic

In fire is magic. The cliché of tossing fireballs in videogames, while tiresome in many respects, is linked to a genuine connection between fire and a primal sense of wonder. As the independent film maker David Lynch observes in an interview, "Fire is so magical," evoking thoughts of "magic, the unexplainable." The ancient Greek philosopher Heraclitus agreed, arguing that the entire cosmos is made of "ever-living fire," which manifests in the universe through the tendency of all objects to change in constant flux.

How then, can we as game designers use fire in a way that intensifies rather than diminishes its magic? The term "pyromancer" may hold a clue. A pyromancer is, literally, one who speaks with the fire. The term is the name of a character class in *Dark Souls* as well as a faction in *A Song of Ice and Fire*. In both cases, fire has larger metaphysical implications— as the place where the primal beings found the souls of Lords in *Dark Souls*, and as the element of the Red God R'hllor in *A Song of Ice and Fire*. The pyromancers of King's Landing appear to be chemists who have mastered the art of incendiary explosions, but the Red Priests of R'hllor wield fire in a more mysterious and magically charged manner connected to their religion.

Fire becomes more interesting as a game mechanic when it is more than a projectile attack or an area of effect napalm strike. A pyromancer is one who *communicates* with fire: as so often in magic, the paradigm of communication and conversation are keys to metaphysical depth of gameplay. Fire becomes a more interesting game mechanic when players are able to speak with the fire, to conjure it, and perhaps to see visions within it. The practice of gazing into fire to divine the future is ancient, and is also at the heart of the Red Priests' magic in *A Song of Ice and Fire*.

Technologically, fire in games tends to be comprised of particle emitters and particle effects, sources which emit bursts and swirls of colored sprites that simulate flames. Fire may also be comprised of various shaders that create glowing and smoldering effects, producing the appearance of guttering embers or simmering magma. Tech demos for many current-generation games often feature gorgeous and realistic renditions of fire; yet, in some ways, this graphical pyrotechnics is part of the problem. A preoccupation with graphical fidelity often comes at the expense of simulation and, more importantly, metaphor (or the best of both worlds: simulation charged with metaphorical implications).

As usual, the *Dwarf Fortress* designer Toady One offers a strikingly different vision of what fire magic could be in "Dwarf Fortress Talk 7.2":

> You don't want to say something like "it's a +3 flaming sword" but if in effect the sword is just on fire and burns things and stuff, that's certainly a fair artifact to put in; just because it's a cheesy Dungeons and Dragons thing doesn't mean that it's the end of the world. But it could be the end of the world if having the artifact sword is somehow drawing your fortress closer to some kind of world of fire and then suddenly it like sucks into some kind of fire plane and your whole fortress catches on fire and then everyone wonders why there's a new volcano.

Toady One's vision of possible fire magic reinforces his overall commentary on magic: "it's kind of depressing in a way if magic isn't mysterious." This aphorism is doubly true of fire magic. Since ancient cultures revered fire because it is both useful and mysterious, fire is cheapened if it is only a form of damage. Fire becomes more exciting if its results are unpredictable and even cosmic. An approach to fire can start by modeling the dynamic chemistry of fire: the way that it can spread and multiply exponentially, the capacity of objects to catch fire and ignite other objects, the effect of variables like dryness, wind, and available fuel on the shape of fire. Ignition could be modeled as a burning state that can toggle as a Boolean, or more richly as relative degrees of intensity and temperature.

Toady's comments suggest an even richer vision of flame that is tied to an alternate plane of fire (a common element in *Dungeons & Dragons* cosmology). The idea that using fire for mundane purposes would bring the player closer to this fire plane resonates strongly with the linguistic origins of pyromancy as speaking with the fire. If the algorithms governing fire generation also incorporated shadowy images or visions, this would be even closer to pyromancy. If gazing into the fire could transport the mage to the fire plane temporarily, fire would take on an even stronger metaphysical resonance. Not all fire is created equal. *Dark Souls* features both ordinary fire and chaos fire, the latter of which is both visually different (a deep crimson instead of orange) and vastly more damaging, with increased power and a lingering magma pool that inflicts damage over time for those within its radius. Chaos fire comes at a price, since the associated spells can be gained only in exchange for the all-important resource of humanity.

4.10.18 Connection Magic

Much occult and mythic magic belongs to a worldview in which everything is connected by mysterious links. Like affects like: similar things can influence each other, as when a tribesman shakes a rain-stick, full of seeds that sound like rain, to cause rainfall. The magical technique of controlling objects through related objects is called sympathetic magic. Anthropologist Sir James George Frazier gives a classic analysis of sympathetic magic in *The Golden Bough*: *A Study of Magic and Religion*, in which he distinguishes two related laws of sympathetic magic: The Law of Similarity ("like produces like, or that an effect resembles its cause") and the Law of Contagion ("things which have once been in contact with each other continue to act on each other at a distance after the physical contact has been severed"). Poking a voodoo doll with needles or burning someone in effigy are both familiar examples of sympathetic magic.

There is perhaps no more elegant example of sympathetic magic modeled as a game mechanic than the Lavori d'Aracne, the magical technique used by players in Emily Short's interactive fictions *Savoir-Faire* and *Damnatio Memoriae* (see Chapter 3, Section 3.4). Because the magic system is semantically based, Inform7's natural language coding creates these mechanics much more elegantly than Inform6. The Lavori d'Aracne is slightly different than sympathetic magic in that the magician actively establishes abstract magical connections, called links, between objects rather than exploiting natural resemblances between them. At the same time, once a connection has been established between objects, the two objects affect each other in much the way that two natural objects linked by sympathy would. Short expresses the Lavori d'Aracne in a few lines of efficient code.

The first block of code defines the concept of linkages as game mechanics.

RECIPE 29:   THE LINKING RELATION IN *LAVORI D'ARACNE* (EMILY SHORT, INFORM7)[*]

```
Volume 1 - Linkages
Book 1 - Two Kinds of One-to-One Relationship
Chapter 1 - Affecting
The blank is a thing. A thing can be important or
  unimportant. A thing is usually important. The blank is
  unimportant.
Affecting relates one thing to one thing.
The verb to affect (he affects, they affect, he affected, it
  is affected, he is affecting) implies the affecting
  relation.
Definition: a thing is linked if it affects something or
  something affects it.
Definition: a thing is unlinked if it is not linked.
```

The second block of code defines the linking action, specifies what should happen when the action is carried out, and defines the relationships of affectedness that result from linking.

---

[*] Used with permission of Emily Short.

RECIPE 30:   THE LINKING ACTION IN LAVORI
             D'ARACNE (EMILY SHORT, INFORM7)[*]

```
Book 3 - Link Actions
Chapter 1 - Link
Understand "link [something] to [something]" as linking it
to.
Linking it to is an action applying to two things.
Carry out linking it to:
now the noun protects blank;
now the second noun protects blank;
now the noun affects the second noun;
now the second noun affects the noun;
Report linking it to:
say "You build a mutually-effective link between [the noun]
   and [the second noun].".
Linking something to something is labor.
```

The Lavori d'Aracne is a complex system that results in multiple solutions to many puzzles as well as humorous and emergent possibilities for connection. The system requires many more pages of code, but its essence is contained in the two blocks above. Both of these blocks are labeled as books, a designation that in the Inform7 programming language refers to rulebooks (collections of related rules that govern groups of in-game behaviors).

Regardless of the language in which one implements sympathetic magic, the game designer needs to plan out the objects in the world that can be linked, how they can be linked, and how these linkages will affect one or both objects. Inform7 has the advantage of being written in rigorously structured natural English, so rulebooks written in this language clarify the underlying logic of rules in a way similar to tabletop role-playing books. Writing code in Inform7 forces designers to define precisely the logic of their rules in a way that a computer can understand, with none of the ambiguity that players of a tabletop role-playing game could tolerate. Modifying Short's Lavori d'Aracne code or writing one's own Inform7 code to perform a similar function would be a useful exercise.

4.10.19 Meta-Recipe: Reality Warping

One of the most powerful recipes at the heart of all magic is the ability to warp reality. "I reject your reality and substitute my own," says the programmer protagonist of *The Dungeonmaster*, a mantra later adopted by

---

[*] Used with permission of Emily Short.

MythBusters. All magicians echo this claim when they cast a spell, because all magic involves transforming reality through the will. However, some spells involve a wholesale transformation of the game-world's state—a formula which is much easier if the game world is already procedurally generated through a set of rules rather than authored in a predetermined way. The *Magic: The Gathering* card Warp World is one example of a complete alteration of game state. The recipe for this effect is:

> Each player shuffles all permanents he or she owns into his or her library, then reveals that many cards from the top of his or her library. Each player puts all artifact, creature, and land cards revealed this way onto the battlefield, then does the same for enchantment cards, then puts all cards revealed this way that weren't put onto the battlefield on the bottom of his or her library.

In keeping with the card's title, this spell alters the entire playing field by forcing both players to relinquish the parts of the game that are ordinarily most stable (permanent cards) and reshuffle them, to be replaced by an equal number of new permanents. The effect of Warp World is to completely change the game state for both players, a strategic move that is potentially useful to the player who plays the card if she has reached a strategically disadvantageous point in the game. However, the spell is a risky gambit and effectively a form of chaos magic, since the new game state is randomly generated and could potentially be worse than the previous one. Decks that feature Warp World often also involve ways to retrieve the card repeatedly, allowing the deck's player to re-set the game state at will. Such decks also rely on a plethora of useful permanent cards, so that the caster has a better chance of arriving at an advantageous game state randomly than her opponent does.

"Alter Reality" is a similar spell in the roguelike *Zangband*, in the realm of Chaos Magic. Alter Reality resets an entire level, and the underlying mechanism of this transformation is surprisingly simple. A glance at the source code for this spell reveals:

RECIPE 31:   ALTER REALITY SPELL (*ZANGBAND, C*)[*]

```
void alter_reality(void)
{
        if (p_ptr->depth)
```

---

[*] Used with permission of Topi Ylinen.

```
        {
                msgf("The world changes!");

                if (autosave_l) do_cmd_save_game(TRUE);

                /* Leaving */
                p_ptr->state.leaving = TRUE;
        }
        else
        {
                msgf("The world seems to change for a moment!");
}
```

The Alter Reality spell resets a given level simply and elegantly: by calling the save game function, then treating the player as if he has left a given level by setting the state.leaving flag to true. (The *Hellband* variant of this spell resets the level slightly more explicitly by resetting two variables: "new _ level _ flag = TRUE;" and "came _ from=START _ RANDOM;"). This flag resets the level because all levels in *Zangband* are procedurally generated. Whenever a player leaves a level by a staircase, a new level is generated. By saving the game and setting the state.leaving flag to true, the Alter Reality spell causes a new level to be generated even though the player has not left via a staircase. Such an effect resonates powerfully with the Chaos Realm of magic to which it belongs, as well as the larger game fiction of the *Chronicles of Amber*, in which the Amberite royalty can shift between realities by traversing a labyrinthine pattern called the Logrus (see Chapter 8, Section 8.8).

4.10.19.1 Nobilis: The Game of Sovereign Powers

Also inspired indirectly by *Amber*, the tabletop role-playing game *Nobilis: The Game of Sovereign Powers* offers players a powerful experience of warping reality through a unique diceless mechanic in which players can spend points to bid over whose attempt to change reality succeeds. Not surprisingly, *Nobilis: The Game of Sovereign Powers* features one of the most flexible and rich schools of magic around. In the game, players take the role of Nobilis, Powers who control various aspects of reality (called Estates), such as Love, Computers, Waves, or Doors. The Nobilis are incarnations of abstract ideas (or aggregates of concrete objects abstracted into larger concepts). *Nobilis* is essentially a rule-based game adaptation of Neil Gaiman's graphic novel *The Sandman*, in which seven powerful beings known as the Endless incarnate the principles of Dream, Death, Desire, Delirium, Destruction, Despair, and Destiny. Tabletop designer Kenneth Hite has memorably described the game as "Neil Gaiman's Sandman and Clive Barker's Hellraiser on an absinthe bender. With flowers," emphasizing the game's surrealism and metaphysical depth. The game is diceless, since the Nobilis have absolute control over their particular domain, removed from randomness. The diceless element of the game is reminiscent of Albert Einstein's comment that "I do not believe God plays at dice."

Nobilis was created by R. Sean Borgstrom (sometimes also known as Jenna K. Moran), who holds a Doctorate of Computer Science from Johns Hopkins University. Her computer science background pervades *Nobilis*, especially in the concept of the domains over which the Nobilis rule, reminiscent of the use of the term "domain" in mathematics and computer science to describe an ordered set connected to the range of meanings that can be expressed in a given programming language. The game exhibits a computer scientist's perspective on metaphysics and meaning, making it an ideal and largely untapped inspiration for what videogame magic could be.

Magic as performed by the Nobilis consists of miracles. Because the Nobilis can rule over any concept, their schools of miraculous magic are infinitely varied, rich, and quirky. Rather than being restricted to the four elements or the seven planets, Nobilis could choose as their estate "Spheres, Division, Stasis, Bridges, Death by Sea, Summer, Fall, Heat, Cold, Storms, Butterflies, the Road, Bronze, Doorways, Words, Tremors, Cooking, the Forge, Parasites, Passivity, Mistrust, Growth, Addiction, Magnetism, Blood, Wine, Reflections, Spring, Lava, Disorder, Insanity, and Time" (47). This list, deliberately mixing categories between the tiny and the vast, the concrete and the abstract, the somber and the frivolous, is a reminder of just how diverse and deep our schools of game magic can be if we open our imaginations and challenge conventions and clichés. One might object that few game worlds model the path of butterflies, the drunkenness of wine, the chains of addiction, or the minutiae of parasites and that therefore constructing magic systems to modify these aspects of reality would be equally challenging. But this is precisely the lesson that *Nobilis* can teach us as videogame designers: to enrich our magic, we must deepen our simulated models of the world, marshaling the variables and algorithms at our disposal to represent the quirky and the sublime alike. A game like *Dwarf Fortress*, with its dizzying layers of simulation that model drunkenness and man-eating carp, has a sufficiently rich world to accommodate a magic system like that of *Nobilis*.

At the heart of *Nobilis'* rich magic system is a refusal to use magic for the primary aims for which it is often exploited: combat. *Nobilis* does not forbid combat but makes clear the absurdity of fist fighting among all-powerful immortals. As one section heading announces, "DIRECT PHYSICAL OR MAGICAL CONFRONTATION IS RARE." The rationales for the rarity of open combat are both practical and magical and can be summed up in the aphorism: "if it comes to blows, both sides have already lost" (11). Nobilis can draw more magical energy from an enemy if they destroy his estate while he is alive rather than killing him. Since the estates are deeply abstract, any form of confrontation or conflict will be equally abstract, since undermining the power of Passivity or Reflections would take more than blasting someone with a fireball or bashing them with a mace. *Nobilis* renders the issue of power moot by granting its player characters almost infinite power over aspects of reality and themselves, thereby making physical conflicts silly. By eschewing combat, *Nobilis* can focus its complex magic system on other aspects of altering reality.

In keeping with the quirky and non-violent magic of the game, the various laws and rules that govern the magic of *Nobilis* are associated with a variety of flowers. There are over a hundred flowers listed in the Appendix, associated with estates and powers (294–98). These flowers take on an eerie tone in that they involve using something very concrete, specific, botanical (flowers) to symbolize something very abstract. If schools of magic constitute a taxonomy of reality, then the use of flowers in *Nobilis* returns taxonomy to its roots in the biological sciences, especially botany. The use of flowers rather than more traditional classification schemes (elements, planets, zodiacal signs) forces our imaginations outside of traditional taxonomies. Like all richly developed and systemic languages, the language of flowers is also internally consistent, so that the meaning of a flower in character generation will be consistent as that flower's meaning in naming rules or laws. For example, the appendix translates the Monarda flower with the phrase "Your whims are unbearable," helping to clarify the rule that the "Monarda Law," which states that the Game Master should never say "no" to a player. This use of flowers has historical precedents in the Victorian language of flowers, by which messages could be communicated through the arrangement of bouquets.

Another chapter lists traits associated with various features of flowers (number of petals, color, open/closed), causing combinatorial possibilities to explode. Other flower-based rules in the game outline the protocol for handling aspect miracles (feats of superhuman strength and reasoning). These rules include: The Mountain Laurel Law (*"If a human can do something, Aspect can do it... a thousand times better.*"), The Primrose Law ("*If a mythical character can do something without magic, Aspect can do it*"), and The Nasturtium Law ("*If it makes good myth, and fits Aspect's style, then Aspect can do it*") (86). The philosophy of the Chamomile Law ("*There is Energy in Adversity*") translates into gameplay as the rule "when a Handicap makes life difficult for a Power, they gain miracle points" (127). In keeping with the metaphysical and mind-bending qualities of *Nobilis*, the flower laws operate on several levels of gameplay, ranging from the meta rules governing game master behavior (such as the Monarda Law), to the rules governing the extent of aspect's powers (such as the Nasturtium Law), to very localized rules pertaining to the acquisition of Miracle points (such as the Chamomile Law).

For all of its abstraction and flexibility, *Nobilis* is a rigorously rule-based game. Indeed, the game is unusually aware on a meta-level of its status as a game, since (as the title suggests) the powers are themselves engaged in a game of competition between each other and their nihilistic antagonists, the Excrucians, who seek to destroy the domains of meaning over which the Nobilis rule. Nobilis also features a sophisticated set of rules for performing miracles of various types. Players manipulate reality through the use of various attributes. Rather than re-skinning the standard six *Dungeons & Dragons*-derived attributes of strength, dexterity, intelligence, wisdom, charisma, and constitution, *Nobilis* includes four attributes: aspect, domain, realm, and spirit. Character attributes correspond to a particular type of miracle: aspect (physical and mental prowess), domain (control over one's Estate), realm (control over one's Chancel, an otherworldly sanctuary consecrated to the Estate), and spirit (capacity to work various forms of magic). Miracles have difficulty levels from 0–9. If the relevant attribute equals the miracle level, a player can perform that miracle. Otherwise, the player must spend miracle points to make up the difference between attribute level and miracle difficulty level. In addition to attribute ratings, players begin the game with five miracle points associated with each attribute. They may also purchase additional miracle points or gain them, paradoxically, by experiencing the challenges associated with an irksome weakness (47).

Domain miracles, through which the Nobilis shape something associated with their Estates, are in some ways the most developed and the most similar to spells as conventionally defined in other games. The seven types of Domain miracles are effectively seven sub-schools of magic, the verbs that act on the infinite variety of nouns associated with the Estates.

Each of these domain miracle types has an associated flower. The domain miracle types are as follows:

- Divination (Hawkweed)
- Preservation (Amaranth/Guilder Rose)
- Creation (Witch Hazel/Angelica)
- Destruction (Hemlock)
- Change (Pimpernel)
- Gating (Stephanotis)
- Mastery (Crown Imperial)

The domain miracles of *Nobilis* are an extraordinarily rich and flexible system for shaping reality. The domain miracles constitute a language with far more classes of nouns in it than *Ars Magica*, though very similar verbs. The classes of nouns can be any Estate over which a power has dominion, which includes any aspect of reality. Because the symbols which stand for these aspects of reality are flowers rather than elements or planets, the set of possible symbols is much larger. (In reality, the number of species of flowering plants is estimated to be between 250,000 and 400,000, not counting fantastic, imaginary flowers.)

Nobilis players can do almost anything, fulfilling the promise of infinite possibility associated with magic. The ranking of cost for miracle difficulty is connected to the way that the player desires to influence her domain, since in order from lowest cost to highest cost are divination, preservation, creation, destruction, and change. These levels of cost repeat themselves cyclically through the miracle levels of 0–9, so that the first four levels are lesser divinations, preservations, creations, and destructions. Lesser destructions and major divinations both overlap at level 5, lesser changes and major preservations both overlap at miracle level 6, followed by major creations, major destructions, and major changes for levels 7–9.

In addition to domain, aspect, and realm miracles, the Nobilis have a set of rites, magical rituals dependent only on the spirit that burns within them. The rites include:

- The Servants' Rite (binding a mortal servant called an anchor to the Nobilis)
- The Witch Hunt Rite (detecting the magical activity of another Power)

- The Redtooth Rite (excising and consuming the heart of a dead power)

- The Rite of the Last Trump (convert miracle points from one type to another, at a conversion rate whose efficiency or lack thereof depends on the Power's spirit level)

- The Rite of Passage (affords constant protection from mortal attacks, with need of renewal)

- The Nettle Rite (removing a power from a Nobilis or Excrucian by destroying a mundane focal point of that power)

4.11 SCHOOLS OF MAGIC AND MAGICAL CHARACTER CUSTOMIZATION

Customizable mage characters are as important as schools of magic, and often inseparable from them. By offering many customization options, designers allow players to create a magical persona, a magical self that makes sense to them. In order for various character builds and classes to adequately reflect their associated flavor and enable player expression, it is vital that each character class have a different way of casting magic. The standard way of varying magical flavors between characters is to have a different spell list for each class, but this approach can result in character classes that are too similar to each other.

More interesting approaches involve character classes with radically different magical mechanics, such as in *Dungeons & Dragons*, the Vancian magic user versus a point-based Warlock. In original *Dungeons & Dragons*, the mage class is simply a magic user, with few options for customization. There are various terms for this vanilla spellcaster: mage in second edition *Dungeons & Dragons* and wizard in third edition *Dungeons & Dragons* onward. First edition *Advanced Dungeons & Dragons* introduces the possibility of role-playing a distinct type of magic-user, a specialist in weaving phantasms called an Illusionist. Playing an Illusionist is an extra challenge, given that illusion spells tend to allow for mental manipulation but not actual alteration of physical reality. In second edition *Advanced Dungeons & Dragons*, the nine schools of magic each acquire an associated sub-class that specializes in a given school. *The Complete Wizards Handbook* also outlines the idea of wizard "kits," including unique classes such as Anagakok (a primitive shaman) and the Witch (a precursor of the 3.5 edition Warlock).

The Warlock himself is introduced in the *Complete Arcane* supplement of 3.5 edition *Dungeons & Dragons*, and both Warlock and Sorcerer are core classes in fourth edition. Both Warlock and Sorcerer are notable in their departure from the Vancian magic system, since each can cast spells without memorization. The limitations and affordances of their spells also stem from different sources, so that a Sorcerer's spells depend on the Charisma attribute instead of intelligence, and a Warlock's spells depend on Pacts with entities that grant him powers and liabilities. The Palladium fantasy RPG takes this approach a step further with its Diabolist and Summoner classes, which create unique spellcasting requirements for the player which performatively mimic the fictional actions of his character.

Tabletop RPGs teach us that magical character classes are most vivid and memorable when each class has effectively its own magic system, or at least a set of mechanics sufficiently distinct to create its own unmistakable feeling of magic. Character customization, like schools of magic, is a place where flavor and mechanics can join seamlessly and are, indeed, difficult to separate. Supporting this idea, Andrew Doull's blog series about designing roguelike magic systems begins by dismissing flavor as a distraction and then admitting that flavor is of paramount importance—the overriding consideration—in designing the mechanics of the various spell classes.

MMOs like *World of Warcraft* and *Age of Conan* offer examples of conveying unique opportunities for magical character customization, despite the severely limited palette associated with spells primarily intended for combat. These games allow for unique choices of magic in part through a range of character class choices, and in part through opportunities to customize during gameplay, such as skill trees. *World of Warcraft*'s mage is a standard offensive caster, with the option of specializing as an ice mage or a fire mage through various skill trees. The *World of Warcraft* warlock, on the other hand, is heavily focused on damage over time, poison, and summoning pets. In keeping with the overall dark sword and sorcery tone of *Age of Conan*, there are no vanilla mage options, only equally diabolical Demonologists, Heralds of Xotil, and Necromancers. Demonologists are hybrids of *World of Warcraft*'s fire mages and warlocks, since demonologists can unleash devastating flames as well as summoning demonic pets.

In conjunction with character classes, magical skill trees in MMOs allow players to customize their characters as they progress, typically through the selection of progressively more powerful spells that in turn unlock other spells. Skill trees look like vertically organized fishbone diagrams, in which choices of skills are represented as branching paths down which players can proceed as they develop. At the extreme of magical character customization is the PlayStation Vita game *Soul Sacrifice*, in which players use magical tears called Lachrima to rewrite any character decision, including spell builds and life-altering Black Rites as well as the main character's name and appearance. Lachrima plays into the central trope of the game, which is that players are reading and rewriting their own story in a sorcerer's interactive journal. The card-based Tarot decks of *Kingdoms of Amalur: Reckoning* offer another vision of magical character customization, in which the player activity of character customization is represented in the game's narrative as a magical ability. *Soul Sacrifice* and *Kingdoms of Amalur* both offer a narrative rationale for the process of re-specing characters (reassigning skill points), in which character customization is itself a magical ability.

A skill-based approach to magical identity allows for greater flexibility than one that depends on initial character class selection, but too much flexibility at too little cost can also lead to generic Swiss Army knife character builds that are jacks of all trades or, worse, masters of all. The absence of constraint associated with purely skill-based builds can lead to diminished role-playing opportunities, based partially on the principle that constraints spur creativity.

There is a great deal of charm to the pre-built classes of early *Elder Scrolls* (Nightblades, Battle Mages, Spellswords) versus the amorphousness of the late installments.

Because of the connections between character build, schools of magic, and color, the goal of the designer is to allow players to choose their own particular color based on their strengths and philosophies. (This is the opposite of the sorting hat from Harry Potter, which presumes to make the choice for characters.) Metaphorically and literally, it is as if designers have been working with a reduced spectrum, a crayon box with four colors, when there are boxes of 256, 512, and 1024 hues available—including seemingly impossible Lovecraftian colors out of space and Prachett-style colors of magic. By allowing players more options of schools of magic to pursue, we also allow them more opportunities for self-expression. Another way of looking at the magical character customization option is that it allows players to find their own octarine, the color of their own magical self in Peter Carroll's vision of things. Octarine is a fictitious eighth color of magic invented by Terry Prachett in his novel *The Colour of Magic* and later used by occultist Peter Carroll in *Liber Kaos* to describe the color of a magician's rebellious, mischievous sorcerous self (Carroll 109–10).

To allow for true magical character customization is to open up a broader and more nuanced spectrum of colors, including shades like Alizarin crimson as well as red and orange.

4.12 MAGICAL COMBAT

Magical combat is overused, especially when modeled as magical artillery or bullets. It is, however, possible to model combat as magic, if similar principles of ritual, language, symbolism are followed. As Huizinga argues in *Homo Ludens*, much medieval fighting (such as duels or trials by combat) was highly stylized and formalized, bound by rules and observances in order to allow for demonstrations of competitive prowess: in other words, a game. It is not surprising, then, that the occult and mystical theories collided with views of combat in this age. The Knights Templar—a sect of holy warriors who were eventually burned at the stake—were accused of participating in occult rituals, an idea at the heart of much conspiracy theory and many games that explore Templar lore, including *The Secret World*, *The Cursed Crusade*, and *The First Templar*.

The intersection of combat and the occult occurs at the level of system as well as lore. A classic example is *The Academy of the Sword*, a fencing manual by Gérard Thibault based on a geometrical design called the mysterious circle. The mysterious circle is a design representing geometrical proportions relevant to fighting, such as the length of blade relative to the swordsman's body. The mysterious circle intersects with Hermetic and Pythagorean ideas of mystical geometric proportions inherent to the universe—the same schools of thought that revered the golden ratio, the golden rectangle, and the pentagram. Cementing the book's relationship to magic, *The Academy of the Sword* was translated in modern times by John Michael Greer, a scholar and practitioner of the occult.

On the other side of the globe, Japanese traditions of the samurai code, bushido, and its historically dubious ninja counterpart, ninjutsu, also cast combat as a ritualized and sometimes mystical art form.

Templar lore and *The Academy of the Sword* both foreshadow a few videogames in which combat is elevated to the level of magic. For this to occur, combat takes on the feel of an arcane skill and a ritual language. It is not enough for combat to be realistic or even deep in order to be magical, nor is it sufficient to dress up combat with flashing particle effects and magic projectiles. These games include *Bushido Blade* and the *BlazBlue* series, in which combat is a form of magic called the Ars Magus, learned from a tome called the Azure Grimoire.

CHAPTER 5

Magic as Programming, Programming as Magic

M AGIC IS PROGRAMMING, AND programming is magic. This central idea shapes the entire structure and content of this book. The process of programming magic systems in videogames is itself a magical act. Such an analogy does not have to doom designers to a maze of infinite regression and meta-level self-reflexivity. Rather, we as designers who program will be better able to create rich, intricate magic systems if we recognize the underlying technological framework of these systems as based on codes that themselves resemble magic. Recognizing the magic of programming can help keep our motivation and morale high when the daily routine of design becomes difficult. Thinking of magic as programming can also assure that our designs are rigorous and susceptible to implementation through the mathematically-based logic of programming languages.

This book is a grimoire in the classic sense of sorcerer's manual or spellbook. Abelson and Sussman, in their classic programming textbook *The Structure and Interpretation of Computer Programs*, express this idea as a compelling and subtle metaphor. Their book is commonly referred to as "The Wizard Book" because of the picture of a wizard on the cover. Abelson and Sussman write:

> People create programs to direct processes. In effect, we conjure the
> spirits of the computer with our spells.

> A computational process is indeed much like a sorcerer's idea of a
> spirit. It cannot be seen or touched. It is not composed of matter
> at all. However, it is very real. […] The programs we use to conjure
> processes are like sorcerers' spells. They are carefully composed
> from symbolic expressions in arcane and esoteric *program-*
> *ming languages* that prescribe the tasks we want our processes to
> perform (1).

Abelson and Sussman create a powerful analogy between spirits and
computational processes, both of which are disembodied, potentially
powerful, and difficult to control. The authors also note a powerful resemblance between spells and programs, both of which are comprised of combinations of symbols that give instructions to ethereal entities. Abelson
and Sussman also note the demanding rigor of the symbolic languages
associated with both spells and programs, which can produce unexpected
and dangerous results if the magician or programmer is not careful. As
they wryly note, "like the sorcerer's apprentice, novice programmers must
learn to understand and to anticipate the consequences of their conjuring" (1). The unintended consequences of spells are legendary in works
of fantasy and occultism, as Mickey Mouse's struggles with hundreds of
rebellious buckets and brooms suggest.

Yet, as Frederick P. Brooks explains in *The Mythical Man Month*, the
exacting requirements of technical perfection are actually part of what
makes programming magical. Under the heading "the joys of the craft,"
Brooks argues, "The magic of myth and legend has come true in our time.
One types the correct incantation on a keyboard, and a display screen
comes to life, showing things that never were nor could be" (7–8). Like
Abelson and Sussman, Brooks believes that the magic of programming
is the ability to use symbolic utterances to cause powerful effects in the
real world, as well as conjuring "things that never were" out of the human
imagination and into representation or simulation. It is not a far jump
from Brooks' axiom about the magic of programming computers generally to the magic of programming computer games specifically, since
computer games are entirely dedicated to representing and simulating
imaginary situations. Yet in order to make these miraculous effects occur,
Brooks recognizes that programming itself is highly demanding and
difficult. He explains, "First, one must perform perfectly. The computer
resembles the magic of legend in this respect, too. If one character, one
pause, of the incantation is not strictly in proper form, the magic doesn't

work" (8). Like Abelson and Sussman, Brooks connects the exacting rigors of programming to the notoriously detailed and demanding nature of casting spells, in which not only the chant but its every rune and rhythmic pause must be correct.

In keeping with both Brooks' and Abelson and Sussman's analogies between magic and programming, the spells in this book are computer programs, written sometimes in actual programming languages and sometimes in pseudocode (the general structure and pattern of a piece of code which can be implemented in many specific languages). While some of these programming examples are derived from hypothetical examples, many are adapted from my own project, *Arcana*.

5.1 *ARCANA: A CEREMONIAL MAGICK SIMULATOR*

This book includes a companion website with examples implemented in a variety of engines. Many of the code examples and their downloadable implementations on the website are based around an ongoing project called *Arcana: A Ceremonial Magick Simulator*. The long-term goal for *Arcana*, its end-game as it were, is an open-source, extensible magic simulator. Simply put, the goal for *Arcana* is to create the *Minecraft* of magic systems. *Minecraft* is a game that offers users the opportunity to create worlds of great complexity and richness out of the simplest of geometrical shapes: cubes. *Minecraft* features an adventure mode in which players can mine resources and fend off monsters called creepers, just as *Arcana* has a story mode in which a French noblewoman named Eliza Knossos summons and questions demons in order to find her lost brother. But the true appeal of *Minecraft* (as with many games that have user generated content) is creative mode in which users can build their own worlds.

Similarly, the primary appeal of *Arcana* is the capacity for players to create their own magic systems. The system in *Arcana*'s story mode is based on a variety of Western ceremonial magic derived most directly from the Hermetic Order of the Golden Dawn, but creative mode allows you to construct your own system based on a variety of historical esoteric systems (such as voodoo, chaos magic, or the traditional witchcraft of the Cultus Sabbati) or rulesets derived from fiction (such as Lovecraft's Cthulhu mythos, Barker's *Abarat*, or Miéville's Bas-Lag trilogy). The artist-poet William Blake said "I must create a system, or be enslaved by another man's." *Arcana* allows you to create your own magic system, inspired by any fictional or actual system you desire, and enslaved by no man's system. But for this goal to occur, *Game Magic* and *Arcana* require a community.

Arcana is a transmedia project developed by the author and a team of students and other collaborators over a period of many years. At the heart of the project is *Arcana: A Ceremonial Magick Simulator*. The purpose of the simulator is to provide the richest, most authentic experience of magic possible, in much the same way that a flight simulator provides the most realistic and nuanced experience of flight. In *Arcana*, players perform rituals to summon and converse with daimons (the Greek word for spirit from which "demon" is derived, originally without the connotations of wickedness suggested by "demon"). The rituals obey a multimodal ritual language consisting of combinations of Tarot cards, gems, artifacts, colors, and sounds. Players ask daimons questions through phrases, which in turn consist of words.

The rituals in *Arcana* are modeled first of all as finite state machines. A finite state machine is a device that can be in a finite number of possible states. For example, a traffic light is a finite state machine with three states: red, yellow, and green. A guard bot in a stealth game like *Metal Gear* or *Thief* could be in three states: searching, alerted, and attacking. Finite state machines switch between states based on triggers, such as the timers that regulate a stoplight or the movements of a player within lines of sight that alert guards.

In *Arcana*, the states of a ritual are tracked by a variable which is incremented (increased by one) every time the ritual enters a new state, shown in the list below. Figure 5.1 shows the states in the finite state machine of *Arcana*.

0 = *Out of ritual* (clean-up state): In this state, the player cleans up from a previous ritual so that he can start a new one, by gathering all of the implements and artifacts and placing them back in drawers beneath the altar.

1 = *Summoning trigger* (all elements cleaned up and put away): When the player has successfully cleaned up all ritual elements, a new state is triggered.

2 = *Summoning state*: The new state triggered by successfully cleaning up is a pre-ritual preparation, which first begins by summoning a spirit. Spirits are summoned through the mastery of symbolic correspondences, through which the magician selects and arranges elements that are congenial to the spirit. Figure 5.2 illustrates the number, color, and shape correspondences for each figure. For example, if

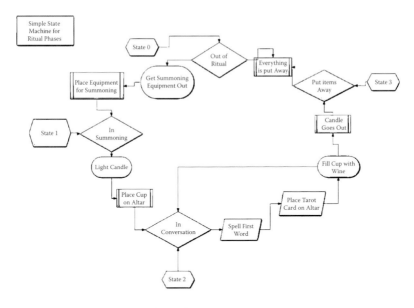

FIGURE 5.1   Ritual State Machine for *Arcana*.

FIGURE 5.2 (See color insert.)   Demon Profiles in *Arcana*.

the player wishes to summon Bartzabel, a spirit of Mars, then he must consult traditional correspondences to know that the fifth branch of the Tree of Life, the number five, the color red, the pentagram, and the trumpet all correspond to Mars and the idea of aggression that it represents. Consequently, he should place five red candles in the form of a pentagram around the circle.

The summoning phase is governed by a set of demon profiles in a two-dimensional array which stores the correspondences most related to particular spirits. These profiles include the demon as well as his or her associated planet, path, Tarot card, color, perfume, number, lineal figure, and gem—as displayed in Table 5.1.

3 = *Begin ritual trigger* (light candle on the altar): When the player has finished placing ritual elements, he signifies the intention to begin the ritual proper by lighting a large candle on the altar. If he has successfully summoned a spirit, the smaller candles around the circle spontaneously burst into flame with the appropriate color of the summoned spirit. (If the color of the candle flames is unexpected, the player should beware, as he may have inadvertently evoked the wrong spirit, and the consequences of mistaking Beelzebub for Michael could be dire.)

4 = *Phrase trigger*

5 = *In ritual state*

6 = *In phrase state*

TABLE 5.1   The Demon Profiles in *Arcana*

Demon	Planet	Tarot Card	Color	Number	Lineal Figure	Gem
Ophiel	Mercury	Magician	Yellow	8	Octagram	Opal
Phul	Moon	High Priestess	Blue	9	Nonagram	Quartz
Hagith	Venus	Empress	Emerald Green	7	Heptagram	Emerald
Bethor	Jupiter	Wheel of Fortune	Violet	4	Square	Amethyst
Phaleg	Mars	Tower	Scarlet	5	Pentagram	Ruby
Och	Sun	Sun	Orange	6	Hexagram	Topaz
Arathron	Saturn	World	Indigo	3	Triangle	Star sapphire

FIGURE 1.1   A Symbolic Key of Intended Audiences. (Pentagram image from Clickr.com)

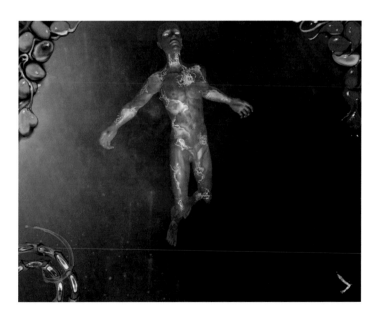

FIGURE 3.10   Hearts and Nerva in *The Void*. (Image by Ice-Pick Lodge.)

FIGURE 4.1 Seven Schools of Magic. (Original image by Giles Timms.)

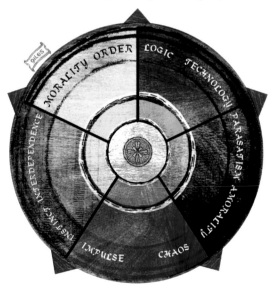

FIGURE 4.2 An Abstract Representation of Five Influential Schools of Magic. (Original image by Giles Timms.)

FIGURE 4.3   The Schools of Magic in This Chapter. (Original image by Giles Timms.)

FIGURE 4.21   Tree of Life with Color Scales.

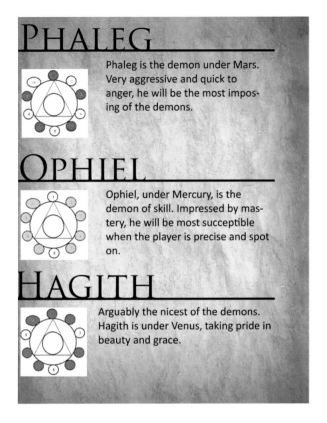

FIGURE 5.2   Demon Profiles in *Arcana*.

FIGURE 6.2   Schools of Occult Magic. (Original image by Giles Timms.)

FIGURE 6.3   Pie Chart of Voodoo Loa. (Original image by Giles Timms.)

FIGURE 6.7   Rose Cross. (By the Order of the Golden Dawn. Public domain due to age.)

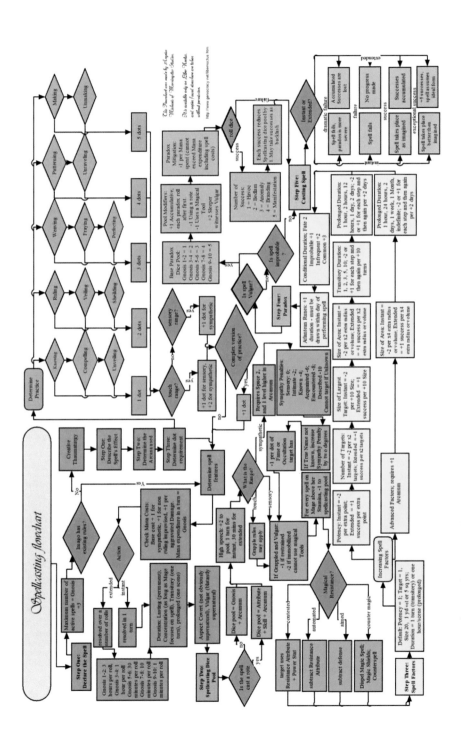

FIGURE 7.2 *Mage: The Awakening* Spell Flowchart. (Image by Angelus Morningstar. Used with permission.)

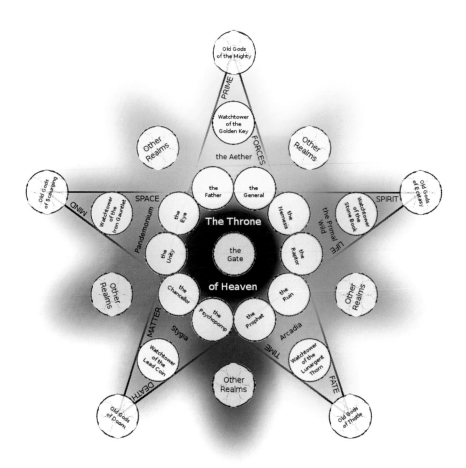

FIGURE 7.3 The Ten Arcana of *Mage: The Awakening*. (Image by Dataweaver. Used with permission.)

7 = *Phrase end trigger*

8 = *In ritual state*

9 = *Word trigger* (place elements of a certain type): Words are formed by stringing together elements of a particular type, such as gems or cards. The transition between words is signified by using a different type of element. For example, one word may consist of gems, while another might consist of Tarot cards. As soon as the player transitions from placing gems on the altar to placing cards on the mosaic, they have begun a new word.

10 = *Phrase end trigger*: When a phrase ends, the player signifies this by filling a cup with wine. The demon drinks the wine, signifying that the phrase has ended.

11 = *End ritual state*: To end the ritual, the candle on the altar must be extinguished, either by the player when she wishes to end the conversation or by the demon when he has finished delivering material.

12 = *Back out of ritual state*: Once the ritual has ended, the player is now in cleanup phase.

These states are stored in global variables inside the file `global.js`, where they are listed along with several other global variables accessed during the course of the game.

RECIPE 32:   GLOBAL VARIABLES TO STORE RITUAL STATE
             IN *ARCANA* (ORIGINAL UNITY/JAVASCRIPT)

```
static var state = 0;
//state is used for the 4 states of the ritual

//out of ritual (0)
//summoning phase (1)
//communication phase (2)
//clean up phase (3)
```

The following code is attached to each of the candleholders (triggers where players can place candles to summon demons). The code checks which color of candle (red [R], yellow [Y], or green [G]) has been placed at a given spot and then assigns a point to a given score for a particular demon, depending on which demon likes a specific color. Figure 5.3 shows a sorcerer summoning a demon.

FIGURE 5.3   An Evocation Ritual to Summon a Demon. (Original image by Giles Timms.)

RECIPE 33:   CANDLEHOLDER SCRIPTS TO TRACK
SUMMONING CANDLE PLACEMENT IN
ARCANA (ORIGINAL UNITY/JAVASCRIPT)

```
//this script is used to check when a candle enters the
//trigger of one of the candleholders.
//candleholder1 goes on the first candleholder. The
//candleholders start at 1 and go to ten, clockwise. If you
//are standing at the altar,
//the candleholder that is farthest from you is the first
//1. Think of it as a clock, with candleholder1 being like
//the 12

var once : boolean = true;        //once is a boolean used
//for the Clear function
//when a summoning is botched, the clear function is called
//to wipe out
//whatever is in the trigger
//once makes sure that this only happens once in a botched
//summoning
var isfull : boolean = false; //isfull checks whether or not
//a candle is already in place in the trigger

function Start()
{
    global.PhalegCheck[0] = 'E';
    global.HagithCheck[0] = 'E';
    global.OphielCheck[0] = 'E';
```

```
        global.ChoronzonCheck[0] = 'E';
}


function OnTriggerEnter(myTrigger : Collider)
{

        global.cor_count = global.cor_count + 1; cor_count is
//a static variable found in the global script
//cor_count keeps track of how many correspondences are
//currently being used
//when an object enters the trigger, cor_count is
//incremented by 1
        isfull = true;          //when a single object enters the
//trigger,isfull is set to true, indicating that only one
//object can be set in the trigger

        if(myTrigger.gameObject.name == "RedCandle(Clone)")
//checks to see if the gameObject that has entered the
//trigger is called RedCandle(Clone)

        {
                global.PhalegCheck[0]  = 'R';
                global.HagithCheck[0]  = 'R';
                global.OphielCheck[0]  = 'R';
                global.ChoronzonCheck[0] = 'R';
                //global.PhalegScore = global.PhalegScore + 1;
        //if the candle is a clone of RedCandle, the
//PhalegScore is incremented by 1
                //global.ChoronzonScore = global.ChoronzonScore
//+ 1;
        //the ChoronzonScore is also incremented by 1
        }
        else if(myTrigger.gameObject.name == "GreenCandle(Clone)")
        //checks to see if the gameObject that has entered the
//trigger is
//called GreenCandle(Clone)
        {
                global.PhalegCheck[0]  = 'G';
                global.HagithCheck[0]  = 'G';
                global.OphielCheck[0]  = 'G';
                global.ChoronzonCheck[0] = 'G';
                //global.HagithScore = global.HagithScore + 1;
        //if so, the HagithScore is incremented by 1
        }
        else if(myTrigger.gameObject.name == "YellowCandle(Clone)")
        //checks if the gameObject in the trigger is called
YellowCandle(Clone)
        {
                global.PhalegCheck[0]  = 'Y';
                global.HagithCheck[0]  = 'Y';
```

```
                  global.OphielCheck[0] = 'Y';
                  global.ChoronzonCheck[0] = 'Y';
     //if so, do nothing, because no point is scored for having a
     //yellow candle at this location
            }

      }


      function OnTriggerExit(myTrigger : Collider)
      {
            global.cor_count = global.cor_count - 1;   //when an
      object exits the trigger, cor_count is decreased by 1
            isfull = false;        //the only object in the trigger
      //has been removed, so isfull is false

            if(myTrigger.gameObject.name == "RedCandle(Clone)")
      //checks for gameObject called RedCandle(Clone) leaving the
      //trigger
            {
                  global.PhalegCheck[0] = 'E';
                  global.HagithCheck[0] = 'E';
                  global.OphielCheck[0] = 'E';
                  global.ChoronzonCheck[0] = 'E';
                  //global.PhalegScore = global.PhalegScore - 1;
            //if so, decrease PhalegScore by 1
                  //global.ChoronzonScore = global.ChoronzonScore - 1;
            //also, decrease ChoronzonScore by 1
            }
            else if(myTrigger.gameObject.name == "GreenCandle(Clone)")
            //checks for gameObject called GreenCandle(Clone)
            //leaving the trigger
            {
                  global.PhalegCheck[0] = 'E';
                  global.HagithCheck[0] = 'E';
                  global.OphielCheck[0] = 'E';
                  global.ChoronzonCheck[0] = 'E';
                  //global.HagithScore = global.HagithScore - 1;
            //if so, decrease HagithScore by 1
            }
            else if(myTrigger.gameObject.name == "YellowCandle(Clone)")
            //checks for gameObject called YellowCandle(Clone)
            //leaving the trigger
            {
                  global.PhalegCheck[0] = 'E';
                  global.HagithCheck[0] = 'E';
                  global.OphielCheck[0] = 'E';
                  global.ChoronzonCheck[0] = 'E';
      //if so, do nothing, because no point was scored for having
      //a yellow candle
```

```
//at this location
     }

}

function Clear ()   //this function is used to reset the
//trigger when a summoning has failed
{
     global.cor_count = global.cor_count - 1;   //since only
//one object could be in this trigger, simply decrease the
//cor_count by 1
     isfull = false;      //reset isfull to false,
//indicating there are no objects in this trigger
     once = false;       //once is set to false, so the
//Clear function only gets called once
//otherwise, the Clear function would get called multiple
//times and the cor_count would go down by more than 1
}
function Update ()
{

     //this if/else statement will reset the values of the
//script when a summoning is failed, and set them up again
//so objects can again be placed
     //at this location
     if (global.failedsummoning == true && isfull == true)
//checks if the summoning has failed and if there is an
//object inside the trigger
     {
          if (once == true)     //if so, check if once is
//true
          {
               Clear();        //if once is true, then
//the Clear function can be called to reset the values of
//the script
          }
     }
     else          //if either failedsummoning is false or
//isfull is false, set once to true
     {
          once = true;          //resets once to true, so
//when a summoning is again failed, the Clear function can
//be called
     }
}
```

5.2 RECIPE: COMBINING LINGUISTIC ELEMENTS THROUGH AN ARRAY

A magic system in which spells are combinations of symbols requires the following features in its underlying programming:

- A table of spells and the strings of symbols associated with them

- A mechanism for evaluating what symbols have been placed to form a string

- A function to match the symbols currently placed against the available spells.

In order to create a sense of ritualistic interaction, it helps to have multi-modal feedback in response to the placement of symbols and the matching of spells, including both valid placements and spells as well as miscastings. The code that follows is written in a scripting language called Actionscript for the multimedia program Adobe Flash. The code snippet is part of a larger two-dimensional, drag and drop interface based on the symbolic correspondences associated with the kabbalistic tree of life, in which the player places Tarot cards, gems, and letters onto the twenty-two paths and ten branches of the tree. When a player places a card, gem, or letter that corresponds to a particular path or branch, the path lights up with the corresponding color and plays a corresponding musical tone.

RECIPE 34:   MATCHING SPELL COMPONENTS AGAINST AN ARRAY (ORIGINAL FLASH ACTIONSCRIPT)

```
if (e.target.dropTarget! = null) {
trace (e.target);
theDrop = e.target.dropTarget.parent;
//registerLetter determines if a tarot card has been placed
//on a target
//and then feeds the corresponding Hebrew letter to a text
//field
     function registerLetter() {
     for (var q:int = 0;q < Cards.length;q++) {
          if (e.target == Cards[q]) {
          //alphabetText.text = alphabet[q];
          trace(alphabetText);
          spellWordArray.push(alphabet[q]);
          alphabetText.text = spellWordArray;
          trace(spellWordArray);
```

```
      //set letter equivalent of dragged element
            } //close if
             }//close for loop
             }//close registerLetter function
function changeColor() {
            for (var q:int = 0;q < Cards.length;q++) {
            if (e.target == Cards[q])
            {
var myColor:ColorTransform = pathsArray[q].transform.
colorTransform;
//myColor.color = 0xCC0000;
myColor.color = colorArray[q];
//trace(myColor.color);
pathsArray[q].transform.colorTransform = myColor;
                   //return;

            }//close if
            }
            }
     function playNote() {
            for (var s:int = 0;s < soundArray.length;s++) {
            if (e.target == Cards[s])
            {var noteChannel:SoundChannel =
soundArray[s].play();
            return;
             } //close if
            }
            }
            }
else {
            theDrop = null;
            }

            if (theDrop == targ) {
                   e.target.onTarget = true;
                   targ.gotoAndStop(2);
                   //spellText.text = "Abracadabra.";
                   //spellText.text = spellArray;
                   counter++;
                   //trace(counter);
                   //play a sound if an element is
//correctly placed
                   //change the color of the path if the
//element is correctly placed

                   //var myColor:ColorTransform =
targ.transform.colorTransform;
                   //myColor.color = 0xFFFF00;
                   //targ.transform.
colorTransform = myColor;
                   //Each time an element is dropped on a
//target, add that element to the spell array
```

```
                              spellArray.push(e.target);
                              //trace(spellArray);
                     spellText.text = spellArray;
                              registerLetter();
                              changeColor();
                              playNote();

                              //matchSpell();
                              matchGrimoire();
            }
            else {
                     e.target.onTarget = false;
                     targ.gotoAndStop(1);
                     spellText.text = "Wrong spell target.";
            }
            if(counter == 3){
//spellText.text = "Spell complete (" + spellArray + "}";
            }
            }
```

RECIPE 35: CODE TO TRACK TAROT CARD PLACEMENT FOR DIVINATION (ORIGINAL UNITY/JAVASCRIPT)

```
//this script is placed on all of the placeholders on the
//paths
//it will check which path it is placed on, and if a certain
//card is placed there, which will then be placed into an
//array for checking which question has been asked

var once : boolean = true;        //variable for doing the
//Clear function only once
var isfull : boolean = false;     //checks if the
//placeholder is full

//this function will check if an object has entered the
//trigger
function OnCollisionEnter(myTrigger : Collision)
{

     global.cor_count = global.cor_count + 1;   //increment
//the cor_count by 1 (number of correspondences currently
//being used)

     isfull = true;        //the placeholder is full

     //checks if we are in the 1st state
     if (global.state == 1)
     {
```

```
                //checks if the object has entered the trigger
//for the 11th path
            if (gameObject.name == "Card_holder_11")
            {
                //checks if the object is the Fool card
                if (myTrigger.gameObject.name ==
"Fool(Clone)")
                {
                        global.Tarot[6] = 1;  //location 6
//of the Tarot array becomes 1, indicating that the correct
//card has been placed for a question
                        Debug.Log("fool");
                }
            }
            //checks if the object has entered the trigger
//for the 15th
//path
            else if (gameObject.name == "Card_holder_15")
            {
                //checks if the object is the Emperor card
                    if (myTrigger.gameObject.name ==
"Emperor(Clone)")
                    {
                        global.Tarot[4] = 1;
//location 4 of//the Tarot array becomes 1, indicating that
//the correct card has been placed for a question
                        //Debug.Log("emperor");
                    }
            }
            //checks if the object has entered the trigger
//for the 20th path
            else if (gameObject.name == "Card_holder_20")
            {
                    //checks if the object is the Hermit card
                    if (myTrigger.gameObject.name ==
"Hermit(Clone)")
                    {
                        global.Tarot[8] = 1; //location 8
//of the Tarot array becomes 1, indicating that the correct
//card has been placed for a question
                    }
            }
            //checks if the object has entered the trigger
//for the 23rd path
            else if (gameObject.name == "Card_holder_23")
            {
                    //checks if the object is the Hangedman
//card
                    if (myTrigger.gameObject.name ==
"Hangedman(Clone)")
```

```
                    {
                            global.Tarot[7] = 1; //location 7
//of the Tarot array becomes 1, indicating that the correct
//card has been placed for a question
                    }
            }
            //checks if the object has entered the trigger
//for the 27th path
            else if (gameObject.name == "Card_holder_27")
            {
                    //checks if the object is the Tower card
                    if (myTrigger.gameObject.name ==
"Tower(Clone)")
                    {
                            global.Tarot[20] = 1; //location
//20 of the Tarot array becomes 1, indicating that the
//correct card has been placed for a question
                            //Debug.Log("tower");
                    }
            }
            //checks if the object has entered the trigger
//for the 32nd path
            else if (gameObject.name == "Card_holder_32")
            {
                    //checks if the object is the World card
if (myTrigger.gameObject.name == "World(Clone)")
                    {
                            global.Tarot[22] = 1; //location 22
//of the Tarot array becomes 1, indicating that the correct
//card has been placed for a question
                    }
            }
      }
}
//this function checks if an object is leaving a trigger
function OnCollisionExit(myTrigger : Collision)
{
      global.cor_count = global.cor_count - 1;   //increment
//the cor_count by 1 (number of correspondences currently
//being used)

      isfull = false;              //the placeholder is full
      Debug.Log(isfull);

      //checks if we are in the 1st state
      if (global.state == 1)
      {
            Debug.Log("pick up");
            //checks if the object has entered the trigger
//for the 11th path
```

```
            if (gameObject.name == "Card_holder_11")
            {
                    //checks if the object is the Fool card
if (myTrigger.gameObject.name == "Fool(Clone)")
                    {
                            global.Tarot[6] = 0; //location 6
//of the Tarot array becomes 1, indicating that the correct
//card has been placed for a question
                            Debug.Log("remove fool");
                    }
            }
            //checks if the object has entered the trigger
              for the 15th
//path
            else if (gameObject.name == "Card_holder_15")
            {
                    //checks if the object is the Emperor card
if (myTrigger.gameObject.name == "Emperor(Clone)")
                    {
                            global.Tarot[4] = 0; //location 4
//of the Tarot array becomes 1, indicating that the correct
//card has been placed for a question
                            //Debug.Log("emperor");
                    }
            }
            //checks if the object has entered the trigger
//for the 20th path
            else if (gameObject.name == "Card_holder_20")
            {
                    //checks if the object is the Hermit card
if (myTrigger.gameObject.name == "Hermit(Clone)")
                    {
                    global.Tarot[8] = 0; //location 8 of the
//Tarot array becomes 1, indicating that the correct card
//has been placed for a question
                    }
            }
            //checks if the object has entered the trigger
//for the 23rd path
            else if (gameObject.name == "Card_holder_23")
            {
                    //checks if the object is the Hangedman
//card
if (myTrigger.gameObject.name == "Hangedman(Clone)")
                    {
                    global.Tarot[7] = 0;  //location 7 of the
//Tarot array becomes 1, indicating that the correct card
//has been placed for a question
                    }
            }
```

```
                    //checks if the object has entered the trigger
        //for the 27th path
                    else if (gameObject.name == "Card_holder_27")
                    {
                            //checks if the object is the Tower card
        if (myTrigger.gameObject.name == "Tower(Clone)")
                            {
                                    global.Tarot[20] = 0;//location 20
        //of the Tarot array becomes 1, indicating that the correct
        //card has been placed for a question
                                    //Debug.Log("tower");
                            }
                    }
                    //checks if the object has entered the trigger
        //for the 32nd path
                    else if (gameObject.name == "Card_holder_32")
                    {
                            //checks if the object is the World card
        if (myTrigger.gameObject.name == //"World(Clone)")
                            {
                            global.Tarot[22] = 0;//location 22 of
        //the Tarot array becomes 1, indicating that the correct
        //card has been placed for a question
                            }
                    }
            }

        }
        //function for clearing the contents of a trigger if a
        //question is failed
        function Clear ()
        {
            global.cor_count = global.cor_count - 1;   //decrement
        //the cor_count by 1
            once = false;          //once is set to false, so it is
        //only cleared once
            isfull = false;        //the trigger is not full
        }
        function Update ()
        {

            //checks if a question has failed and if there is an
        //object in the trigger
            if (global.failedquestion == true && isfull == true)
            {
                    //checks if the Clear function has not yet been
        //used
                    if (once == true)
                    {
                            Clear();        //calls the Clear function
```

```
            }
     }
     else
     {
            once = true;          //once is set to true, so
//the Clear function can be used when a question is failed
//again
            }
}
```

CHAPTER 6

Game Design Lessons from Occult Magic

6.1 OCCULT RITUAL FLOWCHARTS

For a game designer, the purpose of studying occult magic is to develop recipes for rituals, which can inspire spellcasting mechanics and related puzzles. Each system of magic—whether voodoo, ancient Egyptian heka, grimoire-based goetia, or traditional witchcraft—has its own procedures for altering reality and transforming consciousness. These procedures can be represented in part as flowcharts, and flowcharts can be used to help guide the programming of magic systems. Figure 6.1 is a flowchart representing a voodoo ritual.

While voodoo encompasses many diverse practices, the flowchart in Figure 6.1 illustrates a template of common steps. Before any other steps of the ritual can be completed, Papa Legba (a loa, or spirit, sometimes equated with the Catholic Saint Peter) must be called upon to open the gate to the spirit world. This step is a preliminary invocation that makes the other steps possible, so it is the first node in the chart. The remaining steps, which involve the preparation of the temple space in order to invite a loa to appear and temporarily possess one of the congregants, are at the same level of priority and can be performed in the order that best suits a particular invocation. The priest must draw a vevé, or sacred symbol, representative of a particular loa on the ground using chalk or flour. The priest must also light a candle, arrange offerings on an altar, and hang sequined banners on the room's walls in order to balance the spiritual

FIGURE 6.1   Flowchart of a Voodoo Ritual. (Original image by Giles Timms.)

forces designated hot and cold. If all these preconditions are met correctly, a loa might manifest by riding its horse, i.e. temporarily controlling the body of one of the congregants.

Such a flowchart is a simplification and abstraction of the ritual process, but this abstraction is precisely what a game designer needs from any given tradition: a set of symbolic actions that can constitute the mechanics of ritual gameplay. The tone of such a ritual does not have to be overly solemn: the Talking Heads' song "Papa Legba" outlines all of the phases of the ritual, and the accompanying comedy movie *True Stories* depicts them vividly. Ritual can be a form of joyous, even humorous, play. As game designers, we first construct the underlying logical flow of a ritual, then make sure that all of its elements come together to create the experience we want to evoke for our players.

6.2 MAPPING THE DOMAINS OF RITUAL TRADITIONS THROUGH PIE GRAPHS

In addition to flowcharts that represent process, pie graphs can be used to represent the connection between various occult traditions and schools of game magic. Many systems of occult magic are especially concerned with a particular domain of reality, such as Wiccans' reverence for nature or goetic magicians' preoccupations with death, so the various systems can be divided into color based pie charts much like those used to represent schools of game magic. Wiccans see the world through the green-tinted glasses of nature worship, while goetic mages tend to view reality as an extension of a shamanic voyage through the darkness of the underworld. Crowley's Thelemic magic celebrates the red hues of "force and fire," while the famous Guédé Loa adopt the purple hues of pleasure. Figure 6.2 represents several occult traditions as a pie chart resembling the diagrams often used to represent schools of magic in games.

Each tradition of magic is itself highly varied and complex, often applying a particular perspective to many aspects of reality, so each slice of the pie chart could be further subdivided into its own pie chart. For example, the voodoo pantheon includes several groups of loa, each of which can be invoked to affect a particular domain of reality, represented traditionally by a color reflective of the loas' character. The fiery, red Petro loa govern war and aggression, the lascivious Guédé loa rule over sex and death, while the benevolent, white Rada loa control moral law and kindness. Figure 6.3 shows the voodoo loa in a color-coded pie chart.

Occult Traditions

FIGURE 6.2 (See color insert.)   Schools of Occult Magic. (Original image by Giles Timms.)

FIGURE 6.3 (See color insert.)   Pie Chart of Voodoo Loa. (Original image by Giles Timms.)

Such pie charts remind us that occult traditions are rarely monolithic or simple, but rather multiple and complex. By drawing on a fuller range of beliefs both between traditions and within them, game designers will have more and richer material available. For example, the term "witch" sometimes becomes translated into a single character class that is hardly distinguished from the standard magic-user. When popular culture does reference witches, they often refer to a vague Wiccan tradition involving nature worship, reverence toward a goddess, pentagrams with point upright, and emblematic use of the color green. This mainstream version of witchcraft is in fact only one of many traditions, including Gerald Gardner's Wicca but also the lesser known but imaginatively richer strains of Traditional Witchcraft influenced by Robert Cochrane's Clan of Tubal Cain, as well as Andrew Chumbley and Daniel Schulke's Cultus Sabbati.

Chaos magicians adopt a playful meta-perspective on such diagrams through their tendency to accept and include multiple perspectives on magic as belief systems to be temporarily adopted for convenience and consciousness alteration. Consequently, chaos magicians like Peter Carroll often include color-based radial diagrams, accepting red war magic, purple sex magic, and black death magic as useful subdivisions of the ultimate underlying force of chaos (Carroll, *Liber Kaos* 113–41; see Chapter 8, Section 8.5). Carroll himself adopts the concept of an eighth invented color, called octarine, from the short story *The Colour of Magic* by Terry Pratchett, as his own magical shade (Carroll 109–10, see Chapter 4, Section 4.6).

6.3 OCCULT MAGIC AND GAME INTERACTIVITY

The wealth of flowcharts, pie charts, and colors associated with occult magic suggest that magic has been defined in many ways by many individuals and cultures. The words for magic in various languages provide clues about a given culture's attitude toward magic. Given the magical power of incantations, we as game designers should choose our words carefully, whether they are used to describe character classes, schools of magic or just to set the stage of a given simulated magical universe.

According to the *Oxford English Dictionary*, the English word "magic" descends from the Middle French "magique," which in turn stems from the Latin "magica" (short for "ars magica," the magic art) and the ancient Greek "magikos." The linguistic transformations that lead to the word "magic" imply a cultural journey from ancient Greek shamans and the witches who appear in ancient Roman poetry all the way to the medieval sorcerers of England and France. The Greek word "magikos" descends from "magos," an Iranian word meaning "sorcerer" or "wise man," which in turn descends from the Old Persian word "magus." The Iranian and Persian cultures are significant because they were the home of Zoroastrianism, an ancient religion based on the war between light and darkness. As classical scholar George Luck explains in *Arcana Mundi*, the ancient Greeks regarded Zoroastrianism as exotic and mysterious, and hence they associated the priests of this religion with secret knowledge and rites (36).

Two related terms for magic are sorcery and wizardry. The word "sorcery" comes from the Latin "sors," which refers to a lot or other item used in random selection, as in drawing lots. Sorcery is etymologically related to the word "sortilege," which refers to divination through the mechanisms of apparent chance, such as drawing lots from a vessel or rolling dice. Ironically, a sorting function in programming, used to organize the elements of an array, might have been seen by classical and medieval thinkers as a form of sorcery. Sorcery enters modern vocabulary through the popularization of a subgenre of fantastic pulp fiction called sword and sorcery (see Chapter 8, Section 8.3).

In addition to sorcery, wizard or wizardry originates from the Middle English word "wisard," which refers to a wise man. "Wizard" is a common term used in the fantasy narratives of J.R.R. Tolkien and J.K. Rowling, in both cases used to refer to someone with an inborn, hereditary capacity for magic (see Chapter 8, Sections 8.2 and 8.12). In contrast to this fictive emphasis on heredity, the word "wizard" equates magic with wisdom: acquired learning and the ability to apply it judiciously. A sorcerer sorts; a wizard is wise. One term tends to suggest divination and an acceptance of the role of chance, while the other evokes a reverence (and perhaps also fear) toward scholarly study and learning.

Unlike sorcerer and wizard, the term "warlock" has distinctly negative and demonic connotations, descending linguistically from the word for "traitor," literally an "oath-breaker." The term was originally applied to the Devil and later extended to refer to male witches. The use of warlock to denote dark or demonic magic-users, as in *World of Warcraft* and late *Dungeons & Dragons*, is entirely appropriate. The term "witch" is more neutral, descended from the Old English word "wicca," which also simply meant "witch" and was later adopted by contemporary occultist Gerald Gardner as a term for his invented neo-pagan faith. The term "warlock" was originally also gender neutral, referring to either a male or a female magician.

For the purposes of this book, occult magic is the ability to alter reality according to the will. This definition is a compound of many famous axioms and concepts from the history of magic. Perhaps the most famous is the famous occultist Aleister Crowley's definition of magic from his masterwork *Magick*, in which he defines magick as "the Science and Art of causing Change to occur in conformity with Will" (126). This definition is echoed in the avant-garde tabletop game *Mage: The Ascension*, in which magic is defined as "the act of dynamically altering reality through force of will, knowledge and an Awakened Avatar" (9).

Cornelius Agrippa defines magic in terms of the sympathies and resemblances between entities in the natural world, which the magician can harness in order to produce miraculous effects, sometimes by controlling a subordinate thing through something superior. He explains:

> Magic is a faculty of wonderful virtue, full of most high mysteries, containing the most profound contemplation of most things, together with the nature, power, quality, substance, and virtues thereof, as also the knowledge of whole nature, and it doth instruct us concerning the differing, and agreement of things amongst themselves, whence it produceth its wonderful effects, by uniting the virtues of things through the application of them one to the other and to their inferior suitable subjects, joining and knitting

them together thoroughly by the powers, and virtues of the superior bodies (5).

Heinrich Cornelius Agrippa (1486–1535) was a German Renaissance occultist most famous for his work *Three Books of Occult Philosophy*, widely regarded as one of the foundational texts of Western occultism. Agrippa makes cameo appearances in the Harry Potter series, as well as *Amnesia: The Dark Descent*.

This definition of magic can be broken down into its parts to arrive at a clearer picture of magic.

Reality is everything: physical, metaphysical, social; animal, vegetable, mineral; violent, erotic; logical, emotional; infinitesimally small, cosmically large. Reality is more than just the physical world, yet many philosophers limit their definition of reality to the physical, resulting in the belief that magic is false. Reality, in this view, cannot be altered through ritual or supernatural means, which have no direct effect on matter or energy.

But there are as many ways of effecting change as there are facets of reality. We can change things by choosing to see them in a different way, or by feeling a different way toward them. We may not be able to cause rain, but we can view rain in different ways: chemically, as a combination of hydrogen and oxygen; mythologically, as the tears of the gods; emotionally, as an overflowing of our own sorrow (or joy); agriculturally, as nourishment for crops. Each time we look at the rain differently, we change it. It could be argued that we only change our perception of reality, but the line between perception and reality is a thin one. Human beings may or may not be able to access reality independently of their senses.

To change reality, magicians use their will. The will is the human capacity to choose and to set action into motion. The will is a great mystery and a subject of longstanding debate, including the debate over free will. People argue about whether human beings are ever able to choose. In everyday life, though, we can choose to act. When I drink a glass of water, I am carrying out my will. I experience a desire to drink the water, and I exert a focused mental effort to lift the cup to my lips. Viewed from the outside, there is a chain of causal events that leads to this outcome: neuroelectrical impulses are passing from my brain to my arm, causing my muscles to contract. But the mystery is in the first link of this chain: the decision that I make to reach for the glass of water and the mental energy that sets into motion the chain of events. No one fully understands the mystery of the will. It is at the heart of magic.

Magic is, of course, many other things—illusion, wonder, strangeness, the ability to work miracles. But the definition of magic that focuses on altering reality through the will is especially well suited to games, in which a player's ability to affect a simulated reality or virtual world is at the heart of interactivity.

6.4 THE OCCULT HISTORY OF SYMBOLIC CORRESPONDENCES

The heart of magic is symbolism. A symbol is one thing that stands for another thing, but it is more than that. Symbols resonate. They feel charged with mystical energy, because what they represent is somehow beyond the ordinary world of matter. A pentagram is a symbol standing for (among other things) the four classical elements of water, air, earth, and fire and a fifth mystical element of spirit. A hexagram, or six-pointed star, is a symbol, standing for the seven planets known to the ancients, including the sun and the moon. The sun and moon themselves are symbols, resonating with the energies of day and night, male and female. A rose can be a symbol, as can a cross: if the two are conjoined, they produce the rosy cross, revered by the mystical society of the Rosicrucians. Almost anything can be a symbol, including colors, planets, plants, animals, stones, perfumes, Tarot cards, and weapons.

One symbol alone does not a system make, nor does a jumble of symbols constitute a system. Rather, symbols function together in relationships of correspondence, and symbols are integrated with sets of rules (see Chapter 2, Section 2.5). As Skinner observes in *The Complete Magician's Tables*, correspondences are "the basis of magic" (15). Correspondences emerge from a fundamental tenet of the magical worldview: the idea that apparently disparate entities are actually connected in hidden ways. The word "occult" originally means hidden, emphasizing in part the secret nature of the hidden connections. James Wasserman states in his *Art and Symbols of the Occult* (quoted in the beginning of *The Complete Magician's Tables*):

> The basis of occultism can be summed up in a word *correspondence*. The theory of correspondence recognizes an implicit interdependence of all things with all other things, the existence of multiple relationships between various aspects of Nature's kaleidoscopic richness (6).

Wasserman is alluding in part to the theory of sympathetic magic, by which things affect similar things; in this theory, by waving a rain stick, we can make it rain. As Skinner further explains, "correspondences not only form the basis of communication, but they are also the basis of magic" (15).

Symbols correspond to each other. One stands for another, which in turn stands for another. For example, the planet Mars corresponds to the color red, the number five, the pentagram, and the sound of a trumpet blast. Venus corresponds to the color green, the number seven, and the heptagram. Correspondences are best expressed through tables because this format can display multiple symbols of the same kind in columns (e.g. planets in the example above) and long chains of correspondences in rows (e.g. all the associations with Mars in one row, all those for Venus in another). Crowley's *Liber 777* is a compendium of such correspondences, which are derived from a mystical society called the Hermetic Order of the Golden Dawn. These correspondences are in turn derived from *Three Books of Occult Philosophy* by Renaissance occultist Cornelius Agrippa.

Traditionally, in Western occultism the Kabbalistic tree of life is often used as a framework for the correspondences (see Chapter 2, Section 2.5). One doctrine of the Kabbalah is that God created the universe through emanation: by allowing his light to shine outwards, and by speaking mystical words comprised of the Hebrew alphabet. The Tree of Life consists of ten branches representing fundamental ideas—building blocks of the universe such as wisdom, understanding, and victory. There are in turn twenty-two paths connecting these branches, each corresponding to one letter of the Hebrew alphabet.

Fragments of Kabbalah and the Tree of Life have appeared in video-game lore, but the correspondences are rarely used as the basis for a magic system. The branches of the Tree are called Sephiroth, a name familiar to any player of *Final Fantasy VII* as the name of the game's main villain. A mysterious sidequest in *Shin Megami Tensei: Nocturne* involves the collection of the ten sephiroth in the form of candelabra, and the characters in *Shin Megami Tensei II* are based on letters from the Hebrew alphabet. These allusions to kabbalistic tradition add atmosphere to a game, giving it a sense of potential depth or mystery for those familiar with the game or willing to look up the references.

But correspondence could be used much more effectively than mere atmospheric allusions if they were integrated with rule systems. Rules are the means by which symbols are combined in order to affect gameplay.

Since a set of correspondences is a table, which in turn is an array or matrix in programming terms, rules are the basis of the programs that manipulate these tables, arrays, and matrices. There are many functions whose purpose is to cycle through tables, sometimes to match a given string of values against the table. This can be easily done with a while loop (in programming terms, a command that executes repeatedly while a condition remains true, e.g. while items still remain to be counted in a list). For example, a table of correspondences could form the basis of material spell components. In order to cast a frenzy spell designed to cause aggression in monsters, a player might need to assemble materials that correspond to the planet Mars. Based on the example mentioned earlier, the player would need to have a ruby, a trumpet, a red cloth, and an iron sword (see Recipe 34: Matching Spell Components against an Array [Original Flash Actionscript]).

6.5 VIDEOGAMES AND THE HISTORY OF RITUAL

The history of magic is ultimately a history of ritual, and the usefulness of this history for game designers is inspiration to construct our magic systems. For a ritual is a system: a complex system of gestures, words, statues, incense conducted within a carefully consecrated space at a precise time in order to invoke or evoke particular spiritual forces. Just as Jesse Schell argues that the ultimate goal of game designers is to create an experience in a player's mind, so the ultimate aim of ritual is to create a spiritual experience in the mind of a practitioner. The most effective way to engineer an experience is by addressing all of the senses and mental faculties. Consequently, ritual from an outside perspective often closely resembles a complex artistic performance, a massive production probably closest to opera. The great German composer Richard Wagner famously sought to create a gesamtkunstwerkt, a fusion of all existing art forms (music, poetry, drama, painting) into a single, coherent, majestic, and mythic experience (see Chapter 2, Section 2.5). Wagner's work often contains strong ritualistic and magical elements, whether the mysteries of the Holy Grail in *Parzival* or the enchanted rings that would inspire Tolkien's work and, by way of Tolkien, countless games (see Chapter 8, Section 8.2). Wagner's vision has also often been adopted as an ideal anticipating virtual reality through its profusion of multimedia in order to create a coherent and immersive environment. Given the elements of magic ritual and proto virtual reality in Wagner, it is no coincidence that Silicon Knights—the creator of one of the richest and most ritualistically charged magic systems in *Eternal Darkness*—adopts a neo-Wagnerian vision of videogames as the "eighth art," synthesizing the seven previous arts of architecture, painting, sculpture, dance, poetry, cinema, and music in order to produce a final enchanted product that is more than the sum of its parts (Grant).

6.6 IAMBLICHUS AND NEO-PLATONIC MAGIC

This Wagnerian vision of multimodal ritual has its origins in much earlier, ancient history: specifically, the ancient Greek Neo-Platonist Iamblichus. Iamblichus was a philosopher of the school of Neo-Platonism, a set of beliefs that stemmed from the Greek philosopher Plato. At the heart of Plato's doctrines is a belief that the visible and material world is only a shadow or reflection of a spiritual realm of Ideas, which comprise the models and templates from which every created thing has its origin. Plato advocated an extreme devotion to reason and rationality, and magic is largely foreign to his worldview. The Neo-Platonists, however, extended Plato's ideas in a direction that is very favorable toward magic. The Neo-Platonists saw creation as a series of emanations from the divine, which they referred to as the One. As the One emanated its light, it formed the multiplicity of our daily existence, including an intricate array of spirits, demons, heroes, and gods.

Some of the Neo-Platonists belonged to Hellenistic culture, a name for cultures influenced by the Greeks in the late period of their society, when Alexander the Great had founded an empire that included ancient Egypt and Babylon (referred to as Chaldea). Iamblichus observed the exotic rites of the Egyptians, who worshipped a pantheon of deities like Osiris, Isis, and Horus that became combined with traditional Greek gods to form combinations like Serapis (an underworld god fusing Osiris and Hades) and Harpocrates (a god of silence). For a Neo-Platonist, magic is referred to as theurgy: literally, "working with the gods." For Iamblichus, the gods are not indifferent to human actions. On the contrary, the gods can be summoned, petitioned, and even influenced by properly arranging symbols that are harmonious with their natures. Ritual is an organized and deliberate configuration of symbols according to strict and logical rules. In this way, Iamblichus' vision of magic is profoundly similar to the arrangement of a game, which also consists of a set of symbols (tokens, avatars, dice) arranged in complex configurations according to rules.

As Iamblichus himself explains in *On the Mysteries of the Egyptians*, "the theurgist, by virtue of mysterious signs, controls the powers of nature" (51). These mysterious signs are also known as symbols, and they are mysterious because they appear to point to realities beyond the ordinary realm which are in turn able to control the material realm of nature. Scholar of classical magic George Luck further explains, "In the latter case, no medium is needed; only certain 'symbols' and magical formulas are required. The 'symbols' could be an herb, a stone, a root, a seal, or an engraved gem, and the formulas might include the seven vowels of the Greek alphabet, representing the seven planetary gods" (51).

Iamblichus' view of magic ritual as fundamentally symbolic later inspired Crowley, whose books on magic are characterized by a deep attention to the metaphorical significance of each minute aspect of each ritual. Crowley advocates the theory of symbolic correspondences that runs from Iamblichus through the medieval grimoires to the Renaissance magician Cornelius Agrippa and the tables of Stephen Skinner. As Crowley explains: "There is a certain natural connection between certain letters, words, numbers, gestures, shapes, perfumes, and so on, so that any idea, or (as we might call it) 'spirit,' may be composed or called forth by the use of those things which are harmonious with it, and express particular parts of its nature" (142). Crowley articulates in particularly concise and eloquent terms the notion that there are natural linkages between particular symbols, which address a variety of senses (perfume addresses smell, gestures address touch and movement, shapes and letters address sight, words address sight and hearing). Contrary to modern linguistics, the connections between these symbols are not arbitrary but rather natural, and these natural connections are mysterious. Furthermore, the purpose of configuring these symbols together is to conjure up a spirit, which Crowley characterizes as primarily a metaphorical way of describing an idea. By describing spirits as ideas that are summoned through symbols, Crowley is firmly in the Neo-Platonic tradition of theurgy.

6.7 WRITING GAME INCANTATIONS AND THE BARBAROUS NAMES OF EVOCATION

Key to ancient and modern understandings of magic is the power of language, specifically magic words, which survive in contemporary stage magicians' performances as "abracadabra." A recurrent phrase in ceremonial magic is the "barbarous names of evocation," referring to a line from a fragmentary ancient magical text called the *Chaldean Oracles of Zoroaster*: "Change not the barbarous Names of Evocation for there are sacred Names in every language which are given by God, having in the Sacred Rites a Power Ineffable" (Westcott 57). "Barbarous names" means exotic and primitive-sounding words, perhaps even nonsensical gibberish syllables. In *Arcana Mundi*, classical scholar George Luck argues that the barbarous names are characteristic of Hellenistic magic. He explains, "magical power is linked to certain words that are clearly differentiated from normal language; they are pronounced in a certain way or written on gems, papyri, and the like, along with certain signs and diagrams" (56).

Magical texts, such as the Greek magical papyri, are filled with such words. In admonishing magicians not to alter these words, the *Chaldean Oracles* suggest that the barbarous names are powerful despite their primitive, nonsensical qualities and perhaps *because* of these qualities. Crowley explicitly makes this argument in the chapter of *Magick in Theory and Practice* called "On the Barbarous Names of Evocation," in which he argues that the purpose of exotic, bizarre verbiage in spells is to alter the magician's consciousness (187–194). As Crowley explains: "the long strings of formidable words which roar and moan through so many conjurations have a real effect in exalting the consciousness of the Magician to the proper pitch," a process Crowley compares to the operation of music on the emotions (188). As a poet, Crowley's advice on the meter of magical spells is even more specific, as he advises "iambic tetrameters enriched with many rimes both internal and external" (187). Iambic tetrameter refers to lines of poetry consisting of four feet (i.e. four pairs of one accented and one unaccented syllable).

Because it is likely that game writers involved in developing a magic system might be called upon to write poetry in order to bring an atmosphere of mysticism to their games, a few examples of effective conjurations might be useful. Crowley's own "Hymn to Pan" is extremely eerie and charged with energy, and it exemplifies Crowley's own metrical advice, as does any sample from the witches' spell in *Macbeth*:

> Double, double toil and trouble;
> Fire burn, and caldron bubble.
> 2 WITCH. Fillet of a fenny snake,
> In the caldron boil and bake;
> Eye of newt, and toe of frog,
> Wool of bat, and tongue of dog,
> Adder's fork, and blind-worm's sting,
> Lizard's leg, and owlet's wing,—
> For a charm of powerful trouble,
> Like a hell-broth boil and bubble.

Another powerful example of iambic tetrameter in a magical invocation appears when Dream is summoned in *The Sandman* (see Chapter 8, Section 8.15.4).

The barbarous names of evocation are often written in equally mysterious secret alphabets, including runes and the Enochian language.

6.8 VIKING MAGIC AND RUNES

The actual historical basis of runic magic is dubious, based on scant and ambiguous passages in *The Poetic Edda* and other Norse sagas. We do not know for certain if the ancient Norsemen actually ascribed magical powers to the runes or used them in divination. Early New Age and occultist thought on this subject was often based on speculative fancy without solid historical basis, resulting in an academic backlash in which scholars rejected any esoteric application of runes and regarded them purely as a functional alphabet. The pendulum continues to swing back and forth on this subject, as Mindy MacLeod and Bernard Mees conduct a rigorous historical investigation of authentic runic magic.

For our purposes as game designers, however, whether the ancients actually used runes in this way is less important than the ways that various mystics, starting in the Renaissance and continuing into the twentieth and twenty-first centuries, have created systems of runic magic. Perhaps the most influential of these runic scholars was Guido von List, a German mystic who wrote *The Secret of the Runes*. These systems often have little to no basis in the cultural practice of ancient Norsemen, but these systems of runology and runic divination are internally coherent because the mystics who invented them believed them to be true. As with many of the systems of mysticism in the book, what matters is the belief and imagination of particular visionaries, which lends coherence to systems that can then be adapted as rule systems in games.

Runic mysticism finds its way into games by way of other media, including fantasy literature and even heavy metal (symphonic black metal specifically). Tolkien famously inscribed his maps of Middle Earth with runes in *The Hobbit* and *The Lord of the Rings*, and some of these runes operate as a hidden script that can be used as a mystical password to open a door. Heavy metal band Therion built their concept album *Secret of the Runes* around the supposed divinatory and magical powers of runes. Systems of runes drive the magic systems of *Dungeon Master* and *Ultima Underworld* (see Chapter 3, Sections 3.6 and 3.11).

While Scandinavian runes have great potential to inspire game magic, an alphabet and language from the Judeo-Christian tradition of angels and demons is emerging as an equally powerful tradition: the Enochian language of John Dee.

6.9 ENOCHIAN

Enochian is a magical language named after the Hebrew patriarch Enoch, who was taken by God directly in a chariot to heaven where he received divine, esoteric wisdom and spoke with angels. Hence Enochian is a language for communicating with angels. The language was developed or discovered by John Dee, the court mathematician, astrologer, and magician of Queen Elizabeth I, who worked with Edward Kelley to document the language and use it to communicate ritualistically with angels. Enochian is a central component of the Golden Dawn system of magic, where the Forty-Eight Enochian keys are used to summon visions of angels in particular heavens known as aethyrs (from the same root as ether, the cosmic substance once thought to transmit light). Aleister Crowley popularized Enochian based on visions he experienced while scrying in the desert, and Anton Szandor LaVey (founder of the Church of Satan) published a demonic inversion of the Enochian keys in *The Satanic Bible*. Enochian has entered popular culture through several routes, including the television show *Supernatural* as well as several games, including *Bayonetta* and *Dante's Inferno*. Enochian elements pervade *Bayonetta*¸ a fast-paced action game in which the witch player character executes fatality moves that require the player to press buttons in time with a whirling Enochian wheel. Bayonetta's artifacts, such as a ribbon she wears, are decorated with Enochian letters, so that the game is pervaded by angelic lore. Similarly, the choral soundtrack of the videogame *Dante's Inferno* is sung entirely in Enochian, as the soundtrack's two composers explained in their GDC talk "Scoring Hell."

Enochian is most likely a fabricated language. While this could be disappointing or frustrating to a mystic looking for literal communication with angels, the constructed nature of Enochian does not make it less interesting for game magic, but more so. Game designers are in the position of creating internally consistent languages that resonate with virtual worlds, so the truth or falsity of Enochian as a real language spoken by actual beings is less important than its richly developed alphabet, vocabulary, and syntax. As with many aspects of magic, the *belief* in the authenticity of Enochian as an angelic tongue has led magicians and scholars to study and develop it with the rigor of a real human language.

As a sign of its rich development, Enochian has an alphabet, a vocabulary, and a grammar. The alphabet consists of letters, their names, and their phonetic equivalents. Figures 6.4 and 6.5 show the Enochian alphabet and its English equivalents. As Laycock explains in *The Complete Enochian Dictionary*, the language was developed in several stages, each of them representing a phase of supposed angelic revelation. The first phase involved revelations from archangel Uriel, who delivered instructions for the preparation of a mystical sign called the Sigil Ameth (22). The sigil has shown up in popular culture in places as diverse as Marilyn Manson album liner art and Rob Zombie t-shirts, as well as closely resembling the Ae'lanoic Rosette of *Shadow of the Eternals* (see Chapter 4, Section 4.5). Using the sigil as the basis for talismans, altars, and other ritual equipments, Dee and Kelley invoked angels who communicated squares of letters, derived from or yielding the names of many angels (24–27). These squares resemble crossword puzzles, word searches, and a variety of other linguistic puzzles and could hence provide inspiration for many magically charged ciphers and codes analogous to those in Dan Brown's popular novel *The Da Vinci Code* (or for, that matter, *Uncharted 3*, in which the player character Nathan Drake receives puzzles from the explorer

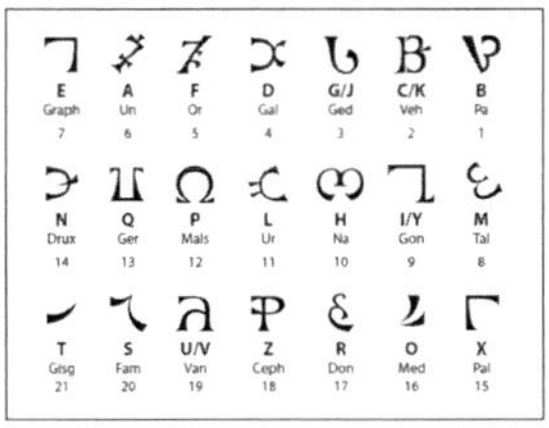

FIGURE 6.4 Enochian Alphabet.

FIGURE 6.5 Enochian Alphabet 2.

Sir Francis Drake). As a mathematician and a self-taught renaissance man, Dee was himself an expert on codes and ciphers.

Continued conversations with angels yielded an alphabet and, eventually, a language. The language is highly musical and sonorous, with patterns that are characteristic of poetry or speaking in tongues during a trance-like state, such as switching between one-syllable words and two-syllables words, as well as "monosyllables containing *o* or *u*" alternating with "dissylables containing the same vowel (mostly *a*) repeated with a nasal consonant" (33). An example of this hypnotic speech can be found in the first famous lines of the first Enochian Call, "Ol sonf vors g, gohó Iad Balt, lansh calz vonpho; Sobra zol ror I ta nazpsad, graa ta malprg" ("I reign over you, says the God of Justice, in power exalted above the firmaments of wrath; in Whose hands the sun is as a sword, and the moon as a penetrating fire") (248). Both the original Enochian and the English translation are poetic and entrancing, though the Enochian is especially rapturous; as the angel Castiel remarks in the television show *Supernatural,* "It's funnier in Enochian." The Enochian Calls must be recited or heard in order to absorb their full impact. (Early, rare recordings of Crowley reciting the first two Calls can be heard on the album *Aleister Crowley: The Order of the Silver Star,* available on iTunes through Red Cab Records.) In addition to the musical qualities associated with the Enochian language, the individual letters of the Enochian or runic alphabets can be combined into visually and symbolically intense magical circles and designs, some of which are known as sigils.

6.10 SIGILS

The history of occultism can provide inspiration for gestural magic systems through the study of magical symbols called sigils (Latin for "seals"). Sigils are extremely common in grimoires, where they are often associated with particular angels or demons, who can be summoned or controlled by drawing the sigils on parchment or other talismanic objects. Most medieval and Renaissance grimoires contain some sigils, with the *Lesser Key of Solomon the King* being a particularly memorable example of sigils for summoning seventy-two demons. Aaron Leitch's *Secrets of the Magical Grimoires* synthesizes many of these sigils collecting them from many different texts and collating them together (263–71), Cornelius Agrippa's *Three Books of Occult Philosophy* suggests a rationale for constructing sigils based on magic squares (grids of numerologically significant digits or the Hebrew letters associated with them) (321–28).

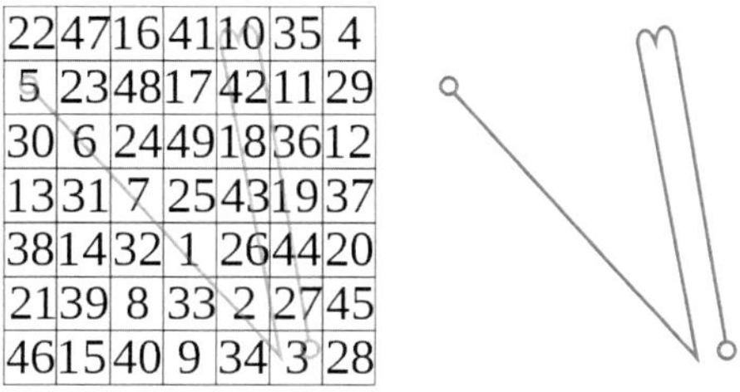

22	47	16	41	10	35	4
5	23	48	17	42	11	29
30	6	24	49	18	36	12
13	31	7	25	43	19	37
38	14	32	1	26	44	20
21	39	8	33	2	27	45
46	15	40	9	34	3	28

Hagiel = הגיאל = 5; 3; 10; 1(10); 30(3)

FIGURE 6.6 Hagiel Magic Square (Kamea). (Ben Whitmore, a.k.a. fuzzypeg. Released into public domain.)

Magicians trace zigzagging lines over the numbers or letters associated with a spirit's name, sometimes with loops to indicate the starting and end points of the sigil. For example, Figure 6.6 illustrates the derivation of the sigil of the spirit Hagiel from the magic square of Venus, his governing planet. The process begins by finding the numerical equivalents of the Hebrew letters in Hagiel (Heh = 5, Gimel = 3, Yod = 10, Aleph = 1 (converted to ten for convenience in the square), and Lamed = 30 (converted to three, also for convenience in the square). The magician then traces line segments and curves between these numbers on the square, after which the background of the square can be removed to yield the sigil by itself. Figure 6.6 shows a sigil based on the magic square of the spirit Hagiel.

The Hermetic Order of the Golden Dawn used a similar sigil generator in the form of a mystical rose, whose twenty-two petals contained the letters of the Hebrew alphabet, which could be traced over to form many sigils. The Rose Cross also encodes a vast amount of magical color symbolism in the form of a spectrum of color called the Queen Scale, which equates certain branches of the Tree of Life with particular hues (see Chapter 4, Section 4.6). The backgrounds of the petals in the rose are colored according to the shade that corresponds to a given path associated with a particular Hebrew letter. By contrast, the Hebrew letters themselves are painted in so-called flashing colors, the complementary colors to the Queen scale, so that they appear to scintillate or flash. Figure 6.7 shows the Rose Cross painted in flashing colors based on the Queen and King scales. Figure 6.8 shows a set of assorted sigils with numerological and symbolic relationships to the Tree of Life.

Occultist tradition includes a dizzying array of similar seals and sigils for individual spirits in the angelic and demonic hierarchy, including

FIGURE 6.7 (See color insert.) Rose Cross. (By the Order of the Golden Dawn. Public domain due to age.)

FIGURE 6.8 Assorted Sigils. (Original image by Giles Timms.)

archangels, angels, demons, spirits, and intelligences. In particular, the *Lesser Key of Solomon the King* is famous for its set of seventy-two seals representing individual demons of the goetia. Such methods of producing sigils are useful from a game design standpoint because they provide a rigorous, systematic, and mathematical way to produce a wide variety of sigils, which can be extracted from practically any word or name. Because sigils are created from a set of mathematical rules, these rules provide the basis of computer programs that allow sigils to be procedurally generated (i.e. created on the fly during a particular gameplay session), thereby creating replay value and preventing players from simply memorizing a single particular set of sigils. The principles of sigil construction, both individual and procedurally generated, are a branch of sacred geometry that applies on a larger level to the spatial layout of a magician's temple.

6.11 MAGICAL LEVEL DESIGN AND RITUAL SPACE

Much historical magic involves the configuration of spaces, something that game designers will recognize as a type of level design. Many magical grimoires consist of verbal descriptions and pictorial layouts of the spatial arrangement of a magician's temple, the place where he performs his magical rituals. An aspiring magician builds a temple, and the layout of this temple resonates with the symbolic correspondences underlying his ritual. Figure 6.9 shows the temple from *Arcana: A Ceremonial Magick Simulator*, in which the level architecture is based on symbolic correspondences.

The role of level design in the construction of magic systems manifests partially in temple architecture, but more so in the creation of a cosmology. A cosmology is a map of the structure of the universe, including alternate planes, dimensions, and realms of thought. Magic is predominantly

FIGURE 6.9   The Magician's Temple from *Arcana*.

metaphysical rather than physical, so its spaces tend to be conceptual, symbolic, and psychological rather than concrete. One of the strengths of *Mage: The Ascension* and *Mage: The Awakening* is the development of elaborate cosmologies from which the various aspects of a spell draw their energy and form (see Chapter 4, Section 4.9). Locations like the Umbra, the Gauntlet, the Silver Ladder, and the Watchtowers are not physical locations, but rather mental placeholders for a particular type of energy or effect. The same is true of the Invisible Labyrinth in Neil Gaiman's *Books of Magic*, the Fade in *Dragon Age*, or the planes in *Dungeons & Dragons* and *Magic: The Gathering*. To map out these locations is to work out the relationship between the types of energy associated with them; spatial relationships are diagrams of mechanics.

Ideally, the architecture of a magician's temple mirrors the cosmology of his internal and external universe, an idea implied in the foundational alchemical text *The Emerald Tablet of Trimegistus* when it famously opines "As above, so below," implying a symmetry between the cosmic patterns of the celestial realm and the physical architecture of the material universe.

In keeping with this symmetry, the first book of Crowley's *Magick* describes the objects in the magician's temple as elaborate metaphors for the metaphysical aspirations of the magician. As Crowley explains, "the temple represents the external universe" (49). In other words, the temple is a metaphorical representation of the macrocosm (a word for the universe as a whole, with which the magician aspires to unite). The temple is of great importance in Crowley's system because it is a symbolic map of the cosmos. Crowley's particular temple blueprint, developed over sixteen chapters, derives from the Western, European tradition of ceremonial magic as described in medieval and renaissance grimoires. Crowley's contribution is a lucid, poetic, and profound interpretation of the objects in the temple as metaphors about magic. Other temples, such as the peristyles of voodoo described by Arthur Métraux, have similar but differing layouts aligned with a given culture's cosmology. An awareness of both the physical layout of the temples and their many metaphorical suggestions can help designers enchant the spaces of their games and integrate these spaces with their magic systems. Too often, mage's guilds and towers are mere storehouses of alchemical ingredients and spellbooks, as is the case in both *Dragon Age* and *Skyrim*. By investigating the occult significance of space, designers can re-invest the lairs of their mages with sanctity and significance.

The general layout of a temple of Western ceremonial magic consists of the following parts:

- A *circle*, in which the magician stands, to protect him from the spirits he summons. The circle represents the totality of the universe. Classic game theorist Johan Huizinga uses the magic circle to denote the self-contained nature of games as conceptual spaces, in which rules, rewards, and fictions apply that have no power outside the limits of the game. He explains:

> Just as there is no formal difference between play and ritual, so the "consecrated spot" cannot be formally distinguished from the play-ground. The arena, the card-table, the magic circle, the temple, the stage, the screen, the tennis court, the court of justice, etc., are all in form and function play-grounds, i.e. forbidden spots, isolated, hedged round, hallowed, within which special rules obtain. All are temporary worlds within the ordinary world, dedicated to the performance of an act apart (10–11).

  Huizinga's concept of the magic circle is part of a larger argument in the book *Homo Ludens* that games operate according to the same cultural rules as rituals. Huizinga devotes much of his book to addressing the question of "how far every ritual act falls within the category of play" (19).

- A *triangle*, into which to evoke spirits
- A *mirror or crystal ball* for receiving otherworldly visions
- An *altar* in the center of the circle, upon which the magician places his ritual implements
- A *cross* of ten squares, representing the kabbalistic tree of life, in which the magician stands

Like game spaces, a magician's temple is re-configurable through interactivity in that the magician can change and shift its arrangement in order to reflect a particular ritual goal. One key purpose of symbolic correspondences is to govern how the parts of a temple should be arranged. Crowley gives an example of the use of symbolic correspondences to shape one's temple when he explains how to arrange a temple to summon a spirit of

Mercury, a god who corresponds to the number eight, the octagon, and the color orange. In *Liber O* (included as an appendix in *Magick*), Crowley writes:

> You would then prepare your Place of Working accordingly. In an orange circle you would draw an eight-pointed star of yellow, at whose points you would place eight lamps. The Sigil of the Spirit (which is to be found in Cornelius Agrippa and other books) you would draw in the four colours with such other devices as your experience may suggest (614).

Crowley's explanation shows that the symbolic correspondences of Mercury shape the lineal figures that are drawn on the floor (an eight-pointed star) as well as the number and placement of lamps. The sigil of the spirit is a particular curvilinear sign that is drawn inside of the triangle to represent the spirit being summoned.

Because the temple space is interactive and re-configurable, the lay-out of a temple to evoke a different spirit would follow a similar pattern but reflect a different set of correspondences. For example, to evoke the spirit Bartzabel, a planetary spirit of Mars, the magician would draw a five-pointed red star instead of an eight-pointed orange star, and the magician would place one red lamp at each point of the star. Figure 6.10 shows a magician's temple arranged to summon Bartzabel, with the sigil of Bartzabel painted in the center of the triangle. Both the circle

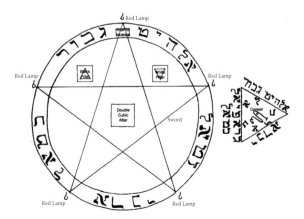

FIGURE 6.10   Temple Configuration for Bartzabel.

and the triangle are surrounded by Hebrew names for God and spirits corresponding to Mars. Ceremonial magic revolves around the arrangement and construction of a consecrated space as well as spiritual voyages into alternate planes of existence, environments that might be referred to collectively as ritual space. The construction of ritual space has strong analogies to many aspects of game design connected to the development of magic systems, including not just level design but the development of various dimensions of programming, such as the status of multiple state machines envisioned as a metaphorical state space. Ritual space is defined by the configurations of objects that could be referred to as spell foci.

6.12 GAME SPELL FOCI AND RITUAL OBJECTS

Ritual spaces are rarely empty. Foci, material components, reagents: the world of magic is brimming with strange and exotic ingredients that lend the power of objects to enchantment. While magic deals in metaphysical forces, human beings are accustomed to living much if not most of their lives in a material realm. Consequently, they need physical objects as symbols and reminders of the spiritual forces they invoke. These symbols serve as sacraments in the classic Catholic Christian understanding of the word: an outward and visible reminder of an inward and spiritual reality. In the case of game magic, these objects have a three-part nature, in that they are digital representations of physical objects meant to symbolize and command spiritual realities. Plato might be appalled (or delighted) by this threefold philosophical puzzle, but as designers all we need to know is how the magical tradition of enchanted objects can help us design better spell foci.

Gary Gygax originally used the word "material component" in describing the ingredients of spells, though the more philosophically nuanced game *Mage: The Ascension* tends to use the word "foci" (the plural of "focus") (*Mage* 181–84). Occultist tradition has long included an elaborate repertoire of ingredients and tools, from the ritual implements of a ceremonial magician to the eldritch recipes of witches' brews. In *Secrets of the Magical Grimoires*, Leitch devotes three chapters to ritual implements described in the grimoires, including wands, pentacles (magical symbols inscribed on parchment or carved into materials such as wood or wax), altars, robes, headbands, ointments, and incense (183–209, 285–91, 355–63). As Leitch points out, aspiring magicians must actively engage in quests for these sacred objects and the materials that make them: "the grimoiric instructions make it very clear that one must go out into nature, and quest for the materials to construct the tools" (186).

Gemstones, because of their shining purity and their vivid, saturated colors, lend themselves to magic systems, as evidenced by the many systems in which players can slot gems into armor and weapons as enchantments (such as *Final Fantasy* and *Kingdoms of Amalur*). Carved or inscribed gems played a key role in ancient Egyptian, Hellenistic, and Gnostic magic as amulets and talismans, as Luck acknowledges in passing (51, 56). In game magic, all too often gems are restricted to inventory items that can't be directly interacted with, perhaps in part because gems are such small items that they are difficult to work with in an inventory screen or in a third-person viewpoint. The *King's Field/Shadow Tower* games, precursors of *Dark Souls* and *Demon's Souls*, are exceptions to this rule. In particular, the game *Eternal Ring* builds its entire magic system around the consecration of gems in magical rings, which are prominently visible in the game's interface and first-person view. Gems and uniquely carved rings are central to the magic of *King's Field*, where they are prerequisites to casting spells, and *Demon's Souls* and *Dark Souls*, where the rings are directly tied into the games' mythologies.

The insistence on a need to go on quests to search for ritual materials ties occult tradition closely to videogame structures, since quests for rare items are extremely common in many videogames. As I argue in my book *Quests*, one key to constructing more meaningful quests is to design richly symbolic quest items, in opposition to the profusion of monster tusks and hooves that predominate in many role-playing games (77–83).

As always, Crowley's *Magick* provides richly metaphorical interpretations of all the standard accoutrements of a ceremonial magician, thereby helping game designers to design magical items with greater meaning. A brief summary of the main items described by Crowley, along with their meanings, could assist designers as they think about their spell foci. After describing the temple and the magic circle, Crowley provides rich and poetic analyses of the following objects.

Object	Meaning
The Altar	"the solid basis of the Work, the fixed Will of the Magician; and the law under which he works" (55)
The Scourge, the Dagger, and the Chain	"the three alchemical principles of Sulphur, Mercury, and Salt" (58)
The Wand	"the Will, the Wisdom, the Word of the Magician" (73)

The Cup	The Understanding of the Magician, understood as "the structuralization of knowledge" (75)
The Sword	"the analytical faculty" (86)
The Pantacle	The "earthly food" of the Magician, understood as the ideas, experiences, and memories that fuel his work (95)
The Lamp	"the light of the pure soul" (102)
The Crown	"the Attainment of [the Magician's] Work" (104)
The Robe	"that which conceals, and that which protects the Magician from the elements; it is the silence and secrecy with which he works, the hiding of himself in the occult life of Magick and Meditation" (106)
The Book	"the record of every thought, word, and deed of the Magician" (107)
The Lamen (breastplate)	"the secret keys of [the Magician's] power" (111)
The Magick Fire	"the absolute destruction alike of the Magician and the Universe" (113)

6.13 ANCIENT EGYPTIAN MAGIC

Many of the conventions of spell foci and temple arrangement are derived directly or indirectly from ancient Egypt, in which ritual actions with symbolic significance intersected with the intricate symbolic vocabulary of hieroglyphics. Ancient Egyptian magic carries with it all the lure of exotic pyramids, vast deserts, and ancient sorcery, yet magic in ancient Egypt (called Heka) was very much a part of everyday life. An especially reliable account of ancient Egyptian magic comes from Oxford Egyptologist Geraldine Pinch in her book *Magic in Ancient Egypt*.

Ancient Egyptian magic exhibits several traits that could be useful to designers of videogames, such as its verbal emphasis. Egyptian magic is highly ritualistic: the line between priestly magic and sorcery is thin, if existent at all. Egyptian magic also places heavy emphasis on the sorcerous power of language, both written and spoken. As Pinch explains, "the spoken word, the power of creative utterance, is an essential part of summoning gods and people into being" (24). Because Egyptian magic was chanted, it was often written down as a guide or script for the magician, along with an accompanying rubric or set of instructions of ritual actions for the magician to perform while casting the spell (68). Egyptian magic also exhibits several traits in common with grimoire magic: magical timing, ritual purification, and the use of enchanted staffs and rods to manifest magical authority (76–79). Emphasizing the magical importance of color but also its cultural relativity, Egyptian magic has a unique magical color palette (see Chapter 4, Section 4.6). For example, red stands for both the crimson of the sun goddess as well as for the chaos and evil associated with the wicked god Seth (81). This emphasis on red results in a unique textual feature that could be used in an in-game spellbook or manuscript, whereby the names of chaotic entities are written in red, while the rest of the text is black. Black was an especially charged color from a magical point of view, resulting in reverence for the "blood or milk of a black animal"—a spooky quest item that could be used as a spell ingredient (81). Indeed, one of the most vivid aspects of Egyptian magic is its wild and exotic ingredients, which Pinch vividly subdivides into categories of "bizarre, such as bat's blood or the hair of a murdered man; some exotic, such as Syrian honey or Indian nard; and some expensive, like frankincense, gold leaf, or real lapis lazuli" (80). Egyptian magicians wielded human figurines, especially for lust charms, as well as amulets in the form of the famous Wedjat eye or eye of horus, in addition to the djed pillar and the tyet knot, often formed out of jasper and carnelian to associate it with the goddess Isis. Many of these general forms of Egyptian magic appear in the White Wolf RPG *Mummy: The Resurrection*, with enough detail to suggest that the game's designers consulted Pinch or a similar authority. The designers' research pays off in a richly cohesive tabletop game, suggesting that videogame designers could make equally productive use of similar research. In addition to classic Egyptian magical texts like *The Book of the Dead*, a vast catalog of grimoires from many different cultures, both modern and medieval, can impart similar depth and sophistication to magic systems.

6.14 MAGICAL BOOKS: GRIMOIRES

At the heart of the history of magic is the idea of magic books, referred to as grimoires. These books are key tools in the arsenal of the magician, who uses them both as guides in casting spells and talismanic objects. Because magicians often rely upon the sorcerous power of words, compendiums of magical language in the form of books become repositories of magical power. At the same time, the books of the magical tradition contain multimedia and interactive elements that prefigure videogames. Grimoires anticipate multimedia in that they are often filled with images, tables, and diagrams illustrating symbolic correspondences, the images of spirits, and talismanic magical seals. Moreover, grimoires prefigure interactivity in that they are not meant to be simply read passively, but rather to be used as guides for ritual and implements that are directly a part of the ritual. Figure 6.11 shows the occultist Aleister Crowley using

FIGURE 6.11   Aleister Crowley with Magic Book.

a grimoire in a ritual. Actual occult texts can help designers create in-game grimoires, which are already beginning to play a powerful role in many games. The *Tome of Eternal Darkness* in *Eternal Darkness* is one key example (see Chapter 4, Section 4.5). The Grimoire Weiss, a magical talking book in the cult action-RPG *Nier* serves a similar breadth of function as spellbook, character, and interface. In cult RPG *Vagrant Story*, grimoires also serve a key role, in which the Gran Grimoire (a magical book whose title echoes the historical *Grand Grimoire*, minus one letter) turns out to be synonymous with an entire city. Various hidden passageways in this city are blocked with glowing Hebrew letters behind which are hidden various puzzles, alluding to the symbolic correspondences contained in medieval grimoires that have literally been built into the architecture of the city.

A working knowledge of the most famous and influential grimoires is useful to game designers of magic systems because it allows them a source of inspiration. The two strongest guides to the grimoires are *Secrets of the Magickal Grimoires* by Aaron Leitch (an impressive synthesis and survey of many Renaissance and medieval grimoires from a practicing occultist) and Owen Davies' *Grimoires: A History of Magic Books* (a more skeptical account from the perspective of intellectual history). Writers tend to invest more work in giving a system coherence and logic if they believe that it is true on some level, and the authors of many grimoires do strive for coherence. It is this coherence that Aaron Leitch seeks amid a bewildering array of primary texts. In addition, many grimoires—especially modern ones—are elaborately executed hoaxes with dubious and falsified claims to authority. The many versions of H.P. Lovecraft's fictional grimoire the *Necronomicon* is a prime example. As Owen Davies subtly and skeptically argues, the *Necronomicon* qualifies as a grimoire not in spite of its falsifications but because of them and the way they resemble the elaborate fictions of ancient grimoires (286). Regardless of one's skepticism or credulity toward grimoires, a well-executed hoax can also provide inspiration for game designers because a successful hoax must ultimately be detailed and historically accurate in order to convince readers of its authenticity.

6.14.1 *Papyri Graecae Magicae*

The starting point for a discussion of magical texts is necessarily somewhat arbitrary, since fragments of spells and conjurations have been floating around since human beings first learned to write. Many historians agree, though, that ancient Egypt is one crucial early source of magical texts, one of the richest of which is the *Papyri Graecae Magicae* (the Greek magical papyri, often abbreviated *PGM* by scholars of magic). These spells were written on papyrus (a material for producing thin scrolls), and they are referred to as Greek because they come from the Hellenistic period of Greek culture, in which Alexander the Great had extended the Greek empire into Egypt. Magic was central to Egyptian mythology and folklore, because as Egyptologist Geraldine Pinch explains, "Ancient Egyptian heroes were usually magicians rather than warriors" (161, see Chapter 6, Section 6.13). These texts exhibit many of the features of ceremonial magic that would later be incorporated into medieval, Renaissance, and modern occultism, including the barbarous names of evocation (elaborate conjurations in exotic and sometimes nonsensical language) and the assumption of god-forms (in which a magician pretends to be a god, like Osiris or even Yahweh, in order to intimidate and coerce lesser spirits). Comparatively few games make use of ancient Egyptian magic in any deep or authentic way, despite the deep popularity of ancient Egypt in films like *The Mummy*. Games tend to feature the most obvious elements of the Egyptians, such as pyramids and mummies, but a deeper investigation of ancient Egyptian magical texts reveals ways that Egypt can shape gameplay through magic systems. The *Papyri Graecae Magicae* emerges from the same branches of magical philosophy espoused by Iamblichus, theurgy, as well as another related branch of magic called hermeticism (see Chapter 6, Section 6.6).

6.14.2 *The Lesser Key of Solomon the King*

Another key grimoire is *The Lesser Key of Solomon the King*, also known as the *Goetia*. Goetia has many potential etymologies but seems to descend from the Greek word for "howling," because of the noises made by magicians or the demons that they summon. There is a traditional distinction in classical thought between theurgy and goetia that roughly corresponds to white and black magic—working with the gods versus evoking demons to do one's bidding. However, many occultists have questioned this black and white distinction. In *Geosophia*, Jake Stratton-Kent argues that goetia is a coherent system that encompasses all the deities of the underworld and the dead, connecting its practitioners with primal energies and giving them a means of confronting their own mortality.

Regardless of its moral classification, the *Goetia* is one of the best-known grimoires containing the instructions for many of the procedures of ceremonial magic. The *Goetia* provides directions for the magician to assemble his temple and his implements for evoking seventy-two demons, which the book describes in vivid and often surreal detail. Many of these demons have already worked their way into videogame culture. For example, the crow demon Malphas shows up in the *Castlevania* series, including both *Dawn of Sorrow* and *Lords of Shadow*, as does the goat-footed lion demon named Buer. Demons such as Belphegor and Eligor can be summoned in the *Shin Megami Tensei* series, including *Nocturne*, the core mechanic of which involves summoning and recruiting demons to one's party. At this point, however, elements from the *Goetia* tend to be present primarily for atmosphere. The *Goetia* itself implies a larger system, including classic features such as the magic circle and the demons' sigils (see Chapter 6, Sections 6.10 and 6.11). Figure 6.12 shows an altar in a syncretic ritual.

6.14.3 Grimoires and the Treasure Hunt

In a monumental study of goetic magic entitled *Geosophia*, Jake Stratton-Kent writes about the "magic book, the cave, and the treasure-hunt," referencing the claim of many grimoires to guide the magician to treasure.

FIGURE 6.12 Altar Configuration from Jake Stratton-Kent.

Intellectual historian Owen Davies wryly notes in *Grimoires* that many grimoires purport primarily to sate the practitioner's quest for gold, but Stratton-Kent embraces the treasure-seeking aspect of goetic magic as an integral part of the necromantic tradition, closely connected to ancient Greek mystery rites that involved connecting with the spirits of the underworld. Viewed in this light, the dungeon crawls and treasure hunts of early adventure games and role-playing games become more closely connected to the magical tradition. XYZZY, the first magic word scrawled on the wall of the cave in *Colossal Cave Adventure*, is a teleportation spell designed to help the player locate treasures (see Chapter 3, Section 3.2). *Zork II* makes the connection between treasure-hunting and magic more explicit in that the treasures are scavenged in order to summon a demon. As Nick Montfort quips in *Twisty Little Passages*, "From the standpoint of the adventurer, *Zork II* adds a new and innovative motivation to the usual drive to plunder: Satanism" (131). Not all subterranean scavenger hunts are equally magical, and various designers have done more and less effective jobs in integrating magic with the treasure hunt. Early RPGs like *Wizardry VII* often featured locational and divinatory spells designed to locate items and NPCs in the world: a feature that has largely been replaced with modern features like automapping and quest targets. But retro games like the Nintendo DS *Dark Spire* are reviving magic whose function is to locate items. While the treasure hunt aspect of grimoires is one of the earthiest purposes of magic, the Renaissance philosopher Cornelius Agrippa offers one of the most rarefied and intellectual versions.

6.14.4 Agrippa's *Three Books of Occult Philosophy*

Cornelius Agrippa is one of the major figures of Western occultism, and his influence on fantasy gaming and imaginative literature more generally has been extensive. Many of the taken-for-granted principles and correspondences at the heart of Western understandings of magic derive from his masterwork, *Three Books of Occult Philosophy*, subtitled by Llewellyn Press as "The Sourcebook of Western Occultism." While this subtitle may be a bit of an overstatement, Agrippa's influence is extensive in both technical occultism and imaginative representations of it. Agrippa builds his threefold system of natural, celestial, and ceremonial magic around the ten branches of the tree of life and associated correspondences pertaining to the numbers one through ten. The founders of the influential nineteenth century Order of the Golden Dawn would later adopt many of these correspondences wholesale, and their correspondences would in turn be adopted by Aleister Crowley.

6.14.5 Eliphas Lévi's Dogma and Ritual of High Magic

Many of the concepts of modern occultism are distilled in Eliphas Lévi, a French occultist whose work would influence the Hermetic Order of the Golden Dawn, Aleister Crowley's Thelema, and Gerald Gardner's Wicca. While the concept of the kabbalistic tree of life had been used as a framework for occult correspondences since Renaissance Hermeticism, one of Lévi's innovations was to overlay the twenty-two picture cards of the Tarot (a.k.a. The Major Arcana) onto the twenty-two paths of the Tree of Life. Levi makes this argument in *The Dogma and Ritual of High Magic*, in which the twenty-two paths serve as a structuring device for the book. As Levi explains, "the kabalistic figures of Abraham the Jew, which imparted to Flamel the first desire for knowledge, are no other than the twenty-two Key of the Tarot" (25, 66). This correspondence, like most occultist correspondences, is primarily imaginative on Lévi's part. The Tarot is a deck of playing cards with some allegorical imagery, referred to aptly by Stephen Skinner as a fractured emblem book (417). (Renaissance thought was pervaded by emblem books, collections of images with extended symbolic meanings, called allegories, which communicated lessons about life and the universe.) Traditional Jewish Kabbalists were not familiar with the Tarot, which came into being long after the inception of the Kabbalah. Nevertheless, Lévi's overlay resonates with many later thinkers because the images on the major arcana are so deeply and abstractly allegorical, just like the paths on the tree of life.

The correspondences between the Tarot cards and the paths on the tree have also resonated with some game designers, although designers have not used these correspondences as effectively as they could. In *Silent Hill 3*, the player character finds a book about the Tarot which explains that each of the cards corresponds to one Hebrew consonant. (This is inaccurate in traditional occult lore, since the cards traditionally correspond to vowels as well as consonants.) The player character ends up placing five Tarot cards (one of which is invented by the developers) in order to open the final door from Alessa's bedroom into the cult's inner sanctum. This final puzzle on the inner bedroom door mirrors a similar puzzle based on authentic Solomonic magic in the first *Silent Hill*. *Silent Hill 3* also features the invented card "The Eye of Night," which the in-game book on Tarot implies is from a rare, secret

"Gardnerian" Tarot deck. Gardnerian refers to the founder of Wicca (a branch of modern British witchcraft), Gerald Gardner. Although there are several Wiccan tarot decks, Gerald Gardner is not associated with any secret Tarot decks (unless they truly are secret from modern scholarship). But Gardner did endorse Lévi's association of the Tarot cards with the Hebrew alphabet and its paths in his *Book of Shadows*. If the role of the Tarot in *Silent Hill 3* stopped with a simple lock and key puzzle, the game would have wasted much of the cards' symbolic potential. But the lead designer of *Silent Hill 3*, Hiroyuki Owaku, used the tarot pervasively in developing the game's lore, as he explains in *The Book of Lost Memories*, an analysis of the *Silent Hill* mythos included in Konami's official strategy guide.

Many other games use the twenty-two paths of the kabbalistic tree of life, including sometimes the tarot correspondences, as frameworks for narrative and mechanics underlying magic systems. The *Shin Megami Tensei* games work with these correspondences extensively, as in *Shin Megami Tensei II*, in which each of the characters is named after one of the letters of the Hebrew alphabet. The magic system of the *Persona* games is directly based on the major arcana of the Tarot, which stand for the various personae (alternate identities) summoned by the protagonists to gain powers. Similarly, in *The Binding of Isaac*, Tarot cards function as pick-ups that grant the player character powers, as summarized on the *The Binding of Isaac* wiki. The powers of these cards are loosely and inconsistently correlated with the images and symbolism of the major arcana. Some cards have meaningfully correlated powers, as in the World card, which reveals the entire world map and all items therein, or the Death card, which greatly damages all enemies in a room. The powers of other cards have no apparent relationship to the cards' images, as in the case of the Empress card, which transforms the player into a demon. Because of the tricky and unforgiving nature of *The Binding of Isaac*, it is always possible that some of the more obscure card powers have hidden or subversive meanings. (The power of the Empress card is the same as the Whore of Babylon item, perhaps suggesting anger toward women on the part of Isaac, whose abuse by his mother is the game's central motivator. Such connections can neither be confirmed nor entirely denied because of an absence of evidence, suggesting that the developers made intriguing but spotty use of the Tarot.) Creative use of tarot opens the way for the even more eclectic and freewheeling grimoires of the modern age.

6.15 MODERN GRIMOIRES, MODERN PRACTICES

While an awareness of ancient, medieval, and Renaissance history is key to revitalizing game magic, game designers should also be aware that there are many contemporary occultists who have worked from the 1970s up until the present. Many of these occultists are bravely creating their own systems of magic, influenced by ancient sources but swerving in their own unique directions. The occultists include Kenneth Grant, Jake Stratton-Kent, Andrew Chumbley, Daniel Schulke, and Michael Howard. These occultists find themselves in a position very similar to game designers, as they seek to glean inspiration from a mountain of past source material without being buried in it. By ensuring that our game magic references modern sources and ideas as well as ancient ones, we can keep our magic fresh.

6.15.1 Andrew Chumbley's *Azoëtia*

Andrew Chumbley's *Azoëtia* may be the single most beautiful and mysterious grimoire, the one that lives up most fully to the name. The title of *Azoëtia* alludes to the Azoth, a magical essence sought by the alchemists, which also features prominently in the cult survival horror game *Haunting Ground*. *Azoëtia* balances a thorough knowledge of multiple magical traditions—witchcraft, ancient Egyptian heka, Kabbalah, alchemy, Thelema—with a powerful drive toward innovation. Much of the book is concerned with the letters of a magical alphabet and the magical operations associated with them, a structuring principle called pathworking derived from the appropriation of the kabbalistic tree of life by various occultist groups, including the Golden Dawn. However, Chumbley's particular witches' alphabet is wholly original and massively complex, accompanied by gorgeously ornate, bizarre, and mind-bending pen and ink illustrations, including several original sigils.

Chumbley's twenty-two letters correspond to a compendium of magical practices from the world's occult traditions. Each pair of letters stands for what Chumbley calls an "aat" or "cell"—one of eleven realms of secret knowledge. Each letter pair in turn connects with another pair of letters via the eight pathways that cross the grand azoetic sigil, itself comprised of 484 lines in what Chumbley refers to in quasi-mathematical terms as a "linear matrix" (125). These eight pathways resemble existing schools of game magic, yet their greater subtlety can be inspiration for richer game magic. The twenty-two letters connected by these eight general pathways include specific practices including automatic writing, sacred sex performed in relation to lunar cycles, syncretic invocations of gods and spirits, drawing sigils, consecration of the three alchemical principles of salt, sulphur, and mercury, crafting of a horse-head rod and witch's knot, assumption of bodily postures representing gods in animal form, shape-shifting, and hand gestures. The quirky imaginativeness of each of these practices, culled from the history of magic and spun through Chumbley's unique traditional witchcraft, can help enliven the clichés of game magic.

Chumbley's azoetic sigil suggests the deep interconnectedness of magical practices, reminding designers that a magic system is far more than a compendium of spells, but rather a set of densely cross-referenced practices. As a grimoire, the *Azoëtia* reads more like a web page with hyperlinks rather than a linear narrative or argument: a grimoire is more hypertext than text. In-game grimoires like Librom of *Soul Sacrifice* or the *Year Walk Companion* can and often do take advantage of the hypertextual cross-reference possible in digital media, allowing players to skip around and jump back and forth in their attempts to solve the puzzles of particular ritual practices. Chumbley's eleven Aatic Cells with their associated twenty-two letters constitute an original alphabet that together form a grand sigil that is also a map of ritual practice. Only a few alternate reality games (ARGs) and transmedia game franchises aspire to this level of intricacy and interconnectedness, but through the study of grimoires like the *Azoëtia*, more could. The letters, cells, and practices of the *Azoëtia* are as follows:

Cell 1 (1st and 12th letters)
  1: Meditation on the first letter, the point that opens each path of contemplation
  12: "Spell of the Witches' Ladder and the Horse-Headed Rod" (104)

Cell 2 (2nd and 13th letters)
  2: Prayer, speaking in tongues ("automatism of speech"), sigils (119)
  13: Control and discipline of belief, the ego

Cell 3 (3rd and 14th letters)
  3: Alchemical rites of water, salt, and fire, in conjunction with and correspondence to lunar phases (140)
  14: The rites of congress between the king and queen of the Sabbat

Cell 4 (4th and 15th letters)
    4: Syncretic alignment (i.e. creating composite magical formulae
        out of similar gods' names from multiple cultures (p. 167)
    15: Assuming postures of animals, spells for shape-shifting (183)

Cell 5 (5th and 16th letters)
    5: Mystic interpretation of the hand
    16: Meditation on divine language
    "The Language of the Gods is most suitably understood by
        means of Symbols and Correspondences" (217)

Cell 6 (6th and 17th letters)
    6: Meditations on and through the five senses
    17: Curses

Cell 7 (7th and 18th letters)
    7: Ritualized sexual intercourse between a stone phallus and a
        stone vagina (kteis)
    18: Mantra/chanting/praising the sun

Cell 8 (8th and 19th letters)
    8: Blasphemy (using existing faiths as veils, or outright invert-
        ing existing faiths, e.g. a black mass)
    19: Necrophiliac meditations ("the eroticism of Thanatos")
        (265): crossroads meditation, witch's unguent, forked stave

Cell 9 (9th and 20th letters)
    9: Self-Hypnosis and Automatic Writing
    20: The Octriga: an eightfold sabbatic rite with all eight mem-
        bers of the covine, including but not limited to sexual con-
        gress between pairs of the covine

Cell 10 (10th and 21st letters)
    10: Sacrifice (animal, human, self)
    21: "spells of the sexual daimon" (315)

Cell 11 (11th and 22nd letters)
    11: binding a servitor or famulus to a vessel; belief as a tool
    22: Final summation of rites, the last conjuration

Chumbley's concept of "syncretic alignment" is highly relevant to game magic in a multicultural landscape of modern media. Syncretism means bringing together the gods and spirits of many traditions, as is characteristic both of modern occultism and of especially ambitious or forward-thinking magic systems, such as recent editions of *Shadowrun* or the *Rifts* book of magic. As Chumbley explains, "A Sorcerer not wishing to be bound unto the way of any single land nor unto any mortal system of praxis […] such as He may align the cognate Divine Forms from amongst the World's beliefs in order to give cohesion and aggregate form unto the Universal Arcana" (167). Chumbley then gives an example in which he aligns gods from a variety of traditions: Seth-pa-kharad (Egyptian), Tezcatlipoca (the Aztec "smoking mirror"), Iblis (Persian), Loki (Norse), Guede (voodoo), Lucifer, Phurba (Tibetan) (167). He shows how to phonetically combine these gods' names into a single formula. He also warns against losing the individuality of particular gods in a soup of muddled multiculturalism (a warning which any designer influenced by archetypal or Jungian thought would do well to heed). "Lose not the unique Beauty and Power of any God or Goddess, but rather realize their States of Singular Entity as mutually indwelling" (168).

Chumbley's work belongs to a larger movement known as Traditional Witchcraft, with great potential benefit to game designers. The work of occult publisher the Three Hands Press exemplifies the Traditional Witchcraft movement, which often focuses on very specific, localized aspects of nature rather than the generalized and sentimental worship of "The Goddess" or "Mother Nature" advocated by so-called Wiccans. Traditional witchcraft is also distinct from Wicca in that the roots of traditional witchcraft are older, and the work is more eclectic. Classic works in Traditional Witchcraft include *Children of Cain: A Study of Modern Traditional Wtiches, Arcanum Bestiarum: On the Subtil and Occult Virtues of Diverse Beasts,* and *The Language of Birds: Some Notes on Chance and Divination.*

CHAPTER **7**

A Videogame Designer's Guide to Non-Digital Game Magic

7.1 THE MAGIC OF ANCIENT GAMES

Game systems that simulate magic or communicate intimations of enchantment have existed since prehistoric and ancient times, long before the invention of any videogame. Some anthropologists believe that dice were used as divination tools in order to tell the future, just as many games of chance were viewed as reflective of the gods' will. The ancient Egyptian game of Senet used its mechanics and board layout to represent and simulate the soul's progress through the afterlife. Archaeologist Peter Piccione observes that while Senet began strictly as a board game without religious significance, it involved into a detailed "simulation of the netherworld," in which individual board positions and moves represented particular mythological elements, such as "the square of Thoth." Piccione describes Senet's evolution into a "ritual game," in which players would narrate the progress of their characters through the underworld as they played. This ritual paralleled similar rites in the Egyptian *Book of the Dead*, a collection of magic spells whose purpose was to guide souls through the afterlife (see Chapter 6, Section 6.12).

The investment of traditional board game mechanics and layout with esoteric, magical significance has parallels in ritualistic variants and applications of chess. The Hermetic Order of the Golden Dawn, a Victorian magical society whose members included Aleister Crowley and the mystically-minded poet W.B. Yeats, practiced a four-handed chess variant called Enochian Chess. Enochian Chess synthesized the angelic language and mystical system of John Dee and Edward Kelly with the Golden Dawn's syncretic teachings about tarot, alchemy, and astrology. Enochian chess was also used for divination.

Crowley observes a more abstract connection between chess and magic in that both potentially involve elaborate imaginary visualizations. As he observes in his autobiography, "On the surface, there seems little relation between Magick and chess, but my ability to play three games simultaneously blindfold was now very useful. I had no difficulty in visualizing the astral temple by an effort of will, and of course I was perfectly able to watch the results of the invocations with my astral eyes" (*Confessions* 517). Crowley's observations predate digital virtual worlds, but his remarks suggest that games and magic both entail complex operations that take place in imaginary spaces requiring the active mental participation of players.

A third traditional game with magical elements is the Tarot, which began as a pack of playing cards whose images drew on the allegorical imagery of Renaissance visual teaching tools called emblem books. Stephen Skinner memorably refers to the original tarot as an "emblem book printed on separate cards," emphasizing that the randomization and modularity of playing cards removed emblems from the narrative sequences in which they were typically contextualized (417).

7.2 CHAINMAIL, DUNGEONS & DRAGONS, ADVANCED DUNGEONS & DRAGONS

In 1974 the first magic system in a modern game appeared in *Dungeons & Dragons*, a role-playing game invented by Gary Gygax and Dave Arneson. *Dungeons & Dragons* was itself an outgrowth of a strategy wargame played with miniatures called *Chainmail*. *Chainmail* initially attempted to simulate mostly realistic medieval combat, with catapults, cavalry, and crossbows. Later, a booklet called the fantasy supplement added elements from fantasy literature, including wizards who could hurl magic projectiles. These fireballs and lightning bolts were numerically the equivalent of catapults; the third edition *Chainmail* book describes a fireball as "equal in hit area to the large catapult hit area." The equivalency of fireballs and catapults anticipates a future in which magic users in videogames would be dismissed as glorified artillery, often justifiably. The spells in *Chainmail* do feature some variety and complexity, including specifications of range and complexity level. There are spells of concealment; spells for hastening and slowing action; spells for creating illusions. In the end, though, *Chainmail* spells tend to be primarily aggressive because the central aim of miniature war gaming is to simulate large-scale battles.

As *Dungeons & Dragons* evolves out of *Chainmail*, magic becomes an individual enterprise, cast by particular player characters who may choose to specialize as a magic-user and cast a variety of spells. The original 1974 *D & D* boxed set included a book called *Vol I Men and Magic*, which offered the observation about magic-users: "Top level magic-users are perhaps the most powerful characters in the game, but it is a long, hard road to the top, and to begin with they are weak, so survival is often the question, unless fighters protect the low-level magical types until they have worked up" (Gygax 1974 6). At this point, the rules surrounding magic are still a bit hazy and jumbled, reflecting the overall disorganization of *Dungeons & Dragons* as a whole. The *Men and Magic* book (volume one of the original *Dungeons & Dragons* pamphlets) offers only twelve pages discussing magic, primarily consisting of descriptions of individual spells. Spells often but not always have both duration and range, and the explanation of spells frequently references earlier *Chainmail* materials. Spells are divided into levels, signifying an increase of spell power at higher levels, and some spells are dependent on character level (e.g. the number of dice per fireball spell depends on the number of character levels). The 1983 Red Box Basic Set of *Dungeons & Dragons* succinctly defines a magic user as follows, "A magic-user is a human character who studies the powers of magic. Magic-users find spells, put them into books, and study those books to learn the spells. Magic-users have their own spells, entirely different from cleric spells. A magic-user has poor fighting skills, and should avoid combat" (Mentzer 37).

Advanced Dungeons & Dragons becomes considerably more systematic in its approach to magic. There is still a long list of individual spells, but every spell now includes a matrix specifying spell level, duration, area of effect, components, casting time, and saving throw. In programming terms, spells are now objects with associated properties and variables—some numerical, others Boolean (true/false). Components refer to three categories of prerequisites for casting a spell, classified as verbal, material, and somatic. Verbal components are magic words, material components are physical elements like spell components, and somatic components are arcane gestures of the hand and body.

First edition *Advanced Dungeons & Dragons* features what would come to be known as a Vancian magic system, given this name because it was inspired by Jack Vance's *Dying Earth* series. Gary Gygax himself describes the magic system of *Dungeons & Dragons* as Vancian in his article "The *Dungeons & Dragons* Magic System," in which he places the system along a continuum of magical power and complexity that runs from *Macbeth* and *Conan* at the most complex, Decamp and Pratt as most powerful, and Tolkien as "generally weak and relatively ineffectual." In the Vancian model of magic, magic users must memorize all the spells which they wish to cast. When they cast a given spell, it disappears from memory and must be memorized again if the magic user so desires (*Player's Handbook* 100). The Vancian system is arguably a method of restricting the power of magic users, which runs the risk of becoming too great and imbalancing the game as a result. Gygax explains that if no restrictions are placed on magic users, the game "quickly degenerates into a weird wizard show where players get bored quickly" (4).

The use of verbal, somatic, and gestural components could also be viewed as a way of restricting magical power, but the specific nature of the components also suggests a desire to make magic feel more like an arcane skill. The first edition of the *Advanced Dungeons & Dragons Player's Handbook* insists on the specific skills required to cast spells: "Most spells have a verbal component, and so must be uttered. Most spells also have a somatic (movement of the caster's body, such as gesturing) component. Some spells have a third component, that of material" (40). Magicians in the world of *Advanced Dungeons & Dragons* must exhibit both work and mastery of their craft in order to cast spells. Indeed, the combination of words, objects, and gestures is close to actual occultist practice, perhaps in part because Gary Gygax consulted encyclopedias of the occult in his development of the game, as he acknowledges in his book *Master of the Game*. Most suggestive of the occultist tone in much *Dungeons & Dragons* is the spell Cacodemon, which requires a set of material components as blood-curdling as the darkest of medieval grimoires:

> The components of this spell are 5 flaming black candles; a brazier of hot coals upon which must be burned sulphur, bat hairs, lard, soot, mercuric nitric acid crystals, mandrake root, alcohol, and a piece of parchment with the demon's name inscribed in runes inside a pentacle; and a dish of blood from some mammal (preferably a human, of course) placed inside the area where the cacodemon is to be held. (87)

This is exactly the sort of material that was removed from later editions of *Dungeons & Dragons* or greatly downplayed in response to anxieties that the game encouraged Satanic, ritual behavior. Partially in response to such concerns and partially as a result of the tabletop genre, *Dungeons & Dragons* makes a clear distinction between player actions and avatar actions, i.e. what the player says in order to cast a spell versus what the character does. This disjunct is especially apparent in the basic edition, a.k.a. the Red Box, which contains several admonitions that players do not need to learn any "special words" or possess any enchanted artifacts to cast spells, even though their characters must recite incantations and carry spell components. The rift between player and character (while foundational to the early understanding of an RPG) was heightened in the case of magic because of pressures from fundamentalist Christian groups who denounced *Dungeons & Dragons* as a form of ritual devil worship. By distancing player actions from those of a character, the designers of *Dungeons & Dragons* made a clear distinction between an activity that was just a game and the supernatural fantasy it represented. By making this distinction, the *Dungeons & Dragons* designers also neutered their own magic system, robbing it of some of the metaphysical depth and supernatural thrill that it might have conveyed.

Despite the attempt at separating player and character action, the most thrilling moments in the *Dungeons & Dragons* magic system occur when the arcane techniques of characters slip over into those of players. In first edition *Advanced Dungeons & Dragons*, there actually were moments where player performance and character action intersected, as when players who cast the spell Aerial Servant had to visually show the real-life Dungeon Master which form of ritual protection he uses in the form of a sigil (42). Figure 7.1 shows the Aerial Servant sigils from *Dungeons & Dragons*.

It is these moments, when the magical actions of players meet and mirror those of their characters, which constitute the greatest achievements in magic systems. Developers should strive for these effects, and they can better do so by understanding when other developers in the history of games have succeeded, as well as where they could benefit from improvement.

Second and third edition *Advanced Dungeons & Dragons* bring with them alterations in the magic system, as chronicled in the Wikipedia article "Magic of *Dungeons & Dragons*." In particular, second edition and 3.5 editions both featured a sourcebook called the *Tome of Magic*, which included an increased variety of magic options.

Aerial Servant: The spell caster should be required to show you what form of protective inscription he or she has used when the spell is cast. The three forms mentioned are:

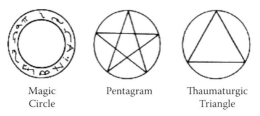

Magic   Pentagram   Thaumaturgic
Circle   Triangle

FIGURE 7.1   Aerial Servant Sigils from *Dungeons & Dragons.*

In a section insightfully titled "Creating a World-View of Magic," *Player's Option: Spells and Magic* describes the relative rarity, mystery, power, and required sacrifice of magic in various settings (10). This section title is meaningful because it acknowledges that magic is part of a fictional worldview (a term coined by sociologists to describe a given culture's framework for organizing beliefs and ideas about the structure of existence). *Player's Option: Spells and Magic* also has an interesting set of alternate magic systems, which constitute ways of using a system of spell points to simulate various alternative worldviews of magic. First, the book uses the spell points to adapt and render more flexible the traditional Vancian magic system of memorizing and then expending spells (Baker 77–80). The spell points "represent the total memorization ability of a wizard character" (80). Other systems place less emphasis on memorization and may break with it entirely. Channelers have access to any spell in their repertoire through free magic that derives from energy, governed by their energy and wisdom but at the cost of fatigue (81). Warlocks also possess a flexible use of spell points to cast spells, with the risk of sliding steadily deeper into the service of the extraplanar forces from whom the warlocks' magic derives. Warlocks' and witches' magic points do not re-charge except through a complex ceremony used to contact another extraplanar demon (83–85). Defilers and preservers are mages who draw upon the power of nearby life, such as plants and animals, to provide magical energy, with associated penalties to initiative simulating charging time. The most common appearance of this magic system is in the *Dark Sun* campaign (85–86). (Alienists and summoners are Lovecraftian sorcerers who operate primarily as wizards with sanity penalties associated with learning spells, as in *Call of Cthulhu* RPG which no doubt influenced it [87–91].)

The *Tome of Magic* has a fascinating table of zany and chaotic side effects of casting spells called wild surges some of which were implemented in the *Baldur's Gate* PC games Sernett (7). Wild surges are associated with wild mages, a class of wizards who hail from the Forgotten Realms, and their spellcasting has unpredictable results simulated through a table of randomized modifiers to spell levels which can also trigger a wild surge (6, table 2). The wild surges in turn are drawn from a randomized table and themselves have random variations, such as the number of days for which the caster speaks in a squeaky voice or the radius for causing hiccupping in adjacent creatures.

Fourth edition *Dungeons & Dragons* generally entailed a simplification of combat and spellcasting mechanics, designed to make *Dungeons & Dragons* feel more like a videogame (and specifically more like an MMO). Fourth edition *Dungeons & Dragons* does away with schools of magic, significantly reducing the richness of its magic system in comparison to the many videogames that have evolved elaborate taxonomies of reality inspired by the *Advanced Dungeons & Dragons* magic systems.

Despite the overall simplification of magic in the fourth edition of *Dungeons & Dragons,* the fourth edition also introduces non-combat spells called rituals, which require time, elaborate preparations, and material components in order to cast. In "4th Edition Excerpts: Rituals," Peter Schaefer argues that rituals are derived from the quest spell in the *Tome of Magic*, itself derived from two high-level cleric spells (Geas and Quest) in original *Dungeons & Dragons* (Cook, *Tome of Magic* 10–14, 122). The fourth edition *Player's Handbook* defines rituals as "complex ceremonies that create magic effects" (296). In terms of flavor and narrative, rituals are indeed complex, involving actions such as "reading long passages out of the ritual book, scribing complex diagrams on the ground, burning incense or sprinkling mystic reagents at appropriate times, or performing a long set of meticulous gestures" (298).

Unfortunately, the gap between player and character performance is large in the case of rituals, since the fourth edition *Player's Handbook* explains that "specific activities aren't described in most ritual descriptions; they're left to your imagination" (298). This somewhat dismissive omission of the particulars of ritual action contrasts strongly with the quest spells of the second edition *Tome of Magic*, which could be used as structuring devices for adventures, in which each ritual action and component could necessitate a unit of the quest. Instead, fourth edition rituals are primarily interesting because of the variety of non-combat magical effects that they bring into focus.

Rituals are classified according to nine categories, which could be viewed as the clandestine return of schools of magic into fourth edition *Dungeons & Dragons*. The nine categories are: binding, creation, deception, divination, exploration, restoration, scrying, travel, and warding. Many of these categories overlap with schools of magic from earlier editions. For example, the category of deception resembles the school of illusion in that both involve creating deceptive appearances in order to trick other characters, while the category of creation resembles the school of enchantment in that both can involve crafting magic items. On the other hand, the categories of divination, exploration, scrying, and travel allow for greater depth and development of spells that were often simply mixed in with other schools haphazardly, such as Dimension Door and Gate. These three categories involve the acquisition of information from supernatural sources as well as the movement through and mapping of complex spaces: activities which computers, as sophisticated information systems, are especially good at simulating. The potential for ritual magic was always present in *Dungeons & Dragons*, as demonstrated by the "Gate" and "Cacodemon" spells, but the fourth edition made this potential explicit in the mechanics.

The fourth edition *Tome of Magic* supplement also complicates and enriches the *Dungeons & Dragons* magic system through the introduction of three new types of magic: Shadow Magic, True Name Magic, and Pact Magic.

7.3 ARS MAGICA

While *Enchanter* is an excellent example of a digitally implemented magical language, the tabletop role-playing game *Ars Magica* (first edition 1987) offers an especially clear example of a magical vocabulary and grammar. The magical language of *Ars Magica* is Latin because of its association with the Middle Ages and the accompanying atmosphere of mystery resulting from its status as a language of learning in the Dark Ages. The language consists of five techniques (magical verbs specifying a particular effect) and forms (magical nouns specifying the target of a particular effect, in the grammatical position of a direct object). The five techniques are Latin verbs in the first person, through which the magician claims "I do this action": Creo (I create), Intellego (I perceive), Muto (I transform), Perdo (I destroy), and Rego (I control). The ten forms are Latin nouns in the accusative form used for direct objects.

Four of these forms are the classical elements of earth, water, wind, and fire (terram, aquam, auram, and ignem), as well as mind and body (corpus and mentem), animal and plant (animalam and herbam), image (imaginem), and power (vim). Combining the five techniques with the ten forms in verb-object pairs yields fifty unique combinations that can serve as spells.

7.4 WHITE WOLF, *THE WORLD OF DARKNESS*, AND *MAGE*

The universe of tabletop RPGs called *World of Darkness* features some of the richest, thematically expressive magic systems, operating in a coherent narrative cosmology that brings together mages with vampires, werewolves, fairies, demons, mummies, and wraiths. Each of these races of supernatural beings has its own flavor of magic, culminating in the authentically occult magic of *Mage: The Ascension* and *Mage: The Awakening*. The basic mechanic of the storytelling system in the *World of Darkness* is simple. Roll a pool of 10-sided dice whose number depends on the character's relevant ability scores. Count number of successes, where success is gauged by the number of dice rolls that score above the difficulty rating of a given task. The number of successes determines how well the player character performs the action. No successes means that the player fails the action. Other factors (such as rolling 1's and no successes) can cause more humiliating or painful failures called botches.

Mage: The Ascension and its third edition successor, *Mage: The Awakening*, both add rules to this simple system that richly simulate magic. Indeed, the spellcasting system of *Mage: The Awakening* can be represented through a flowchart with the complexity of a circuit board, whose forks and loops represent the many player choices and feedback patterns of the system. Figure 7.2 shows a *Mage: The Awakening* spell flowchart.

The magic systems of both *Mage: The Ascension* and *Mage: The Awakening* are so rich that they can be represented at various levels of detail, a term from graphics programming that refers to varying degrees of visual information provided depending on the player's distance from a given object, such as texture or a model. Both *Mage* systems can be examined from a bird's eye view (in which the steps of spellcasting are distilled down to four steps), a more expanded high concept document (in which the steps are expanded to ten steps), an elaborate flowchart (in which each eddy in the flow of the system is mapped), or a full rulebook (in which detailed exposition, charts, and lore fully expands the system). Indeed,

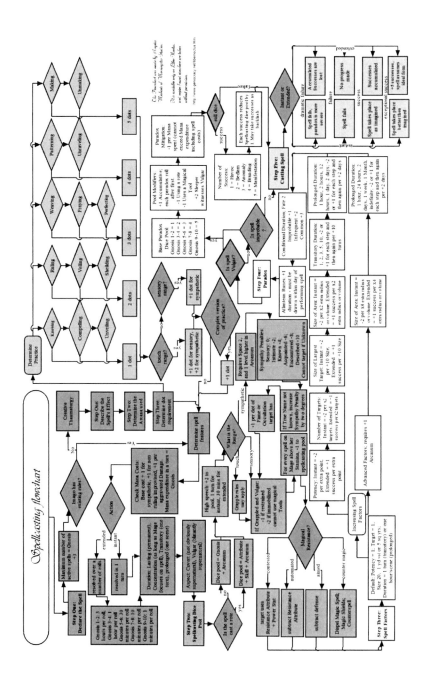

FIGURE 7.2 (See color insert.) *Mage: The Awakening* Spell Flowchart. (Image by Angelus Morningstar. Used with permission.)

the *Book of Shadows: The Player's Guide for Mage the Ascension*, distills the magic system down to four questions:

- "What do you want to do, and how do you want to do it?
- Do you know enough to pull it off?
- Do you succeed?
- If so or if not, what happens?" (Barnes 101).

Mage: The Awakening also has perhaps the richest schools of magic, reclaiming the symbol of the pentagram for five realms and ten associated schools of magic (called arcana) which escape the clichés of the five elements while drawing upon historical occultism. Each point of the pentagram is associated with one plane of existence that, in the manner of *Magic: The Gathering*, represents a fundamental aspect of reality and the cosmos. These five elements are the Aether (heavenly light), Stygia (death), Arcadia (orderly nature), the Primal Wild (untamed nature), and Pandemonium (a realm of the demons). As in the planes of the *Dungeons & Dragons* universe, the domains of *Mage* avoid cliché or restrictive symmetry by distributing forces across multiple planes, so that *Mage*'s Stygia and Pandemonium represent different aspects of darkness in much the same way that Gehenna and the Abyss do in *Dungeons & Dragons*. Figure 7.3 is a fan-made representation of the *Mage: The Awakening* cosmology.

As the *Awakening* rulebook explains, "in the Atlantean configuration, the subtle Arcana form the points while the gross Arcana form the lines between them" (Bridges 130). The rulebook then goes on to outline two different ways of tracing a pentagram—an invocation cycle starting and ending at the top prime point, and a banishing cycle other starting and ending at the bottom left death point. The existence of two methods of tracing a pentagram starting at different points in order to signify invoking and banishing is modeled directly on the Lesser Banishing Ritual of the Pentagram as described and diagramed in Israel Regardie's *The Golden Dawn* (54–55).

As this modified use of the pentagram to transcend the simplicities of the five elements suggests, *Mage: The Awakening* is a rare case in which the depth and subtlety of a game magic system outstrip that of most actual occult systems of belief and practice. Only the system of the Cultus Sabbati outlined in Chumbley's *Azoëtia* (see Chapter 6, Section 6.15.1) comes close to this degree of eclecticism and nuance. For example,

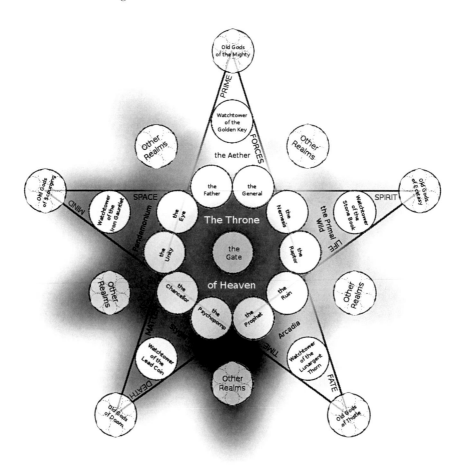

FIGURE 7.3 (See color insert.) The Ten Arcana of *Mage: The Awakening*. (Image by Dataweaver. Used with permission.)

Mage: The Awakening lists a set of "occult correspondences" for each path, based on the law of sympathetic magic and resonating specifically with Chumbley's law of syncretic alignment, in which a magician synthesizes the underlying energies of gods and spirits from diverse magical traditions without overriding their individuality (Bridges 35). The system has a truly rich system of towers, far more evocative than the elemental Watchtowers of Enochian and Golden Dawn symbology.

These five Watchtowers and associated realms are: the Watchtower of the Lunargent Thorn (in Arcadia, Kingdom of Enchantment), the Watchtower of the Golden Key (in Aether, Kingdom of the Celestial Spheres), the Watchtower of the Stone Book (in the Primal Wild, Kingdom of Totems), the Watchtower of the Leaden Coin (in Stygia, Kingdom of Crypts), and the Watchtower of the Iron Gauntlet (in Pandemonium, Kingdom of Nightmares) (Bridges 68). Each of these kingdoms could be thought of as roughly corresponding to another one of White Wolf's *World of Darkness* systems and campaign settings (both old and new), with the fairies of *Changeling* in Arcadia, the wraiths of *Wraith* or *Geist* in Stygia, the demons of *Demon: The Fallen* in Pandemonium, and the werewolves of *Werewolf: The Apocalypse* and *Werewolf: The Forsaken* in the Primal Wild. Given this overlap and the appearance of the Realm names such as Stygia and Arcadia directly in the sourcebooks for these games, *Mage* becomes a kind of meta-game, encompassing each of the other games' settings and magic systems inside its own multiversal cosmology.

These watchtowers are not restricted to the clichéd four elements of the Enochian Watchtowers, but instead even their names are subtly poetic. The Watchtower of the Lead Coin, associated with the realm of Stygia, gently but firmly suggests the coin placed on the tongues of recently deceased to pay the boatman Charon to ferry them across the Styx. The Watchtower of the Lunargent Coin, associated with the realm of fairy enchantment called Arcadia, combines the words for moon (Luna) and silver (argent) with the piercing danger of a thorn. The subtle poetry of these names taps into a larger set of correspondences charged with magical resonance, appealing to the senses of role-players in the ways that rituals appeal to the magical instincts of mages. As the rulebook explains, mages "find that incorporating these Sleeper occult systems into their rituals actually aids their magic, strengthening sympathetic ties to the Watchtowers" (35). The list of these correspondences could almost have been culled from Crowley's *Liber 777* (see Chapter 2, Section 2.5), except that they exhibit a greater range of cross-cultural reference as well as a subtle sensitivity to the deeper meanings of these realms.

Rather than simply describing a particular realm as the source of evil or demonic magic, two different realms encompass different versions of the underworld. Pandemonium includes the demonic in its classic infernal form, including "Goetia, Middle Eastern myths of demons, Zoroastrian devas, Iblis and the nafs, Haitian voodoo" (35). This series of phrases alone ranges over Solomonic magic (goetia), ancient Iranian mythology (Zoroastrian devas), Islamic thought (Iblis as a demon and nafs as impure souls), and Caribbean mythology (Haitian voodoo). In addition, Stygia expresses a related but distinct aspect of the underworld through a range of references associated with death cults that are somber but not necessarily evil: "Egyptian and Etruscan religion, Hades, Greek eidola,

Haitian voodoo, certain forms of Chinese ancestor worship." The rulebook mentions voodoo in relationship to both Stygia and Pandemonium, suggesting a flexibility and nuance in the developers' understanding of occult resonance. Extending the rulebook's logic, the Guede (loa of the dead) could be associated with Stygia, whereas the Petro loa ("hot" spirits often linked to black magic) could correspond with Pandemonium. Building on the correspondences of these realms and their associated arcana or schools, *Mage: The Awakening* truly shines in the rich and unique spells associated with each realm.

White Wolf's *World of Darkness* games exemplify thematically expressive mechanics, to which each game's magic system contributes organically. Each campaign setting showcases a different theme, expressed on the game's title page as "A Storytelling Game of X" (Personal Horror in *Vampire: The Masquerade*, Gothic Horror in *Vampire: The Dark Ages*, Reality on the Brink in *Mage: The Ascension*, Death and Damnation in *Wraith: The Oblivion,* Savage Horror in *Werewolf: The Apocalypse*, Modern Fantasy in *Changeling: The Dreaming*, Righteous Fury in *Hunter: The Reckoning*, and Infernal Glory in *Demon: The Fallen*). Each game also features a different magic system (or a set of abilities which roughly correspond to magic in a particular universe). The mechanics of each system reflect and express the themes of the particular world seamlessly, which is the ultimate aim of a magic system.

Magic is part of the White Wolf system for resolving action, which is always basically the same across gamelines. The player rolls a number of dice equal to the relevant attribute plus ability scores, then counts the number of successes. (The New *World of Darkness* gamelines, such as *Vampire: The Requiem* and *Mage: The Awakening*, adopt a simplified system for counting successes compared to Classic *World of Darkness*, such as *Vampire: The Masquerade* and *Mage: The Ascension*.) In Classic *World of Darkness*, successes are defined by the difficulty of a given action, with six being standard difficulty, whereas any roll over an eight counts as a success in New *World of Darkness*. In practice, the actions attempted by players are often of difficulty seven and eight (difficult and very difficult), since games gain much of their tension and drama from challenge.

The basic *World of Darkness* formula can be used to cast spells, which are a key component of the magic system of each gameline. In *Mage: The Awakening*, casting an already learned spell consists of choosing a spell, then rolling a dice pool based on attribute plus skill plus arcanum (or gnosis plus arcanum if the spell is improvised). The effect of the spell depends on the number of successes. Modifiers determine the enhancements and penalties to a given spell based on magical foci, mana expenditure, and other factors such as paradox, a warping in reality that occurs through misapplied spells. The storyteller rolls for paradox according to whether the magic was vulgar or improbable. The rules surrounding paradox encourage players to cast magic creatively and subtly, in keeping with the occult injunction to "keep silent." Players can spend mana to mitigate the effects of paradox.

In contrast with the metaphysical coherence of *Mage*, *Vampire: The Masquerade* emphasizes several separate clans, each with an individual set of discipline, as befits a game whose primary theme is personal horror. In *Vampire*, each discipline effectively has its own formula, the analog equivalent of what Doull calls a "unique code path," listed under the designation "system" (147). For example, controlling an animal necessitates rolling Manipulation plus Animal Ken, with various difficulties for creatures scaling upward from mammals to reptiles. Aura perception requires players to toll Perception plus Empathy and difficulty 8 (150). By assigning a unique system to each spell, magic has an atmosphere of being both individually tailored to particular characters and somewhat fragmented, reflecting the overall lack of otherworldly transcendence in *Vampire*. Vampires are undead, so their powers are supernatural, yet they often do not understand the source of these powers in the philosophical way that a mage does, nor do they have the metaphysical confidence to warp reality as reliably as a mage. Some vampires do practice ritual magic, which has its own formula. As the sourcebook explains, "Casting rituals requires a successful Intelligence + Occult roll, for which the difficulty equals 3 + the level of the ritual (maximum 9)."

Unlike the individualized fragmentation of magic in *Vampire*, *Demon: The Fallen* themes its magic through a system of theological evocations and lore, a variation on True Names and the linguistic magic of kabbalistic mythology. For a demon, faith is the magical resource, or mana, and it is finite and expendable, after which demons must power their abilities using torment of their victims. Successes rolled must also exceed torment score, or else trigger an alternate spell form called high-torment. Demons possess the magical lore that belonged to them as specific squadrons of angels, including the Lore of Sky, Flame, Portals, Radiance, and Awakening.

Demon also contains a very interesting reverse implementation of ritual summoning, whereby an NPC (or another human player, perhaps a mage from a crossover *Mage* universe) can summon the demon PC. The effectiveness of the summoning is greatly affected by the possession of the demon's True Name, resulting in a fascinating and nuanced formula: "If the summoner knows only the demon's Celestial Name, the demon receives bonus dice to the roll equal to her Faith rating. If the summoner knows the demon's True Name, binding the demon is easy. The summoner receives a number of *automatic successes* on the Willpower roll equal to the demon's Torment rating" (258). This formula is simultaneously simple, elegant, and deep in that it is based around the simple practice of rolling a dice pool and counting successes, but it incorporates a true/false condition based on True Names, which can trigger either a Faith check for bonus dice or an automatic success roll acquired from the weakness caused by the summoned demon's torment level. As pseudocode, this formula might look like the following:

RECIPE 36: FORMULA FOR *DEMON: THE FALLEN*
SUMMONING RITUAL

```
if (hasCelestialName)
{
NumberofDiceinDicepool = Willpower + Faith;
}
If (hasTrueName)
{
NumberofSuccesses = (1d10 * Willpower) + (1d10 *
   DemonsTormentScore);
}
```

In *Wraith: The Oblivion*, pathos is the positive spellcasting resource or mana, while angst is the negative resource that accumulates as a consequence of risky decisions, analogous to Torment in *Demon: The Fallen*. There are 13 Guilds, each associated with one Greater Arcanos. These 13 Arcanoi and their associated guilds are:

- Argos: Harbingers (teleportation in the Tempest)

- Castigate: Pardoners (resist the Shadow)

- Embody: Proctors (possess or "skinride" a human)

- Fatalism: Oracles (read and occasionally alter fate—largely divination)

- Inhabit: Artificer (possess inanimate objects)

- Keening: Chanteur (sing a song that produces emotion)

- Lifeweb: Monitors (detect and manipulate Fetters—dead souls' ties to the earth)

- Moliate: Masquers (shape and sculpt the substance of ectoplasm)

- Outrage: Spooks (use telekinesis to frighten victims)

- Pandemonium: Haunters (unleash eldritch energies of sheer weirdness)

- Phantasm: Sandmen (sculpt dreams and create illusory appearances)

- Puppetry: Puppeteers (move living human beings' bodies)

- Usury: Usurers (trade resources of the Dead)

Changeling: The Dreaming themes magic according to the lore of fairies, as inherited from Celtic and Elizabethan sources as well as modern adaptations such as Neil Gaiman's *Sandman* graphic novel. Spells are manifestations of glamour, the capacity of fairies to bewitch mortals with beauteous but false appearances. Spells themselves are cantrips, a Scottish-derived word that the *Oxford English Dictionary* defines as a witch's mischievous trick. The character of *Changeling*'s magic is primarily defined by its unique realms of magic, which emphasize mischief and deception, such as Chicanery, Legerdemain, Primal, and Wayfaring. The rule system also includes a Table of Mists, a rule-based implementation of the lore of fairy-induced amnesia, used to determine the degree of recall or forgetfulness by a human who witnesses a cantrip.

7.5 OCCULT ROLE-PLAYING: *UNKNOWN ARMIES*, *MALÉFICES*, AND *NEPHILIM*

There is a school of second-generation role-playing games, roughly in the early to mid-nineties, that adopt a more flexible and subtle approach toward magic than the first-generation *Dungeons & Dragons* approach. These subtle and rich magic games include *Nephilim* (1992) and *Unknown Armies* (1998). A French-language game called *Maléfices* (which translates in English to *Curses*) exhibits similar richness and authenticity even though it was published earlier (1985). A much later game, Monte Cook's *Arcana Unearthed* (2003), also puts elaborate ritual at the core of its mechanics. These systems often exhibit a heightened awareness of actual occult systems, possibly inspired by Isaac Bonewits' *Authentic Thaumaturgy*, which suggests ways that tabletop magic systems could be inspired by the history and theory of occult magic.

Unknown Armies is a grim, gritty, and self-consciously postmodern vision of the occult in the late twentieth century. Its schools of magic are quirky and unusual, including dipsomancy (alcohol magic), cliomancy (history magic), epidermomancy (flesh magic), plutomancy (money magic), and pornomancy (lust magic). These schools are in one sense deeply modern and in another profoundly mythological: modern in that they involve the trappings of twentieth century existence like drunken streetcorner bums and pornographic films, and mythological in that their names and core concepts derive from ancient and deeply human archetypes associated with the gods (Clio as the muse of history, Dionysus as the mystical power of wine, Pluto as the chthonic power of buried treasure associated with the god of riches and the underworld).

As the *Unknown Armies* core rulebook explains, magic in the game is based primarily on meaning, in the sense that its underlying logic is semantic and philosophical rather than scientific. The authors link this version of magic to the surreal school of Latin American literature known as magic realism, in which a beautiful and dreamy female character floats away because she has never been practical or "down to earth" (136). As Stolze and Tines eloquently write, "Magick operates according to *meaning*, not logic or reason" (136). Because meaning is the basis of this magic system, it is unusually flexible, permitting and encouraging players to invent new schools based on three loose principles: symbolic tension, transaction, and obedience (102–103). Symbolic tension means that there must be a paradox at the heart of the school (such as drawing power by gaining wealth but needing to hoard), transaction means that all magic has a cost in proportion to its power, and obedience means that the magician must obey taboos by avoiding forbidden actions in order to retain power (76).

Maléfices and *Nephilim* pioneered similarly symbolic and authentic approaches to RPG magic in games that were originally published in French, perhaps reflecting the avant-garde, Bohemian sensibilities of the French and their occultist experimentations in figures like Eliphas Lévi and the symbolist poet Arthur Rimbaud. *Maléfices'* poetic subtitle suggests its preoccupation with infernal forces and black magic: "the roleplaying game with the scent of sulphur," alluding to the odor of brimstone thought to accompany the devil and his minions. Players take the role of members of the Pythagoras Club, a group of ordinary citizens turned hunters of the diabolical in the French Third Republic (1870–1914). The design goal of *Maléfices* is to exude a mood of supernatural menace, heightened by a pack of subversive and surreal Tarot cards unique to the game which players draw as part of character creation. Most of the magic in the game operates according to rules that are known only by the game master, who often makes secret dice rolls and consults tables that are unknown to the players, in order to increase the atmosphere of supernatural mystery surrounding magic in the game.

A later supplement, called *On the Edge of Night*, includes rules for magic, which will nevertheless be seldom used directly by players but rather by their largely unseen adversaries. As in the later *Call of Cthulhu*, magic is extremely dangerous for players to use, resulting in a variety of catastrophic effects to mind and body. Unlike *Call of Cthulhu*, the supernatural forces in the game are hidden, almost invisible, to the point that players may never actually encounter a demon even though the entire game is built around implications of diabolical influence. The metaphor of a faint "odor of sulphur" is a fascinating design goal that might actually be easier for videogame designers to implement than tabletop developers, since computers are extremely effective at concealing rules from players while appealing to a sense of ambience through audio, visual, and tactile feedback.

Nephilim, a later French role-playing game that (unlike *Maléfices*) was translated into English and published by Chaosium, also attempted to create a sense of occult authenticity. The game's text and marketing hinge primarily on the game's accuracy, including the subtitle of "Occult Roleplaying" and a back cover endorsement by Donald H. Frew, identified as "Wiccan Elder, High Priest, & Magus." *Nephilim*'s title alludes to the offspring of fallen angels known as Watchers or the Sons of God, and human women referred to as the Daughters of Men. The player takes the role of one of the Nephilim, understood as a reincarnating elemental spirit with magical abilities that draw on the force of Ka, an Egyptian word for an aspect of the soul. On the plus side, *Nephilim* is extremely accurate in its depiction of magic, especially in its representation of astrological factors as influences on the power of a given magical operation. The Game Master's screen contains an elaborate planetary wheel made of interlocking discs, which can be rotated to input day and time in order to receive an exact set of spell modifiers based on the conjunctions and oppositions of various planets. On the negative side, *Nephilim*'s entire magic system is based on the classical four elements, with all the accompanying problems of excessively concrete, physical, and clichéd magic (see Chapter 4, Section 4.3).

7.6 TAKING PERFORMATIVE MAGIC TO THE NEXT LEVEL IN THE PALLADIUM FANTASY RPG

The Diabolist and Summoner classes in the Palladium Fantasy RPG emphasize performative and linguistic magic, through the construction of wards and circles. Despite their menacing name, Diabolists are primarily masters of magical symbols, especially powerful protective inscriptions called wards (117). For example, the Summoner class calls up demons and other supernatural beings by deciphering circles, drawing them, and speaking a word of power to activate them. Unlike many RPG books, the Palladium sourcebook actually provides comprehensive listings of runes, colors, and seals (130–31). The book insists that players must perform some of the magical actions of their characters. Rather than simply stating that Summoners use a circle and then rolling a die to determine whether it works, players must actually keep a record of the circles in a notebook, then draw them and speak the words. As creator Kevin Siembieda explains, "each time a player wants to discover if his character has deduced the correct creation/invocation of a circle, he must actually create the circle and attempt to activate it with his power word sequence. Then and only then does the G.M. allow the player to roll percentile dice for a successful deciphering of the circle."

Siembieda is aware that the Diabolist and Summoner character classes are fairly unique, to the point that he shifts into the first person to explain his rationale for their invention, saying, "I have also designed them to be very *different* than the traditional 'wizard' and spell casters found in virtually every other fantasy game" (136). Perhaps because of the rarity of drawing circles and wards in tabletop games, these styles of performative magic are especially well-suited to a digital format, in which a computer can track drawing actions in real-time rather than forcing all other players around a table to pause while the party's designated Diabolist draws. The Summoner and Diabolist magics fall firmly within the magic as minigame or ritual puzzle approach advocated throughout this book, and the complexity of the circle magic is approached only by the Sorcery of *Ultima VIII: Pagan* (see Chapter 3, Section 3.12).

The Diabolists and Summoner classes use two different sets of symbols, with some overlap. Diabolists use Ward Symbols in constructing wards (though in theory they understand all runes and mystic symbols), while Summoners use mystic symbols to construct magic circles. In visual appearance, the Summoner's magic circles are clearly inspired by the seals of the Solomonic grimoires (see Chapter 6, Section 6.14.2). The circles' functional meanings are often more transparently logical and coherent than those of the medieval grimoires, in which layers of obscurity and the hazy transmission of learning in the Dark Ages sometimes makes the construction of seals difficult to comprehend. In contrast, Siembieda's system is rare in that the symbols actually add up to a coherent vocabulary in which the words in a given circle make sense in terms of its function. For example, the Protection from Evil circle contains the downward triangle of evil on the left and the cross of protection in the center.

The geometrical designs also have a logic that ties into their function. All circles consist of four quadrants created by two crisscrossing lines that form an X in the center of the circle. Protective circles can either be open (allowing anyone to enter the ward) or sealed (excluding all but the caster from protection). A sealed circle has circular dots representing the Summoner's blood-drops at all ends of the intersecting lines that crisscross the circle, while an open circle has at least one line without a dot (138). A similar geometrical logic governs the creation of Summoning Circles, in which the top quadrant has no rim and is open to hold the symbol of the summoned being (though the circle's intersecting lines must be sealed to protect the Summoner, who is only protected in the bottom quadrant) (145).

CHAPTER 8

Adapting Game Magic from the Literature of the Fantastic

8.1 PROCEDURAL ADAPTATION

The literature of the fantastic revolves around magic. Fantasy literature from Tolkien to Moorcock to George R.R. Martin; horror fiction from Lovecraft to Barker and King; weird fiction and the New Weird of China Miéville and Jeff Van Der Meer; all share a common thematic concern with sorcery and enchantment. At first glance, the role of magic in fantastic literature might seem purely a narrative device, lacking in the rigor necessary to construct game mechanics. In fact, the magic of the literature of the fantastic often obeys rules as complex and rich as any game—so much so that the rules of game magic often derive from fictive magic. A greater understanding of fictive magic can improve the richness of our game magic by allowing us to invest our game mechanics with the thematic preoccupations of our favorite fiction, through a process that game studies scholar Ian Bogost and narrative designer Matthew Weise refer to as "procedural adaptation." As Weise explains in his essay "The Rules of Horror," procedural adaptation is "the concept of taking a text from another medium and modeling it as a computer simulation" (Weise). Weise further clarifies the concept and relates it to Bogost's "procedural rhetoric":

> Procedural translation is the practice of authoring rules and sys-
> tems dynamics in such ways that they model the situational log-
> ics implied by texts from other media. Developing a game system
> that expressed Marxist ideology would be procedural rhetoric.
> Developing a game system that let the user experience what it
> would be like to be Laurie in Halloween (John Carpenter, 1979)
> would be procedural translation (239).

One can easily imagine an extension of the idea of procedural translation (or adaptation, as Weise more commonly refers to it, taking a cue
from one of Bogost's unpublished lectures) into magic systems. Indeed,
such adaptations have occurred with varying degrees of specificity and
self-awareness throughout the history of magic systems. Developing a
magic system that allowed the user to experience what it would be like
to be the protagonist of Raymond Feist's Rift War saga would be procedural adaptation, and precisely this has been done in the CRPG *Betrayal
at Krondor*. *Age of Conan* entails a similar adaptation of the magic in
Robert E. Howard's Conan saga, just as *Champions of Krynn* did much
earlier with the moon-based, alignment-inflected mythological magic of
the *Dragonlance* saga.

Fictive magic systems run the gamut from vast, unified fictional
meta-universes that extend across seemingly unrelated media, as in the
work of Clive Barker, who explains that the magic systems in all of his
stories—from the cosmic sadomasochistic horror of "The Hellbound
Heart" to the fantastic enchantment of the *Abarat* series of young adult
fiction—are part of one vast overarching system. Barker revealed this
in a Twitter exchange in which he was asked if *Weaveworld* and *The
Great and Secret Show* exist in the same universe, since the *Weaveworld*
character Immacolata refers to magic as "the show." Barker replied, "@
SoundOfElegance Yes. All the magic in my books is part of a single
massive system. It is best summarized by the words that open G.A.S.S."
The opening words from *The Great and Secret Show* that Barker
references are:

> Memory, prophecy, and fantasy—
> the past, the future and the dreaming moment between—
> are all one country, living one immortal day.
> To know that is Wisdom.
> To use it is the Art (x).

At the other end of the spectrum is China Miéville, who asserts that each of his novels contains its own self-contained, cohesive magic system functioning according to its own internal logic. Miéville explains:

> Each big magic system [in my books] is self contained and rigorous. They're literalizations of theories of how the world works. But in Kraken, it feels different. The basis of magic in Kraken is about the persuasiveness of metaphor. If you can say to the universe that this thing is like this other thing and slide from simile to metaphor, the universe will listen and will change its nature. I'm taking the making of connections and literalizing that as a magical force... it's sort of a D&Dification of [Thomas] Pyncheon [sic] (Newitz).

For example, in the novel *Perdido Street Station*, Miéville describes an invocation of the Ambassador of Hell, a high-ranking demon in a bureaucratic hierarchy, as a cross between a classic grimoiric ritual and a scientific operation. The summoner chalks "intricate, stylized markings on thick pieces of paper," which he instructs his companions to place "over your hearts" with the "symbol facing out," just as a grimoire magician draws talismanic sigils and wears them on his robe to assert power over a demon (240). The summoner then uses a machine to begin the invocation, explaining that the machine obviates the need for a ritual sacrifice by pulling in an aetheric spirit and then bleeding it into the wires of the machine, producing a "victimless sacrifice" (241). The summoner proudly proclaims that "invocation's automatic now," meaning "no more learning stupid languages" (241). The use of sigils, sacrifices, and linguistic invocations are all present but efficiently mechanized to fit with the book's overall fusion of magic and science in such disciplines as "bio-thaumaturgy," yet the actual ritual is still charged with an atmosphere of risk due to the implication of a possible "transplantronic leap" and the opening up of unstable rifts to other dimensions (241). The conversation with the infernal Ambassador is also governed by strict rules, such as a procedure called Melluary in which the querent can only receive a "True Answer" if the question is asked in seven words in reverse order (243). This scene is one example of Miéville's rigorously systemized magic, derived from accurate occult sources but skewed to fit the highly idiosyncratic universe of New Crobuzon.

Both Barker and Miéville are touchstones of procedural adaptation especially relevant to game magic because of their involvement in game design work: Barker through *Clive Barker's Undying* and *Clive Barker's*

Jericho and Miéville through his work on the *Pathfinder* RPG, specifically his contributions to the supplement *Guide to the River Kingdoms.* Miéville was a dedicated tabletop gamer throughout his childhood, and in multiple interviews he attributes a penchant toward systematization of his fantasy worlds to the influence of *Dungeons & Dragons* and similar games (Gordon, Reed). In Miéville's thinking, systemization refers to rigorous world-building, through which Miéville converts an initial spontaneous image of an exotic setting into a set of rules, including "maps, histories, timelines." Miéville views his fiction as the intersection of images that are bizarre, mysterious, and outlandish—and therefore both resistant to systemization (analogous to the creative goals of the Surrealists) and rigorously systematized (influenced by *Dungeons & Dragons*). The tension between mystery and logical rigor in magic systems is an ongoing theme in the intersection of fictive and game magic.

The key to procedural adaptation of fictive magic is the awareness that each narrative world has its own set of rules, as displayed vividly in the chart "Rules of Magic" compiled by Charlie Jane Anders and the writers at i09.com. In addition to a title column, this chart includes columns that address the following questions in each universe: "Where does magic come from?", "How do you wield it?", "Is there good and evil magic?", "Is magic hereditary, or can anyone learn?", "What's the secret to defeating magic?", "Is magic a secret from a primarily non-magic world?"

There is a basic conflict, or perhaps tension, between the fictional need for magic systems to be mysterious and the gameplay need for them to be transparent. Stephen King indirectly suggests this contrast in his horror manifesto *Danse Macabre*, in which he writes that "the great theme of fantasy fiction is not holding the magic and wielding it (if so, Sauron, not Frodo, would have been the hero of Tolkien's ring cycle); it is—or so it seems to me—Finding the magic and discovering how it works" (370). King's maxim is not universally true in fantasy fiction, since there are many works of fantasy about practicing wizards holding and wielding their power, just as there are many games in which finding and understanding magic are a key component of gameplay. Yet King's comments suggest that magic in the literature of the fantastic serves primarily thematic and dramatic purposes within a narrative. In contrast, players aspire for mastery over a magic system, since core gameplay involves a moment-to-moment engagement with spells. The trick of procedural adaptation is to translate the thematic power of a fictive magic system into a set of mechanics that resonate harmoniously with the narrative themes of a game's world. Fictive magic can be primarily art, whereas game magic must be at least partially a science. Fictive magic can afford to be primarily an art because the most important purpose of magic in this context is to move players' emotions to wonder and awe, whereas game magic needs to be accessible to players as an interactive system.

Even among fictional magic systems, there is a continuum of rigorously scientific magic systems and more open, mysterious systems, with some authors advocating for or exemplifying one side more than another. Fantasy author Brandon Sanderson expresses some of the tension between these two approaches to fictive magic in his essay "Sanderson's First Law," in which he outlines a contrast between hard and soft magic systems. Sanderson's First Law of Magics expresses the relationship between clarity of a magic system's rules and the plausibility of solving problems with magic in a fictive world: "An author's ability to solve conflict with magic is DIRECTLY PROPORTIONAL to how well the reader understands said magic." Hard magic systems are those in which magic has clearly defined rules that both characters and readers understand, allowing characters to plausibly solve problems using magic because magical solutions seem plausible to readers. Soft magic systems are those in which the rules of magic are mysterious and only dimly understood by characters and readers, fostering a sense of mystical wonder (or eldritch unease) toward magic but also making magic an implausible solution to problems.

In an extremely soft system in which magic has few or no rules, magic carelessly used to solve a problem can be a deux ex machina (contrived and implausible solution, breaking the suspension of disbelief for readers and typically indicating poor craftsmanship on a writer's part). At first glance, one might argue that game magic needs to be firmly at the hard end of the spectrum, since the primary purpose of magic in games is to help players solve problems. Yet the insights Sanderson expresses that are most relevant to game magic are actually edge cases exploring how to handle what happens when characters attempt to solve problems with magic in a soft magic setting. Sanderson writes, "If the characters try to use the magic, it shouldn't do what they expect it to as the reader doesn't know what to expect either." This axiom translates into game mechanics as the many random and backlash effects associated with chaos magic and wild magic in tabletop role-playing games and roguelikes.

Sanderson associates soft magic systems with J.R.R. Tolkien and George R.R. Martin, two writers whose fictive magical worldviews are diametrically opposed but equally provocative and challenging for designers of game magic. As Sanderson explains, "Books that focus on this use of magic tend to want to indicate that men are a small, small part of the eternal and mystical workings of the universe. This gives the reader a sense of tension as they're never certain what dangers or wonders the characters will encounter. Indeed, the characters themselves never truly know what can happen and what can't." Game designers have often used Tolkien's fiction as the basis of game settings, though one might argue that an authentic adaptation of Tolkien's magic system is difficult because of its vagueness. George R.R. Martin's *Song of Ice and Fire* is an equally challenging and largely untapped wellspring for game magic. In order to address the challenges and benefits of adapting fictive magic as game magic, it makes sense to start with Tolkien, since he was the entranceway of many game designers into fantasy and fictive magic.

8.2 TOLKIEN

J.R.R. Tolkien, the author of *The Hobbit* and *The Lord of the Rings*, exerted a powerful influence on magic in the literature of the fantastic and games, despite his ambivalence toward magic from a metaphysical and narrative standpoint. The wizard Gandalf is one of the most memorable representations of a magic user in literature before Harry Potter. Consequently, game magic from *Dungeons & Dragons* onward was heavily influenced by Tolkien, despite the vagueness of magic in his fiction. Tolkien's own commentary on his work reveals his awareness that his version of magic is rather unsystematized as a whole. Tolkien writes in Letter 155 of his *Collected Letters* (a draft portion of Letter 154, which he never sent): "I am afraid I have been far too casual about 'magic' and especially the use of the word; though Galadriel and others show by the criticism of the 'mortal' use of the word, that the thought about it is not altogether casual." Another way to say this would be that magic in Tolkien is not particularly systemic in the sense of rigorously developed in a way that could be simulated, but rather invoked by Tolkien primarily for narrative and thematic purposes, i.e. telling a good story with some meaningful thematic undertones.

The mention of Galadriel refers to the "Galadriel's Mirror" chapter of *The Fellowship of the Ring*, in which the powerful elf-lord Galadriel tells Sam "this is what your folk would call magic. I believe; though I do not understand clearly what they mean; and they seem also to use the same word of the deceits of the Enemy. But this, if you will, is the magic of Galadriel. Did you not say that you wished to see Elf-magic?" Tolkien himself elaborates on Galadriel's distinction between elven magic and wicked, deceitful magic as analogous to the medieval contrast between *magia* and *goetia*. Tolkien understands the difference between magia and goetia as the contrast between genuine sorcery, using supernatural forces to modify the world, and deceptive illusions. Medieval philosophers equate magia with white magic (the theurgy that allows magicians to harness natural forces and the holy spirits allied with them) and goetia with black (the summoning of deceptive and demonic forces through acts of necromancy and diabolism). Tolkien rejects this moral distinction, instead arguing that good and evil magic are distinguished from each other by their effects rather than by any inherent moral value of a particular type of magic.

Tolkien foreshadows the difficulties of basing game magic on his work when he remarks, "a difference in the use of 'magic' in this story is that it is not to be come by through 'lore' or spells; but is in an inherent power not possessed or attainable by Men as such." Magic in Tolkien's world does not consist of spells, nor is it mastered through knowledge, whereas game magic consists largely of abilities and the player's mastery of the systems associated with these abilities. Tolkien's magic is an inherent natural power that operates vaguely and inconsistently, making it hard to reconcile with game magic that can be mastered by players because it operates precisely and consistently. This incongruity is at the heart of why games based on Tolkien, such as *The Lord of the Rings Online*, present a weak and bloodless version of magic. The Loremasters of *LoTRO* or *War in the North* do not belong in Tolkien's universe, and when they do appear, they carry neutered, vaguely druidic collections of half-useful spells, or clichéd elemental blasts of fire and electricity.

Despite Tolkien's genius and powerful influence on the settings and tropes of role-playing games, there are other, better, sources for game magic.

8.3 PULP MAGIC: ROBERT HOWARD'S *CONAN*, FRITZ LEIBER

Much post-Tolkien fantasy falls into the category of pulp fiction, so called because of the large percentage of wood pulp in the paper on which the tales were printed. Pulp fiction introduced or codified many of the genres that are well-known today, including fantasy, science fiction, and horror. Much pulp fiction operated in between these genres, which were still in the process of being defined and therefore both flexible and permeable. The umbrella genre of weird fiction included any confluence of these genres intended to create an impression of the bizarre and marvelous. Much weird fiction was published in the magazine *Weird Tales,* which included work by H.P. Lovecraft, Robert E. Howard, and Fritz Leiber. A subgenre of pulp fiction is known as Swords and Sorcery and primarily refers to the work of authors like Robert E. Howard and Fritz Leiber. Leiber uses the phrase "swords and sorcery" directly in the magically poetic introduction to *Swords and Deviltry*, the first volume of the adventures of Fafhrd and the Gray Mouser: "Sundered from us by gulfs of time and stranger dimensions dreams the ancient world of Nehwon with its towers and skulls and jewels, its swords and sorceries" (9). The invocation of "towers and skulls and jewels" could describe the magical locations and implements of countless tabletop role-playing games and videogames. Leiber was deeply influential on game magic, and a return to his wells of inspiration can greatly enrich contemporary game design, like drinking from a pure fountainhead instead of a diluted tributary.

"The Unholy Grail" by Fritz Leiber introduces a vivid contrast between white and black magic through the Gray Mouser, a wizard's apprentice who is suspended between these two extremes. In Leiber, the white magic advocated by the Gray Mouser's benevolent tutor functions through the Law of Sympathy in nature, evoked poetically through the suggestion of connections between "small creatures and stars and beneficial sorceries and Nature's codes of courtesy" (136). The Mouser's wizard had taught him that "the universe has laws of sympathy and love" (139), a phrase which deliberately conflates the law of sympathy (like affects like) with a secondary emotional meaning of sympathy as compassion. Black magic, on the other hand, is driven by hate and pain, poetically evoked by Leiber when he describes "the magic which stemmed from death and pain and hate and decay, which dealt in poisons and night-shrieks, which trickled down from the black spaces between the stars, which […] cursed in the dark behind the back" (136). Leiber's description includes a Lovecraftian touch in the phrase "trickled down from the black spaces," as well as an emphasis on slow and pernicious destruction by poisons (what MMO parlance would describe as damage over time, a power often attributed to darker mage classes such as warlocks). "Cursed in the dark behind the back" suggests deception and stealth, whether through an assassin or a thief who sneaks up behind a victim through magical concealments.

Leiber's black magic is predicated on negative emotions such as hate having a force that can be harnessed mechanically, thereby using "hate as an engine" in a phrase from Leiber's own memorable summary of the story. Black magic also entails a terrible, fearsome risk and cost, as encapsulated in a warning from the Mouser's mentor, who admonishes him that "none can use black magic without straining the soul to the uttermost—and staining it into the bargain. None can inflict suffering without enduring the same. None can send death by spells and sorcery without walking on the brink of death's own abyss, aye, and dripping his own blood into it" (147). Not only does black magic have a cost, but it is a cost specifically of corruption—a gradual sullying of the soul's purity: a trope that appears as a mechanic in a multitude of role-playing games in which the player amasses corruption points as a cost for using wicked magic. Leiber also connects black magic with blood magic and necromancy through the image of dripping blood in death's abyss: a vivid metaphor that suggests terrifying possibilities of bloody sacrifice and underworld journeys without spelling them out (see Chapter 4, Sections 4.10.1, 4.10.2, 4.10.13, and 4.10.14). In the climactic moments of "The Unholy Grail," the Gray Mouser channels his hatred toward an enemy through the eyes of her daughter in order to destroy the enemy. In the process, the Gray Mouser travels imaginatively or astrally into "a whole black universe," in which he hears "wings of stone" and feels "a wild black whirlpool of evil, like a torrent of black tigers" (160). This idea of transmitting hatred through a channel is sympathetic magic stripped of all compassion and infused with the dark mystery of interdimensional evil.

While Robert E. Howard's Conan stories are best known for their barbarian protagonist and his silver screen incarnation as Arnold Schwarzenegger, his work also abounds in dark and haunting representations of sorcery. Many tabletop and videogames have been based directly on the world of Conan, such as the MMO *Age of Conan*, and some of these games' designers have attempted to adapt the spirit of this magic. Much of the magic in the Conan stories is influenced by Ancient Egyptian lore (see Chapter 6, Section 6.13), in part because the inhabitants of Stygia practice demonic magic inspired by their dark god Set, who comes directly from Egyptian mythology as the brother and adversary of the sun god Horus. The magic of Stygia is also Lovecraftian in that its devotees evoke malefic forces from other dimensions outside of space and time. In the 1932 short story "The Phoenix on the Sword," a Stygian priest (who shares the name Thoth with the Egyptian god of writing and magic) evokes a demonic horror through a complex operation involving a magic serpentine ring. The ritual is vividly described and fairly detailed—worth quoting in full as a model for an in-game ritual:

> Stooping, he cupped a handful of congealing blood from the sluggish pool in which his victim sprawled, and rubbed it in

the copper serpent's eyes until the yellow sparks were covered by a crimson mask.

"Blind your eyes, mystic serpent," he chanted in a blood-freezing whisper. "Blind your eyes to the moonlight and open them on darker gulfs! What do you see, oh serpent of Set? Whom do you call from the gulfs of the Night? Whose shadow falls on the waning Light? Call him to me, oh serpent of Set!"

Stroking the scales with a peculiar circular motion of his fingers, a motion which always carried the fingers back to their starting place, his voice sank still lower as he whispered dark names and grisly incantations forgotten the world over save in the grim hinterlands of dark Stygia, where monstrous shapes move in the dusk of the tombs (16).

This ritual exhibits many of the traits that make powerful game magic: an exotic and disturbing ritual artifact, a dark and hypnotic invocation, a set of barbarous names, and a symbolic action—blinding a golden serpent's eyes with the blood of an enemy so that the serpent may see into the dark beyond. The sorcerer's recitation of names in particular foreshadows the work of Ursula Le Guin, a writer who turned the fantasy genre into a philosophical vehicle for a reflection on the nature of identity, morality, and names.

8.4 TRUE NAMES AND URSULA LE GUIN

In the history and fantasy of magic, names have power. By naming something, the magician asserts his understanding of its nature and his claim to control it. Some names have more power than others. In ancient understandings of language, every entity has a True Name, a name that expresses and captures the essence of something. In some Jewish and Christian traditions, the theory of True Names is connected to the idea of the Adamic language, bequeathed by God to Adam when naming things in the Garden of Eden. John Dee thought of the angelic tongue of Enochian as a version of the Adamic language (see Chapter 6, Section 6.9). (The theory of True Names is in stark contrast to modern linguistics, whose theorists assert that the connection between names and things is arbitrary and relative, based on the accidents, whims, and perspectives of a particular culture.) Regardless of the truth or falsity of True Names, the idea is valuable to game designers creating linguistic magic systems.

The fantasy author most directly associated with True Names is Ursula K. Le Guin, whose novel *A Wizard of Earthsea* depicts a young wizard named Ged, gradually initiated into magic and the power of True Names. In Le Guin's novel, the common speech of the islanders is descended from "the Old Speech, in which things are named with their True Names, and the way to the understanding of this speech starts with the Runes that were written when the islands of the world were first raised up from the sea" (19). Here Le Guin conjoins two traditions: the notion of a primordial language, in which words are directly and naturally connected to things themselves, and the idea of magic runes, influenced by Tolkien and originating in the ancient Norse way of writing (see Chapter 6, Section 6.8). Perhaps coincidentally, the True Name of Le Guin's protagonist is Ged, which is also one of the letters of the Enochian alphabet (see Chapter 6, Section 6.9). Because words are directly connected to things, it follows logically that a wizard transmutes one object into another by altering the object's name (53). This idea could lead to a game magic system based on puzzles of linguistic transformation, such as anagrams and rebuses. Another logical consequence of Le Guin's linguistic magic is that animals must approach if a magician calls them by their true names (5), which could be applied in game magic as a mechanic for animal control, with animal names either collected, or learned and inputted through a text parser or other interface. Wizards are wary of sharing their True Names, since the True Name would allow another wizard to control them. Such a scenario could inspire a mechanic akin to charades in a multiplayer format, in which players could take the role of rival wizards attempting to guess and exploit each other's True Names.

Influenced by Le Guin, the 3.5 edition *Dungeons & Dragons* supplement *Tome of Magic: Pact, Shadow, and Truename Magic* explores the magic of true names, and its authors display a nuanced understanding of the challenges of procedural adaptation. In the section "Behind the Curtain: The Roots of Truename Magic," Sernett explains that the original approach to Truename magic in *Dungeons & Dragons* followed fantasy literature tropes closely by giving players knowledge of individual nouns that would allow them to control specific things in the game world. However, the designers eventually diverged from this idea, arguing that controlling nouns would give a given Truename mage limited power over the world, so that a mage with Truename mastery over goblins would be powerless against other creatures (193). In other words, the problem with nouns as Truenames is that they have a one-to-one relationship with things in the world. Verbs, on the other hand, grant a much more efficient, one-to-many relationship, since a given verb like "change" can affect many things in the world. As Sernett explains, "the rules system presented here instead makes verbs the rare and powerful parts of truenames" (193). The emphasis on extending and enriching a vocabulary of game verbs reinforces an argument made by several theorists of games and interactive narratives that games need verb sets with more verbs and greater diversity (see Chapter 3, Section 3.1).

8.5 H.P. LOVECRAFT AND CHAOS MAGIC

The most game-friendly school of modern occultism is chaos magic, a British occultist movement founded by Peter Carroll and most directly incarnated in the magical society called the I.O.T. (Initiates of the Order of Thanateros). Chaos magicians are the most willing to acknowledge that magic is a kind of game operating according to principles of active imagination and arbitrary rules adopted for the sake of particular kinds of play. As Peter Carroll proclaims in *Liber Kaos*, chaos magic appeals to individuals "with a strong suspicion that both reality and the human condition have a game-like quality." He further explains that this game is improvisational, based on the invention of rules spontaneously, and that parapsychology is a form of deliberate cheating (76). Chaos magic is also the school with the most direct influence on digital and non-digital games, surfacing in the *Warhammer* universe of miniature and role-playing games as well as in *The Secret World*, where it appears as one of three available schools of magic, represented by the eight-pointed star of chaos.

In terms of mechanics, chaos magic is best simulated through strikingly unpredictable effects: backlashes, unintended consequences, strange metamorphoses. Random number generators, carefully connected and embedded in one another, help designers to simulate the chaos in magic. For example, Richard Garfield (creator of *Magic: The Gathering*) argues that the element of card shuffling in his game helps to simulate the unpredictable nature of magic. One might argue that chaos and unpredictability are exactly what make magic *magic* rather than science, since *Science: The Gathering* would have been considerably less compelling. The challenge for a programmer is how to create controlled, programmatic chaos that can still form the basis of game mechanics and strategy, which entails meaningful choices with outcomes that can be predicted.

Chaos magic is a confluence of occultism, gaming, and fantasy literature. Chaos magicians treat fiction and games as resources for their rituals and iconography, which in turn influence fiction and games. The weird fiction author H.P. Lovecraft is a powerful influence on chaos magic. Although Lovecraft was an atheist and self-declared scientific materialist, his work nevertheless contains a complicated vision of the supernatural which is closely connected to an equally ambiguous vision of magic. As Lovecraft explains in his essay on supernatural horror:

> Cosmic terror [...] was, indeed, a prominent feature of the elabo-rate ceremonial magic, with its rituals for the evocation of dæmons and spectres, which flourished from prehistoric times, and which reached its highest development in Egypt and the Semitic nations. Fragments like the Book of Enoch and the Claviculae of Solomon well illustrate the power of the weird over the ancient Eastern mind, and upon such things were based enduring systems and traditions whose echoes extend obscurely even to the present time.

Lovecraft specifically highlights the elaborate nature of ceremonial magic, describing it as incarnated in "enduring systems" that are reflected by narrative fragments, including apocryphal scripture and the *Lesser Key of Solomon the King* (see Chapter 6, Sections 6.9 and 6.14.2). Lovecraft thus shows awareness of the concept of magic systems and their connection to his aesthetic goal of cosmic terror. In the essay "Calling Cthulhu," theo-rist of technology and mysticism Erik Davis thoroughly traces the mutual influence of Lovecraft and occultism on one another, discussing the role of games in this magic as a product of the density of Lovecraft's world-building.

Lovecraft's work possesses a cosmological coherence, especially in its representation of fearsome otherworldly deities, which could be described as a mythology. Consequently, Lovecraft's work and the expansions of it by other authors have been dubbed the Cthulhu mythos (named after one of its key deities), even though this was not a name that Lovecraft used. The Cthulhu mythos is associated with magic, especially by way of the *Necronomicon*, an invented grimoire whose name means roughly "The Book of the Dead." In the "History of the Necronomicon," Lovecraft himself connects the *Necronomicon* to historical occultism by imagining that a copy was translated by John Dee, one of the actual inventors of the Enochian system of angelic magic (1).

Because the *Necronomicon* is a grimoire, several writers (including scholars of the occult) have attempted to create actual readable cop-ies of the *Necronomicon*, ranging from an edition in 1977 known as the Simon *Necronomicon* to a tetralogy of grimoires by occult scholar Donald Tyson, who also edited the most reliable version of Cornelius Agrippa's *Three Books of Occult Philosophy*. Such expansions of Lovecraft's fictional grimoire require the creation of elaborate systems in order to create the appearance of a fully functioning magical handbook out of fragmented fictional references. The introduction to the Simon *Necronomicon* consciously places the book within the tradition of magical grimoires, highlighting these books' unique status as compilations of recipes rather than general introductions to magical practice. As the editor explains, "These were the sorcerer's handbooks, and generally not meant as textbooks or encyclopedias of ceremonial magick. In other words, the sorcerer or magician is supposed to be in possession of the requisite knowledge and training with which to carry out a complex magickal ritual, just as a cook is expected to be able to master the scrambling of eggs before he conjures an 'eggs Benedict'" (xv). While one might argue that the *Necronomicon*'s status as a fictional book inside the Cthulhu mythos makes it fundamentally different from cookbooks for ritual practice, one could equally answer that the creation of magical practice out of fiction is not unique to the *Necronomicon*, but a common aspect of many grimoires. Owen Davies explains of the Simon *Necronomicon*, "as a piece of magical literature it, and other *Necronomicons*, are no less 'worthy' than their predecessors. Like other famous grimoires explored in this book, it is their falsity that makes them genuine" (268). Davies' witty paradox originates from a position of historical skepticism likely to be accepted primarily by iconoclastic modern magicians of the Chaos or Discordian school, but game magic is highly compatible with this playful skepticism.

Regardless of one's beliefs about the metaphysical validity or fictional fabrication of magic, the process of developing a set of ritual procedures out of a fictional book is a playful and game-like action that resembles the adaptation of Lovecraft's fictions into various games. An understanding of how Lovecraft's fictional rules of magic have been adapted in both magical grimoires and game rules can help designers infuse an eldritch aura into their own systems, whether directly based on the Cthulhu mythos or no. Many game designers have developed Lovecraftian games that transform the fictional rules of the Cthulhu mythos into a set of rules for play. Several of these games involve magic, notably including *Eternal Darkness* (see Chapter 4, Section 4.5).

For example, the *Call of Cthulhu* RPG adapts the Lovecraftian idea that magic is dangerous to human sanity by imposing penalties derived from learning more about the Cthulhu mythos every time a character casts a spell, thereby diminishing sanity. As the *Call of Cthulhu* rulebook explains, "Mythos magic bewilders, shocks, disorients, and debilitates its human practitioners. With enough exposure, the psychic contradictions involved in using this magic drives humans insane" (89). Spells in this game cost magic points, but also sanity points and potentially POW (power, the statistic governing overall mental strength) (102). In addition, the *Call of Cthulhu* rulebook contains complex rules for learning spells from mythos tomes, each of which takes large and varying amounts of time, effort, and sanity to read. In contrast with Vancian systems, in which memorizing spells is relatively painless from a player's point of view, reading mythos tomes is difficult and costly to sanity. Indeed, the rulebook contains large tables of mythos tomes with corresponding sanity costs (98–99). *Call of Cthulhu* involves an overwhelmingly book-centric approach to magic, with descriptions of tomes and rules for reading them taking up vastly more than the rules for casting spells (90–99).

8.6 JACK VANCE AND VANCIAN MAGIC

Jack Vance's *Dying Earth* series (1950) is the origin of the term "Vancian magic system," popularized as an approach to magic in the original *Dungeons & Dragons* game. In Vance's vision of magic, wizards must memorize spells before casting them. After casting a spell, it vanishes from the caster's memory. In the first story of *The Dying Earth*, entitled "Mazirian the Magician," the titular magician memorizes his spells by studying books before retiring to bed, and he chooses a range of spells that he believes will be useful for the challenges he anticipates. Vance writes: "Mazirian made a selection from his books and with great effort forced five spells upon his brain: Phandaal's Gyrator, Felojun's Second Hypnotic Spell, The Excellent Prismatic Spray, the Charm of Untiring Nourishment, and the Spell of the Omnipotent Sphere" (23). The spell "Excellent Prismatic Spray" later became the *Dungeons & Dragons* spell "Prismatic Spray," and the more general idea of committing a limited number of spells to memory by studying spellbooks became the heart of the Vancian magic system in *Dungeons & Dragons*. Prefiguring *Dungeons & Dragons*, the number of memorized spells is strictly limited by the magician's memory capacity in proportion to the spells' difficulty levels, effectively granting a number of spell slots. Vance writes of "volumes compiled by many wizards of the past, untidy folios collected by the Sage, leather-bound librams setting forth the syllables of a hundred powerful spells, so cogent that Turjan's brain could know but four at a time" (4). Vance even provides an equation for spell slots when he writes that "Mazirian, by dint of stringent exercise, could encompass four of the most formidable, or six of the lesser spells" (19). By this equation, one lesser spell occupies 0.666 as much memory space as a greater spell, though

Dungeons & Dragons would simplify the formula to a number of spell slots scaling with the player character's level. The division of spells into lesser and greater slots also resembles late edition *Dungeons & Dragons'* distinction between major and minor actions, though by that point in the *Dungeons & Dragons* franchise, spell slots had been eradicated. When unsure of the obstacles they face, other magicians choose spells of "general utility," which could apply in many situations. When describing the magician Turjan of Miir's spell memorization process, Vance writes, "What dangers he might meet he could not know, so he selected three spells of general application: the Excellent Prismatic Spray, Phandaal's Mantle of Stealth, and the Spell of the Slow Hour" (5). This need to plan one's spell memorization choices based on upcoming threats (as well as the danger of choosing poorly and being ill-prepared for an unexpected adversary) are familiar as aspects of game strategy to anyone who has played early *Dungeons & Dragons*.

8.7 LARRY NIVEN AND MANA

Fantasist Larry Niven offers a fictive alternative to Vancian magic that exerts a powerful influence on videogames: the concept of a pool of magical energy called mana. "Mana" with one "n" is not to be confused with "manna" with two n's, a mysterious substance eaten by the Israelites during their exodus from Egypt, as described in *Exodus* 16:31. Rather, mana is a word meaning "power" which originates in the cultures of the Polynesian islanders, which were studied by anthropologists such as Robert Codrington in his book *The Melanesians: Studies in their Religion and Folklore*. Codrington defines mana as follows:

> That invisible power which is believed by the natives to cause all such effects as transcend their conception of the regular course of nature, and to reside in spiritual beings, whether in the spiritual part of living men or in the ghosts of the dead, being imparted by them to their names and to various things that belong to them, such as stones, snakes, and indeed objects of all sorts, is that generally known as *mana*. (191)

Niven introduces the fictionalized version of mana in his 1969 short story "Not Long Before the End," a prequel to the *Magic Goes Away* series, a shared world anthology also named the Warlock universe after its protagonist. Constructed as an allegory of the energy crisis, the world of *The Magic Goes Away* represents mana as a non-renewable resource that is being perpetually leached out of the land, resulting in a disenchanted world. The Warlock wields a whirling disc that sucks up all available mana from the land. The trope of drawing mana from the land appears directly as a game mechanic in the *Magic: The Gathering* collectable card game, in which players tap various types of land to produce different colors of mana that power spells. The Warlock's disc also appears directly in the *Magic: The Gathering* artifact card called Nevinyrral's Disk (Larry Niven's Disk spelled backwards), which allows the player to "destroy all artifacts, creatures, and enchantments"—as if emulating the squandering of the precious resource of mana in Niven's stories.

8.8 ROGER ZELAZNY *CHRONICLES OF AMBER* (PLANAR MAGIC AND TAROT)

Roger Zelazny's *Chronicles of Amber* offer a unique contribution to the world of game magic, through their emphasis on magic as planar travel accomplished through enchanted decks of tarot cards. The books have sufficient power to inspire many rich game mechanics, as seen in two direct adaptations, an interactive fiction called *Nine Princes in Amber,* a roguelike called *Zangband* (Zelazny *Angband*), and a diceless role-playing game that is in some ways the ancestor of *Nobilis*. The novel *Nine Princes in Amber,* the first installment in the *Chronicles of Amber*, describes an amnesiac hero named Corwin who gradually recovers his memories as an Amberite noble, including the ability to perform magic. The most striking episodes in relation to this magic are scenes of teleportation, through direct interdimensional travel, the use of tarot cards as a way of contacting others, and the navigation of the Pattern, a labyrinth that allows an Amberite noble to travel across planes and return to the home city of Amber (see Chapter 4, Section 4.10.5). Zelazny lays out the premises of his fictional magic as three formal rules, making them prime for procedural adaptation as game mechanics.

Direct interdimensional travel is called walking in shadows, and practitioners of this art prefigure the Planeswalkers of *Magic: The Gathering* lore as well as echoing traditional shamans, who have long been called walkers between worlds. Zelazny explains, "If one is a prince or princess of the blood, then one may walk, crossing through Shadows, forcing one's environment to change as one passes, until it is finally in precisely the shape one desires it, and there stop" (77). The custom decks of tarot cards wielded by the Amberite nobles are a tool for traveling more directly between dimensions by nullifying perspective, allowing for instantaneous communication between nobles and possible teleportation between them. The cards are early versions of telecommunication technologies, such as video calls and text messaging, along with a dose of mysticism. Zelazny elaborates, "The second means is the cards, cast by Dworkin, Master of the Line, who had created them in our image, to facilitate communication between members of the royal family. He was an ancient artist to whom space and perspective meant nothing" (77). Zelazny is using an accident of art history, that medieval artists did not understand how to render three-dimensional space through perspective, as an inspiration for magical art that bends space through teleportation.

The final means of teleportation through the Pattern is connected to the previous two, as Zelazny makes clear when he writes, "The third was the Pattern, also drawn by Dworkin, which could only be walked by a member of our family. It initiated the walker into the system of the cards, as it were, and at its ending gave its walker the power to stride across Shadows" (77). Zelazny's explanation of teleportation has the logical rigor of three intertwined parts in which the Pattern taps into the cards, described as a system, in order to facilitate walking in the shadows. The scene in which Corwin walks the pattern further clarifies the power and challenges of this magical teleportation method. Zelazny describes it beautifully when he writes:

> It shimmered like the cold fire that it was, quivered, made the whole room seem somehow insubstantial. It was an elaborate tracery of bright power, composed mainly of curves, though there were a few straight lines near its middle. It reminded me of a fantastically intricate, life-scale version of one of those maze things you do with a pencil (or ballpoint, as the case may be), to get you into or out of something (57).

Zelazny is describing the process of walking a labyrinth in the classical sense of a winding pathway, inscribed on the floor in the manner of medieval cathedrals such as the one at Amiens, where walking a labyrinth was a spiritual exercise designed to lead a pilgrim or penitent closer to a mystical experience of divinity. At various points in the walking process, Corwin must push through ethereal Veils: fields of resistance that metaphorically represent the challenges experienced by anyone engaged in an imaginative or mystical vision quest. At the same time, Zelazny directly compares the labyrinth to a maze puzzle such as those sometimes found on the back of breakfast cereal boxes or in the comics sections of newspapers. Zelazny collapses the distinction between symbolic metaphysical voyage and child's puzzle game, thereby opening the way for games that are simultaneously deeply philosophical and entertaining through their puzzle elements. Like a pilgrim walking the Pattern, Zelazny also opens the way for another writer whose vision of the multiverse can provide powerful inspiration for game magic: Michael Moorcock.

8.9 MICHAEL MOORCOCK AND ELRIC'S RITUAL

The moment of fantasy spellcasting that most exemplifies the ideas in *Game Magic* occurs in *Elric of Melnibone*, when the albino sorcerer and emperor Elric summons Arioch, a Chaos Lord who becomes his patron. Moorcock writes:

> He read much in the library, though this time he read only certain grimoires and he read those over and over again.
>
> These grimoires were written in the High Speech of Melniboné— the ancient language of sorcery with which Elric's ancestors had been able to communicate with the supernatural beings that they had summoned. And at last Elric was satisfied that he understood them fully, though what he read sometimes threatened to stop him in his present course of action.
>
> And when he was satisfied—for the dangers of misunderstanding the implications of the things described in the grimoires were catastrophic—he slept for three nights in a drugged slumber (80–81).

Several traits of this fictive evocation could be productively adapted in game form, and some of these features have been adapted in the *Elric!* tabletop role-playing game, also known as *Stormbringer*. This game includes a supplement called *The Bronze Grimoire* that directly bases its magic system on the episode in which Elric summons Arioch. An *Elric* action-adventure titled *Elric the Necromancer* was also planned and partially developed by Psygnosis, the acclaimed avant-garde studio that produced *Shadow of the Beast*, though *Elric the Necromancer* was eventually cancelled. The game's title suggests that Elric's ability to summon spirits of the dead, rather than his skills as a swordsman, would have been a primary focus of gameplay.

The first inspiring feature of the summoning scene is that it is heavily dependent on study—not just memorization, but understanding of magical operations and their consequences. The many Vancian magic systems in which players simply memorize spells (usually by selecting them from a menu) leave out the understanding that is one of the key virtues of a magus, or wise man. The second feature of the system is that mistakes are extremely risky because of the dire consequences they can bring. There are unnamed "implications" of the grimoires that suggest Lovecraftian cosmic secrets so terrible that they cannot be described directly, but could rebound terribly on an unprepared magician.

The next passage in Elric's summoning scene is the most vivid: a description of supremely ceremonial magic that could be a powerful inspiration for many game designers seeking to enrich their game's magic systems. Moorcock writes:

> When he had meditated for more than five hours Elric took a brush and a jar of ink and began to paint both walls and floor with complicated symbols, some of which were so intricate that they seemed to disappear at an angle to the surface on which they had been laid. At last this was done and Elric spread-eagled himself in the very center of his huge rune, face down, one hand upon his grimoire, the other (with the Arctorios upon it) stretched palm down. The moon was full. A shaft of light fell directly upon Elric's head, turning the hair to silver. And then the Summoning began (81).

From the perspective of a magic system, the first feature exhibited in this passage is extreme, intricate preparation. Elric's magic takes days of intensive, focused effort. Elric's painting of the runes is the ultimate sigil-based preparation in that it entails the construction of a fully immersive environment: a sigil that covers not just the floor, but the walls until it almost disappears into visual paradoxes in three dimensions and beyond. Elric begins his summoning by using the grimoire itself as a talisman (in line with the medieval status of grimoires as living magical objects, as described by Aaron Leitch), along with his ruby-colored Arctorios ring (itself a haunting artifact that swirls as if a spirit is trapped inside).

The climactic moment of Elric's summoning depicts planar magic in the form of a voyage through alternate realms of existence whose nature is fundamentally symbolic. Moorcock writes, "Elric sent his mind into twisting tunnels of logic, across endless plains of ideas, through mountains of symbolism and endless universes of alternate truths" (81). The strength of this passage is its conjoining of literal landscapes with abstractions: plains made of pure ideas, mountains crafted out of symbols, universes based on alternate versions of reality. In the strongest game systems, magic ultimately originates out of the planes and allows the magicians to voyage through them. While on the one hand such a process is shamanic, it more closely resembles the "lodge-based, hermetic" magic that Aaron Reid alludes to in *Secrets of the Magickal Grimoires*. Elric's rituals resemble what Reid calls the "gating" rituals of the Golden Dawn Pentagram and Hexagram rituals, designed to formally open the gateways to other dimensions. At the same time, Elric's magic is deeply psychedelic in the 1960s countercultural sense of the word, in its vision of twisted and bizarre alternate dimensions, from which ultimately emerges a chaos lord in the form of a talking fly. As comic book artist and practicing occultist Alan Moore has observed, Moorcock's vision is at its core psychedelic and countercultural: "The Melnibonéan landscape—seething, warped by the touch of fractal horrors—was an anti-matter antidote to Middle Earth, a toxic and fluorescent elf repellent" (xv).

In addition to the psychedelic vision of Elric, Michael Moorcock originated the eight-pointed star of chaos that was adopted by both the occult movement of Chaos Magic and numerous games and popular media. As Moorcock himself explains in *Stormbringer: Fantasy Roleplaying in the World of Elric*, he invented the symbol in 1962, when it appeared on the cover of *Science Fantasy* in an illustration done by Jim Cawthorn, who later incorporated the symbol in a comic book version of *Elric* (Willis). Moorcock emphasizes the symbolic, ideographic character of the image, designed to reflect the openness of chaos to multiple possibilities of reality:

> The origin of the Chaos Symbol was me doodling sitting at the kitchen table and wondering what to tell Jim Cawthorn the arms of Chaos looked like. I drew a straightforward geographical quadrant (which often has arrows, too!)—N, S, E, W—and then added another four directions and that was that—eight arrows representing all possibilities, one arrow representing the single, certain road of Law. I have since been told that it is an "ancient symbol of Chaos" and if it is then it confirms a lot of theories about the race mind (Willis).

Michael Moorcock's iconography influenced the symbolism of Chaos Magic, but H.P. Lovecraft brought it to ghastly fruition. Moorcock's depiction of Elric as an antihero sorcerer also opens the way to another plane of existence: the world of Krynn, in which an equally antiheroic mage named Raistlin Majere weaves his spells underneath a sky with three moons.

8.10 *DRAGONLANCE* AND THE MOON-BASED MAGIC OF KRYNN

The key objective of procedural adaptation is to find what is unique about a particular fictive world's representation of magic and then convert this unique aspect into game mechanics. One prime example of this process is the *Dragonlance* universe, created by Margaret Weis and Tracy Hickman as a transmedia world that spans novels, tabletop role-playing rulebooks and scenarios, and computer role-playing games as well as animations and other media. *Dragonlance* began as a *Dungeons & Dragons* campaign, which Weis and Hickman transformed into a series of novels called the *Dragonlance Chronicles*, representing the party characters' actions in the campaign as a series of narrative events. Among the most vivid of the *Dragonlance* characters is Raistlin Majere, a cynical mage who ascends from the ranks of a neophyte to a warlock of godlike powers, in the process changing both his robe color and his moral alignment to reflect a shift toward darkness. But Raistlin's magic is part of a much larger and systemic understanding of magic based on the three colored moons of Krynn (white Solinari, black Nuitari, and red Lunitari), each of which is associated with a moral alignment as well as a god and a color. In the *Dragonlance* universe, good mages wear white robes, evil mages wear black robes, and neutral mages wear red robes.

When Weis and Hickman adapted their fictive setting as a tabletop rulebook called *Dragonlance Adventures*, they included diagrams of the three moons' phases and rules for how a given moon phase would affect the spells of a mage (27–28). These diagrams and rules are reproduced on the fan page "Moons of Krynn: Moon Tracking Chart." Moons may be in one of four phases at a given time: waxing, waning, high sanction, or low sanction. Each moon moves through these four phases or quarters cyclically, though each moon also has its own cycle, with some longer and some shorter. Moon phases grant enhancements or penalties to the saving throws of mages with corresponding or opposed robe colors, as well as additional spells and even the ability to cast spells at a higher level than normal, provided the mage's alignment matches the color of the current waxing moon. On a single rare night called the Night of the Eye, when all moons are aligned at High Sanction, all mages receive intense boosts to their saving throws, spell slots, and the levels at which they cast spells.

8.11 *DEATH GATE* AND QUANTUM MAGIC

Another Margaret Weis and Tracy Hickman fantasy series, the *Death Gate* cycle, is a very rare case of procedural adaptation in which a direct videogame adaptation of a book series led to what is widely regarded as an excellent game. Part of this game's excellence stems from the coherence and thoroughness of its magic systems, which are so rigorously developed in book form that they can be easily transformed into a set of game mechanics. Casting spells in *Death Gate* entails weaving patterns out of runes. Spells that have already been learned can be cast by pressing a button, which causes the runes to be automatically woven, but some spells must be first learned through trial and error.

Hickman traces back the book version of the magic systems to his researches into quantum physics. He explains:

> Some years ago, I was working on a fantasy series called Death Gate with Margaret Weis. We needed two competing systems of magic that made sense. I remembered a saying of my old friend, Jeff Grubb. He defined quantum physics as "figures, figures, figures, figures, figures... and then God does something... figures, figures, figures, figures, figures." So, in order to create a believable pair of magic systems, I researched what amounted to Newtonian versus Quantum mechanics and, later, competing visions of quantum theory. I read popular science books regarding Relativity, quantum mechanics, Heisenberg's uncertainty principle, parallel universes and chaos theory. The results were a wonderful and sensible pair of magic systems that made sense because they were modeled on quantum and chaos theories.

Dragon Wing, the first volume of the *Death Gate* cycle, contains an appendix that maps out the scientific theory of the book's magic system as well as its linguistic structure. Magic is founded on the idea of possibility and possible worlds, derived from the many worlds interpretation of quantum mechanics in which multiple realities exist adjacent to one another, resulting in a multiverse of possible realities rather than a universe with a single reality.

These possible universes exist as waves with which a magician can harmonize, causing aspects of another reality to become actualized within the current reality. To bypass a stone wall, the magician harmonizes himself with the possibility of a door in the wall. For a frail wizard to protect himself from an armored warrior, he actualizes the possibility of a force shield. This emphasis on multiple possible worlds echoes Michael Moorcock's Eternal Champion multiverse and Roger Zelazny's Amber multiverse (see Chapter 8, Sections 8.8 and 8.9). The multiple realities posited by quantum mechanics are useful as a premise for game magic because they help to explain how reality could be malleable, as well as encouraging designers to increase the flexibility and imagination of their magic systems based on the freedom offered by a multiverse of infinite possibilities. These systems of magic tend to depict the multiverse itself as a magical puzzle whose solution enables planar travel, as in the opening of the Death Gate.

In *Death Gate*, the way to produce a harmonious wave in this sea of possibilities is through a complex multimodal language based on performance. As the *Dragon Wing* appendix explains, "The key to rune (or runic) magic is that the harmonic wave that weaves a possibility into existence must be created with as much simultaneity as possible. This means that the various motions, signs, words, thoughts and elements that go into making up the harmonic wave must be completed as close together as possible" (422). The appendix insists that speech and writing are only one component of the language, "which is not so much spoken […] as it is performed" (423). This explanation elegantly formulates the idea of magical language as multimodal and performative, ideas which Weis and Hickman label as "simultaneous," based on the idea that magical language communicates through multiple sensory channels simultaneously, like a theatrical performance (see Chapter 2, Section 2.6).

In practice, these multiple simultaneous channels take the idea of linguistic structure to a whole new level, since magicians of the Sartan race arrange runes in hexagonal honeycomb matrices whose spatial arrangement communicates complex information about a given spell. *Dragon Wing* provides several elaborate diagrams of these hexagonal rune patterns, whose position carries semantic and grammatical information. At the center of the hexagon is the root or fountain rune, expressing the nature of the spell. To the lower left and lower right of the hexagon are the matriarch and patriarch runes, which form a supporting foundation to the root, and directly below the root is the dom or master rune, which inflects the root toward a spiritual or material manifestation. To the upper left and upper right of the root rune respectively are the dawn and dusk runes, which specify the power and direction of the spell.

Magic as described in the *Death Gate* cycle is an elaborate puzzle (see Chapter 2, Section 2.7). It is no surprise that it translates well into an adventure game, in which puzzles are the core gameplay. Weaving runes together in the *Death Gate* game involves combining their hexagonal tiles together like pieces of a jigsaw puzzle. Because adventure games are founded on a large and varied verb set needed to explore a world and solve challenges within it, the spells in the *Death Gate* game naturally tend to perform a wider range of actions than the heal, attack, and buff commands typically found in an RPG. As one Mobygames review from user Yid Yang enthuses, "Turning a portrait into reality, switching bodies with a dog, setting statues in motion—those are just a few examples of the interesting, creative magic spells of the game." *Dragonlance* and *Death Gate* are two of the most potent, popular, and surprisingly complex inspirations of game magic from the 1980s, before the emergence of a simpler tale of wizards that would command the imaginations of children: Harry Potter.

8.12 HARRY POTTER

There is no question that *Harry Potter* has exerted a deservedly powerful influence on the popular imagination, including the visions of game designers. The books have spawned a multitude of direct game adaptations, ranging from the 2001 *Harry Potter and the Philosopher's Stone* for the PlayStation One to the PlayStation 3 *Miranda Goshawk's Book of Spells*, driven by both the PlayStation Move wand peripheral and the Wonderbook tablet accessory (designed specifically for this game).

Yet, while *Harry Potter* is perhaps the best-known vision of fictive magic in the popular consciousness, it is neither the be-all nor end-all of fictive magic, nor is it the most imaginative basis for game magic. *Potter's* mainstream popularity, especially among children and young adults, weakens its status as magic, since magic by its very nature runs counter to the baseline representation or simulation of a given world. As beat writer and chaos magician William S. Burroughs once said, "Magic is dangerous or it is nothing." There is plenty of physically dangerous magic in *Harry Potter*, with evil wizards like Voldemort and the Death Eaters running rampant, but there is very little magic that shakes readers out of a worldview appropriate for a young adult audience. One antidote to the sometimes mundane magic of *Harry Potter* is another popular series that challenges the limits associated with fantasy for a young adult audience by viewing magic through a starkly adult eye: George R.R. Martin's *Song of Ice and Fire*.

8.13 *A SONG OF ICE AND FIRE*

George R.R. Martin's *A Song of Ice and Fire* series, an incomplete (at time of writing) saga projected to include seven books, comprises one of the masterpieces of modern fantasy, as well as one of the most subtle and foreboding magic systems of modern fantasy. As a work of low fantasy, magic is relatively rare, to the point that many characters doubt its existence.

An offhand comment by Maester Luwin reveals that the Maesters can apply for a Valyrian steel link in their chain to indicate study of magic and the occult, but only one in one hundred Maesters have done this. Maester Luwin believes that magic has passed away along with dragons, and that consequently each Maester who studies the "higher mysteries" fails to cast spells (*Clash of Kings* 441). Luwin poetically sums up the rarity of magic in *Clash of Kings* when he explains:

> Perhaps magic was once a mighty force in the world, but no longer. What little that remains is no more than the wisp of smoke that lingers in the air after a great fire has burned out, and even that is fading. Valyria was the last ember, and Valyria is gone. The dragons are no more, the giants are dead, the children of the forest forgotten with all their lore (442).

Having used Luwin's perspective to establish a foundation of overall skepticism toward magic and mourning of its loss, Martin then takes great pleasure in gradually revealing the return of the dragons, the existence of giants, and the revelation of higher lore. The Targaryens come from Valyria, the erstwhile stronghold of magic, and they carry the blood of the dragon. These clues help explain the connection of dragons to magic, the disappearance of dragons to the vanishing of magic, and the growing dragon's relationship to the return of magic (832).

Indeed, magic is effective in *A Song of Ice and Fire* precisely *because* it is gradually revealed to exist, secretly, in a world that denies its existence. Adapting such a perspective as a set of mechanics is difficult, since it requires entire gameplay systems and sub-systems to be hidden, like Easter eggs. *A Song of Ice and Fire* can teach us as game designers how to gradually reveal magical abilities rather than making them transparent and immediately available. The impact and marvel of magic grows in proportion to its rarity and mystery, provided this mystery is balanced by accessible game systems.

In *A Song of Ice and Fire*, Martin exhibits mastery of just such a slow reveal. Slowly, through a series of intimations and disturbing episodes, magic begins to appear in the book. Mirri Maz Duur, the witch taken hostage by the Dothraki, practices the conjoined disciplines of blood magic and necromancy, through which she summons the dead into a tent and restores the Khal to life (*Game of Thrones* 710). The Warlocks of Qarth practice a mixture of stage illusionism, mind control, and speak of a return of magic along with the dragons. The House of the Undying owned by the Warlocks abounds in labyrinthine spatial paradoxes and a pattern of ascent, as well as a TARDIS-like interior that is larger than its exterior. Most disturbingly, the Red Priestess Melisandre uses false promises of power to convert a king and his people to the supposed god of light, R'hllor, who is also the god of fire and shadow. Melisandre gives birth to a shadowy spirit assassin, suggesting the dark side of her supposed god of light.

As Duur herself explains, "My teacher was a bloodmage from the Shadow Lands" (710). Magic in *A Game of Thrones* comes at a tremendous cost, an idea that Duur reiterates several times before proving it bleakly through Khal Drogo's successful but tormentingly incomplete resurrection. Daenerys sums up the extreme sacrifice required for magic in Martin's world when she chides Duur that "your spells are costly" (759). Duur warns that while a resurrection spell does exist, "it is hard, lady, and dark" since it carries with it great potential for corruption, such that "some would say that death is cleaner" (710). Duur herself paid an ominously unspecified price, having "learned the way in Asshai, and paid dear for the lesson." Not only did she pay for the knowledge of magic, but she insists that the very nature of blood magic demands sacrifice and deadly transactions. As she explains, "There is a price" that is "not a matter of gold or horses." The formula is clear: "This is blood-magic, lady. Only death may pay for life" (710). The school of blood magic appears to be familiar to the Dothraki but absolutely taboo, since Daenerys' follower Jhogo explains "this is bloodmagic. […] It is forbidden" (711). During the spell itself, the nature of this sacrifice becomes clear, as she slits the throat of the Khal's stallion with a glyph-inscribed, red bronze knife and drains the horse's blood into Drogo's tub. The words of the spell that she intones suggest the transference of life energy between an animal and a man: "strength of the mount, go into the rider" "strength of the beast, go into the man." This is a recipe for sacrifice and transfusion (see Chapter 4, Section 4.10.1).

This act of blood magic is a prelude to a necromantic ritual involving burning a mysterious red powder as incense and singing in order to summon the shadows of the dead. Duur's description of the ritual emphasizes its secrecy and danger: "Once I begin to sing, no one must enter the tent. My song will wake powers old and dark. The dead will dance here this night. No living man must look on them" (712). This magic is ideal for game adaptation because it balances extreme precision with enough mystery to allow for the creation of game mechanics (or their concealment behind a virtual game master's screen of rules). Resurrection magic requires a blood sacrifice of a creature closely allied to the endangered human, a glyph-inscribed knife of a particular material, red powder incense, music sung by the caster, and a veil of secrecy. Beyond this, a game designer is free to interpret and add, using mechanics to retain the feeling of extreme costly sacrifices and taboos requiring secrecy.

In addition to blood magic, two opposed schools of magic slowly congeal throughout *A Song of Ice and Fire*, the red magic of the Red God and the shamanic nature magic called Greensight. As in many game and occult magic systems, Martin uses color to communicate the metaphysical character of these two types of magic (see Chapter 4, Section 4.6). These two schools of the Red God and Greensight are opposed, complementary colors on the color wheel because their properties are opposite. The magic of the Red God is overwhelmingly associated with fire, which has equal powers over death and resurrection. Thoros the Red Priest can repeatedly bring Lord Beric back from the dead, and Lord Beric himself can ignite his sword with magic flame by anointing it in his own kingly blood. The Red God's magic is a magic of fire and blood, associations that color theorist Becky Koenig argues caused primitive man to revere the color red (Koenig 26). When Jon Snow encounters the red priestess Melisandre, his observations of her make the nature of red magic clear. Melisandre reminds Jon of the "forge, of the way iron smelled when red-hot; the scent was smoke and blood" (1054). In contrast, Greensight is the magic of nature, growing plants, and shamanistic visions. As with the Red God's sorcery, these qualities are in keeping with the color associations of green, which Koenig identifies as "plants, trees, water, and landscape" (26). The Greenseers had other magic powers in addition to greensight: "the old songs say that the greenseers used dark magic to make the seas rise and sweep away the land" (738).

Magic in *A Song of Ice and Fire* is costly and dangerous, a fact that is reiterated by almost any character who speaks of it. When discussing his reluctance to use a powerful enchanted horn, wildling king Mance Rayder vividly remarks that "sorcery is a sword without a hilt. There is no safe way to grasp it," implying a perpetual risk of harm to the wielder of magic (and echoing Priscilla's scythe, a magic weapon that literally lacks a hilt and cuts the player with every second it is wielded in the RPG *Dark Souls*) (1019). Part of the cost of magic is the difficulty of learning it, directly associated with its rarity. The leader of the Faceless Men, a sect of assassins skilled in magical disguise, emphasizes this rarity to Arya Stark when she seeks knowledge of spells. He explains, "All sorcery comes at a cost, child. Years of prayer and sacrifice and study are required to work a proper glamor" (463). In this context, "glamor" refers to a spell designed to change the caster's appearance, and the kindly man communicates that the acquisition of glamor is far from glamorous, but rather steeped in hard work and scholarship. This requirement of hard work helps explain why magic is rare in the low fantasy world of *A Song of Ice and Fire*, since the kindly man succinctly observes that "if it were easy all men would do it" (463). From a game perspective, easy magic mechanics involving only the press of a button tend to clash with difficult fictive magic demanding skill and precision. *A Song of Ice and Fire* offers an example of a richly mysterious representation of fictive magic that would accommodate any number of puzzling, sophisticated mechanics.

Despite this rich magical source material, the *Game of Thrones* RPG is mediocre, but the challenges of procedural adaptation that Martin's series represents are intriguing. The strongest procedural adaptations are likely to be unlicensed, since they are freed from the constraints of following the IP slavishly, especially the linear events of its storyline. To accommodate the richness of magic in *A Song of Ice and Fire*, a designer would need to create mechanics that fall outside most current magic systems, such as looking into flames for visions or lighting obsidian/dragonglass candles, the latter of which would be a fascinating puzzle. The player might take the role of a Maester studying the higher mysteries in the Citadel, amidst the denials of his peers that magic exists. Magic in the book series derives its power from being dimly understood, even denied, so making the mechanics too transparent would greatly limit the emotional impact of the magic, but making them too opaque would render the game unplayable.

8.13.1 *Demon's Souls* and *Dark Souls* as Adaptations of *A Song of Ice and Fire*

Following the logic of mysterious yet accessible mechanics, there is a procedural adaptation of *A Song of Ice and Fire*, in the form of two games that obey its spirit while having no direct relationship to its events: *Demon's Souls* and *Dark Souls*. These two games are thematically and spiritually a procedural adaptation of *A Song of Ice and Fire*, far more than any of the officially licensed adaptations of the series. The juxtaposition of the *Souls* games and *A Song of Ice and Fire* reminds us that the greatest magic is hidden: a trope and associated mechanic that tends to work best in low fantasy worlds.

Players acquire magic slowly, one spell at a time, trading powerful and eminently valuable demons' souls without awareness of the overall set of

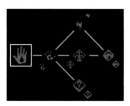

FIGURE 8.1   A Blood Magic Skill Tree in *Dragon Age 2*.

available spells. *Demon's Souls* has nothing so friendly as a skill tree, which would allow players to plan their next acquisition steadily: instead, magic comes in fits and starts, acquired gropingly and in darkness by periodically returning to two or three magical trainers after defeating bosses to see if the player can sell a soul in exchange for power that may well be self-destructive. *Demon's Souls* also contains a secret and staggeringly powerful school of magic, taught by a witch who condemns all magic as dangerous and corrupting. The witch Yuria is an elaborate Easter egg, rescuable only through a set of convoluted steps near the end of the game, and providing magic only in the unlikely event the player has hoarded demon souls (or re-plays the game on New game plus to acquire the souls again). Yuria's hidden school of magic also resembles the school of blood magic in *Dragon Age*, a method of dark compulsion hidden as an Easter egg. Because both *Dragon Age* and *Demon's Souls* are low fantasy worlds, it is plausible that entire schools of magic are hidden. Figure 8.1 shows the blood magic skill tree in *Dragon Age 2*.

Magic in *Demon's Souls* enacts the Faustian bargain as a set of mechanics. In the Faust legend, an aspiring magician sells his soul to the Devil (named Mephistopheles) in exchange for power. Through this legend, which stems back to biblical times and the false apostle Simon Faustus, the term "Faustian bargain" has been coined to denote a dangerous and self-destructive exchange, often of one's soul for occult power. Since souls are the currency of *Demon's Souls*, every exchange in the game is effectively a Faustian bargain, resulting in a chilling economy of harvested souls. It is no surprise, then, that a character who appears to tempt players with black soul tendency is named Mephistopheles.

8.14 CONTEMPORARY MAGICAL WORLD-BUILDING

There is a recent generation of complex fictional magic systems that are part of large epic fictions, including Steven Erikson's ten-book *Malazan: Book of the Fallen* series, R. Scott Bakker's *Prince of Nothing* trilogy, and

Brandon Sanderson's *Stormlight Archive* series, of which *The Way of Kings* is the first installment. These books offer a late-generation view of fictive magic systems at a mature stage of development, often highly abstract, systematic, poetic, and influenced by games.

8.14.1 *Malazan: Book of the Fallen*

As with the much earlier *Dragonlance*, the process of procedural adaptation is a two-way street, in which tabletop gaming campaigns become novels, which are in turn re-adapted into games. *Malazan: Book of the Fallen* was originally based on Steven Erikson's role-playing campaign in GURPS (General Universal Roleplaying System).

Malazan: Book of the Fallen features a complex magic system based on self-contained worlds called warrens, a variation on the familiar notion of magical energy derived from planes and other dimensions of the multiverse. *Malazan* also incorporates a custom tarot pack called the Deck of Dragons, the cards of which mirror large-scale change at the political and mythological level. An even more ancient form of the Deck of Dragons, called the Tiles of the Holds, offers an alternate method of divination closer to scrying or remote viewing. Game magic elements become narrative devices, which could inspire game mechanics again.

Sorcerers in Malazan cast spells by summoning energy from alternate planes of existence called warrens, which Paran thinks of as "the secret paths of sorcery" (37). The warrens appear to have color associations, such as ocher, and they can be used for teleportation and travel as well as sources of magical energy. In both respects, they strongly resemble the planes of *Planescape: Torment* or the Planeswalkers of *Magic: The Gathering*, so much so that they are probably directly influenced by these games.

As with so many schools of game magic derived from planes of existence, each warren corresponds to a powerful cosmic force, representing a deeply archetypal aspect of human existence and the universe. According to the *Malazan* wiki, the warrens accessible by human mages, called paths, are:

- Aral Gamelain—The Path of Demons
- Denul—The Path of Healing
- D'riss—The Path of Stone
- Fener's Warren, bordering Chaos itself
- Hood's Path—The Path of Death

- Imperial Warren
- Meanas—The Path of Shadow and Illusion
- Mockra—The Path of the Mind
- Rashan—The Path of Darkness
- Ruse—The Path of the Sea
- Serc—The Path of the Sky
- Telas—The Path of Fire—Child of Tellan
- Tennes—The Path of the Land
- Thyr—The Path of Light

8.14.2 *The Prince of Nothing*

R. Scott Bakker's *The Prince of Nothing* trilogy features two branches of sorcery: gnostic and anagogic, both of them highly abstract and based on the philosophical and linguistic concept of meaning, much like the tabletop role-playing games *Nobilis* and *Unknown Armies*. "Gnostic" is the adjective form of "gnosis," the ancient Greek word for knowledge—words often used to refer to an early Christian sect called the Gnostics, labeled by the early church fathers as a heresy. The word "anagogic" is the Greek word for an analogy or comparison.

The spells in *The Prince of Nothing*, called cants, are gorgeously abstract, in keeping with the overall philosophical themes of the book and Bakker's own training as a philosopher. *The Prince of Nothing* wiki lists these spells, which often take the form of geometric shapes:

The Bar of Heaven

The Bisecting Planes of Mirseor

The Cant of Sideways Stepping

The Cants of Torment (Agonies)

The Cirroi Loom

The Compass of Noshainrau

The Cross of Arches

The Ellipses of Thosolankis

The First Quyan Fold

The Huiritic Ring

The Mathesis Pin

The Noviratic Spike

The Odaini Concussion Cant

The Scythe of Gotagga

The Seventh Quyan Theorem

The Thawa Ligatures

The Third Concentric

The Weära Comb

Each spell, such as "The Bisecting Planes of Mirseor" and "The Ellipses of Thosolankis," conjures a vivid image of abstract spatial configurations and exotic lore, suggested through Greek and Arabic influenced names. Paradoxically, the intense abstraction of these spell concepts leads to some of the most exciting magical combat written, with competing sorcerers engaged in elaborate duels of arcing light and gem-like precision, each seeking to overwhelm the other's wards. A magical battle in Bakker's world is far more than a clumsy exchange of artillery blasts. When the sorcerer Achamian fights off a horde of enemies, Bakker describes the fight as a cross between a laser light show and a non-Euclidean physics demonstration:

> But Achamian had whispered secrets to his first attacker. Five lines glittered along the gorge of blasted shelves, through smoke and wafting pages. Impact. The air cracked.
>
> His unseen foe cried out in astonishment—they always did at the first touch of the Gnosis. Achamian muttered more ancient words of power, more Cants. The Bisecting Planes of Mirseor, to continuously stress an opponent's Wards. The Odani Concussion Cants, to stun him, break his concentration. Then the Cirroi Loom….
>
> Dazzling geometries leapt through the smoke, lines and parabolas of razor light, punching through wood and papyrus, shearing through stone (270–71).

These lines express a fusion of brutality and intellectual beauty that could deeply enliven any game magic representation of magical combat (see Chapter 4, Section 4.12).

8.14.3 Brandon Sanderson and *The Stormlight Archive*

Sanderson has put his various laws of magic into practice in *The Way of the Kings*, which contains multiple magic systems of sufficient depth such that fans have been able to systematize them into diagrams suggestive of actual occultism and game mechanics. One prominent form of magic in *The Way of Kings* is called Surgebinding, while a darker and more obscure art called Voidbinding bears a possible relationship to a third school of sorcery known as the Old Magic. One of the book's appendices, "Ars Arcanum," contains a chart of mystical correspondences between the Ten Essences and a number of gems, bodily foci, soulcasting ingredients, attributes, and associated gods. Such a chart strongly resembles the compilations of correspondences characteristic of grimoires and other handbooks of occult magic.

Mages work spells by storing and unleashing energy, known as Stormlight, in precious gems.

Sanderson describes three "lashings" characteristic of Surgebinding, all of which involve altering the physical relationships between objects, by reversing their gravity, binding them to one another, or by granting them gravitational pull.

8.15 COMIC MAGIC

Comic books are one of the most common and influential manifestations of magic in popular culture and media, and one which has exerted a powerful influence on game magic. From Doctor Strange to John Constantine, the world of comics brims with sorcerers, enchanters, and magicians, rounding out a universe of superheroes with a metaphysical depth not often found in tales of caped avengers. Moreover, several key comic book artists are practicing occultists, including most notably the magician-artists Alan Moore and Grant Morrison, whose disparate approaches to magic are equally grounded in ceremonial traditions from the Golden Dawn, Crowley, voodoo, and Austin Osman Spare. As Moore observes, "Comics is itself where the magic comes in. The comics medium is one of the few mainstream entertainment industries open to folks who are openly into what is considered to be very weird, spooky and possibly dangerous stuff." More contemporary comic artists, such as Menton3 in the *Monocyte* series, continue to push the frontiers of occultist symbology in comics. With such avid crossover between comics and videogames in our transmedia landscape, comics are rife with possibilities for procedural adaptation.

8.15.1 Alan Moore

The figure most responsible for bringing occult and magical discourse into the field of comic books is Alan Moore, and his applications of ritual techniques and occult lore to popular culture are relevant to any game designer wishing to infuse her medium with depth and richness. As Moore tells the story, he decided to become a magician in his forties, as an alternative to experiencing a midlife crisis. Magical lore had also figured heavily in his work before this point. In an interview with Jay Babcock called "Magic is Afoot" and in the documentary film *The Mindscape of Alan Moore*, Moore teases out the labyrinthine relationship between art and magic. Moore himself explains:

> Comics, it seems, attracts—or breeds—magicians, and magical thinking. Perhaps it's that the form—representational lines on a surface—is directly tied to the first (permanent) visual art: the paintings on cave walls in what were probably shamanistic or ritualistic settings. In other words: magical settings. Understood this way, comics writers and artists' interest in magic/shamanism seems almost logical.

Moore's own early work in comics, such as *Swamp Thing* and *Hellblazer*, were pervaded by occult elements. The Swamp Thing character of the title is a vegetative spirit known as a plant elemental (emphasizing an intriguing departure from the clichéd four elements), and Moore introduced the occult detective John Constantine as a "working-class warlock" whose initial function is to provide lore about the Swamp Thing. The graphic novel *From Hell* explores the Jack the Ripper murders from the standpoint of Masonic conspiracy and includes a cameo appearance by a young Aleister Crowley, who insists on the reality of magic. Moore's series *Promethea,* written after Moore's magical awakening, chronicles the magical adventures of a sorcerer goddess whose name echoes the Greek Titan who stole fire.

Most relevant to game design are Moore's ritual performance art pieces, such as *Snakes and Ladders* and *The Highbury Working*, performed with the Moon and Serpent Grand Egyptian Theatre of Marvels. *Snakes and Ladders* in particular takes its central structuring motif from the classic board game of the same name which, while dependent purely on luck and lacking in strategic depth, aligns well with Moore's themes of cosmic resurrection and evolution. Moore refers to his performances as workings in the classic occultist sense of the word as a ritual operation, and his workings include spoken word poetry, music, circus fire breathers, mimes acting as living statues, and flashing lights. All of these elements are coordinated to create a single impression emotionally and thematically. They are evocative in the sense both of calling up spirits and eliciting emotions and ideas—which, in the best magic systems, are the same thing.

Yet, rich as these performances are, it also helps from the standpoint of procedural adaptation to examine specific comic book narratives and how their magic systems might be adapted as game mechanics.

8.15.2 *Hellblazer*/John Constantine

Hellblazer, a comic book series about a private investigator and occultist named John Constantine, bristles with instances of adapting magical rules from one medium or format to another. The comic book itself draws heavily on genuine occultist lore. The storyline depicting Constantine's failed exorcism of a demon in Newcastle (*Hellblazer* issues 11–12) adapts the rules of magic from the *Grimoirium Verum* and other "white magic" grimoires (and ironizes them through Constantine's failure). Constantine describes grimoire-based magic as "just like cooking," alluding to a common analogy between spellbooks and collections of recipes. Other elements, including the rod of art ("hazelwood, cut at the hour of Mercury"), "parchment flayed from a virgin kid," the "knife of the art, forged from new steel on the day of Jupiter," as well as an authentically drawn talisman used to evoke the demon Sagatana, all come directly from the grimoire tradition (Delano 12–13). According to Jake Stratton-Kent's edition of *The True Grimoire*, Sagatana is indeed one of the goetia or demons in the infernal hierarchy. The talisman depicted in *Hellblazer* issue 12 is the character of Scirlin, authentically drawn in most of its intricate curving sigils and the Latin words for the cardinal directions.

The film adapts similar occult lore as well as inventing its own (such as Constantine's tattoos and incantation of "into the light I command thee") in addition to adapting the "Deadly Habits" storyline from the comics—itself highly concerned with a deadly ritual derived from the *Grimoirium Verum*. As body art editorialist Rae Schwarz explains in her article "The Tattoos of CONSTANTINE," Constantine's tattoos in the film *Constantine* (added for the movie and not present in the comic books) have historical magical significance in alchemical lore. She further speculates that the symbols operate by the laws of sympathy to summon demons. Schwarz explains:

> The symbol is from a group of seventeenth century alchemy designs created by Eugenius Philalethe and means "the sulfur of perfection." It appears that the same design is tattooed on both arms so that when Constantine brings his arms together, the bilateral symmetry forms the whole design again. Given that the manifestation of demons brings a sulfurous aftersmell, it must be something to the theory that "like draws like" that allows Constantine to force Gabriel to appear with the incantation.

A PlayStation 2 videogame adaptation of *Constantine* adds its own links to the chain of transmedia adaptation, this time focusing on procedural adaptation as the game transforms the rules of magic in comic book and film into a system of game mechanics. In *Constantine*, the player presses sequences of buttons within time limits in order to cause the player character to recite incantations in order to cast spells. This method of spellcasting is firmly in the "magic as mini-game" or "magic as quicktime event" school, though several of the spells have unique effects, including a "True Sight" spell that exposes demons masquerading in human form, as well as revealing secret glyphs in the manner of *Clive Barker's Undying*. The game also uses water portals and a gate spell to adapt the narrative rule of the film that Constantine must immerse himself partially in water to travel into hell. Constantine's infernal travels owe a significant debt to the interdimensional voyages of a much earlier comic book mage: *Doctor Strange*.

8.15.3 Steve Ditko and the Psychedelic Dimensions of *Doctor Strange*

Doctor Strange is a comic that provides a unique, surreal vision of magic with great potential for game adaptation. As one of the more cerebral heroes of the Marvel universe, *Doctor Strange* has received few film adaptations and fewer appearances in videogames. Yet, the original Steve Ditko vision of *Doctor Strange* is one of the most psychedelic perspectives on magic, influential on any tale of interdimensional travel and rife with mystical powers. As comic historian Bradford W. Wright explains, surrealism, psychedelia, and Eastern mysticism all converged to produce a mind-bending trip far stranger than *The Hobbit*. Wright explains:

> Steve Ditko contributed some of his most surrealistic work to the comic book and gave it a disorienting, hallucinogenic quality.

Doctor Strange's adventures take place in bizarre worlds and twisting dimensions that resembled Salvador Dalí paintings....Inspired
by the pulp-fiction magicians of Stan Lee's childhood as well as by
contemporary Beat culture. Doctor Strange remarkably predicted
the youth counterculture's fascination with Eastern mysticism
and psychedelia. Never among Marvel's more popular or accessible
characters, Doctor Strange still found a niche among an audience
seeking a challenging alternative to more conventional superhero
fare (213).

Like the later *World of Darkness* and the best fantasy fiction, part of the
appeal of *Doctor Strange* involved a coherent vision of the metaphysical
world, consisting of concentric and interlocking planes. As comics historian Mike Benton explains, "The Doctor Strange stories of the 1960s
constructed a cohesive cosmology that would have thrilled any self-
respecting theosophist" (63). The surrealism of Steve Ditko's landscapes
would be excellent inspiration for magical level design when representing
alternate planes of existence. The colors are bright and psychedelic, rendered even more so by the many black light posters that were produced
based on giant-sized reproductions of full-page or double-page spreads.
Twisting, warped pathways connect abstract geometry of dodecahedrons
in a way that invites traversal by the shamanic equivalent of Sonic the
Hedgehog. But Doctor Strange's planar travel is more than surrealism for
its own sake, since like the planes of occultism and theosophy, these other
worlds have allegorical meanings. For example, the character Eternity is
an entire realm unto himself, described as a microcosm. The microcosm
is a concept from alchemy and hermeticism that involves the idea that
the little universe of each human being reflects the divine order of the
cosmos. The surrealism and cosmic depth of *Doctor Strange* open a portal
into an even more cosmic and game-like vision of the dream realms: Neil
Gaiman's *The Sandman*.

8.15.4 *The Sandman*

Neil Gaiman's graphic novel series *The Sandman* portrays one of the
most vivid visions of magic in any medium. The protagonist of the *The
Sandman* is Dream, one of the Endless, a group of seven beings who incarnate various abstract ideas: Death, Desire, Despair, Delirium, Destiny, and
Destruction. *The Sandman* contains many references to magic, ranging
from Dream's own transformative abilities to the ritual that is initially

used to summon and entrap him. Gaiman's magic walks a delicate line between allusiveness and originality, referencing occultism and mythology but breaking free of any established traditions to create truly surreal and evocative imagery.

In the opening volume of *The Sandman*, Anthony Burgess, a magician based closely on Aleister Crowley, attempts to summon the incarnation of Death in order to achieve immortality. Instead, the ritual accidentally summons and imprisons Dream, who eventually wreaks his revenge after centuries of imprisonment. The ritual, especially its chanted invocation, is one of the most powerful and poetic in Western literature, both for its hypnotic meter and its list of eerie and exotic spell foci (see Chapter 6, Section 6.12). The invocation reads:

> I give you a coin I made from stone
> I give you a song I stole from the dirt.
> I give you a knife from under the hills,
> and a stick I stuck through a dead man's eye.
> I give you a claw I ripped from a rat.
> I give you a name, and the name is lost.
> I give you the blood... from out of my vein,
> and a feather I pulled from an angel's wing.
> I call you with names, oh my lord, oh my lord
> I summon with poison and summon with pain.
> I open the way and I open the gates.

This invocation has a similar meter to Crowley's "Hymn to Pan," which as Internet poster "Thain" observes has many lines in rough iambic tetrameter ending in an anapest ("Re: Crowley's Influence on Wicca"). Each of the items offered in the ritual is uncanny, conjoining ordinary objects made of bizarre materials (a stone coin) or taken from exotic, spooky locations (a song from the dirt, a knife from the hills). The list culminates finally in the most sought-after, wicked, and eerie of feathers: one stolen from the wing of an angel.

The invocation is clearly modeled off the famous "double, double toil and trouble" witches' chant in *Macbeth* with its inventory of grotesque ingredients ("eye of newt, and toe of frog"), but Gaiman allows Burgess to up the ante on the sheer weirdness of these spell foci. The invocation also includes a variety of authentic and obscure mythological names of demons and spirits, many of them from Mesopotamian lore or demonological literature, such as Johann Weyer's *Pseudomonarchia Daemonum*: "Namtar. Allatu. Morax. Naberius. Klesh. Vepar. Maymon." This authentic historical research and the harsh, exotic sounds of the names lend a powerful atmosphere to the conjuration (see Chapter 6, Section 6.7). The scene is as powerful a representation of ceremonial magic as exists in any fiction, with a great deal of potential inspiration for games. Yet, the Sandman himself raises the bar on ritual magic once he has reclaimed his full powers much later in the series, after dismissing Burgess' operation as "petty hedge-magicking" and "a two-penny spell."

As the incarnation of Dream, the Sandman possesses nearly limitless power to draw objects and situations from the minds of slumbering dreamers, an ability which he uses to set the stage for a ritual when he needs to summon the three Weird Sisters known in one of their manifestations as the Fates. The Sandman prepares the ritual as if assembling a tableau, himself repeatedly contemplating how to best "set the scene." Indeed, the Sandman operates as a kind of infinitely empowered level designer who can shape the substance of the world by merely imagining what he needs based on the storehouse of the collective unconscious. The rule by which he is bound is that he must take specific elements directly from the dreams of particular dreamers: not just the idea of a crossroads, but a specific crossroads from the dream of a Cambodian farmer who longs for a new ox cart. He carefully arranges the context for the ritual in terms of time, space, and objects, first setting the stage spatially by placing a gallows at the center of a crossroads. He then places symbolically charged ritual objects onto the stage, including honey, snakes, a crescent moon, and a black she-lamb. His final ritual action is to set the time to midnight, the fabled witching hour, as signified by the tolling of a lonely church bell. In keeping with a well-designed ritual (see Chapter 2, Section 2.5 and Chapter 6, Section 6.5), all of these elements correspond symbolically to the three-fold goddess Hecate, and all of them evoke a mood of somber gloom.

Indeed, the Sandman operates as a kind of infinitely empowered level designer who can shape the substance of the world by merely imagining what he needs based on the storehouse of the collective unconscious. The Sandman's dream abilities could provide great inspiration for game magic, especially the school of Dream Magic (see Chapter 4, Section 4.10.4). The diceless role-playing game *Nobilis*, especially in its first edition, could be viewed as a procedural adaptation of *The Sandman*, in that players incarnate abstract concepts (like the color yellow or the principle of vibration) and act on them. Similarly, the Arcana Ritual Toolset, a work in progress by the author, is intended as a tool for creating ritual tableau akin to the Sandman's dream design of ritual tableaux.

8.15.5 *Monocyte*

Monocyte is an independent comic book by Menton3, which also includes a concept album. Menton3 is no stranger to the occult or to videogames, since he is both one of the artists on the *Silent Hill: Past Life* comic book and a longtime devotee of magic.

8.16 FANTASY, GAMES, AND MAGICAL WORLD-BUILDING

From fantasy to comics, the strength of magic in fantasy literature is the way that magic fits into a larger enterprise of world-building. As fantasy author R. Scott Bakker observes, "One of the things so fascinating about epic fantasy in particular is the way the boundary between plot and setting dissolves, so that learning about the world becomes a kind of narrative revelation." Unlike other genres in which character drives plot, and setting serves as backdrop, the worlds of epic fantasy are often the primary focus, complete with their own geography, weather patterns, cultural anthropology, history, and mythology. In well-constructed fantasy, magic is an integral part of the world, connected to many other aspects of the universe in terms of what domains the magic can affect and the sources of the magic.

Well-written fantasy can teach game designers powerful lessons about how to build worlds in which magic thrives organically. World-building in magic involves modeling the forces at work in the world and how they can modify the world, especially what aspects of a robust simulation they can affect. To model any magic system, whether occult, fictive, or original, we must first create a world. In particular, we must create it at a deep metaphysical level, where magic occurs. We must especially create its other worlds, its reservoirs of magic energy, its planes or warrens in Steven Erikson's terms, as well as the symbols used to represent these forces. These forces need to have a narrative rationale, a mythic coherence, or the magic will fall flat. In order to accommodate powerful magic, a procedurally generated game world would require an algorithm that creates coherent mythologies, because only when we know the metaphysics and the mythology can we know the rituals used to access it. Only when we know the rituals would we know what effects they have.

The difficulties of constructing such an algorithm are part of what has delayed the development of magic in *Dwarf Fortress*. Every time a new game starts up, the algorithms of *Dwarf Fortress* generate a world with thousands of years of history, geologically accurate terrain layers, aquifers, and ancient ruins. There are established algorithms for creating realistic terrain by modeling real-world physical processes, such as erosion patterns. But the patterns of magic are metaphysical, mythological, and psychological, and the algorithms for those domains are less concrete. The game's lead designer, ToadyOne (Zach Adams) has made it clear in design documents and interviews that he wants to simulate deep mythic and supernatural sources for magic. The documentation for 3d RPG Roguelike *Slaves of Armok: God of Blood, Part I* contains elaborate reflections on the relationship between mythology, ritual, and game mechanics, though many of these features were unimplemented when development focus shifted to *Dwarf Fortress* (*Slaves of Armok: God of Blood, Part II*). Though ambitious to incorporate magic into *Dwarf Fortress*, ToadyOne observes that he would like to avoid "the industrialisation [sic] of magic." He explains:

> What we want to focus on is making it so that if there's a magical object that's really a rare special magical object then it should be something that you don't really understand that well and that's not necessarily reliable. It depends on the source; where does the magic come from? Was the dwarf inspired by all those gods that don't actually exist in the game right now, that are just names, or did the dwarf create something so perfect that it just gets infused by magic because it's a perfect thing, or did the dwarf really have some understanding of magical forces and create such a thing. If that's the case you've got to watch out for the industrialisation of magic; why doesn't he just do it seven or eight more times?

ToadyOne's comments emphasize the sources of magic, including its grounding in the gods of the procedurally generated mythology of the game. In a forum thread about magic and other proposed features for the adventure mode of *Dwarf Fortress*, ToadyOne explains, "We don't want another cheap fantasy universe, we want a cheap fantasy universe generator. A lot of fiction sounds computer generated anyway." To create magic that resonates with our game worlds, we must generate fantasy universes that are not cheap. Only poorly written fantasy fiction sounds computer generated in an obvious or awkward way, because in this usage ToadyOne seems to be using computer-generated to mean random and clichéd—in other words, cheap. It is possible for aspects of one's world-building and mechanics to be systemic and perhaps even procedurally generated without being cheap, but to do so requires an understanding of what distinguishes worlds with powerful and compelling fantasy magic from dull and trite ones.

Works Cited

38 Studios and Big Huge Games. *Kingdoms of Amalur: Reckoning*. 38 Studios and Electronic Arts, 2012. PlayStation 3, Windows PC, Xbox 360.

Aarseth, Espen. *Cybertext: Perspectives on Ergodic Literature*. Baltimore: Johns Hopkins UP, 1997.

Abelson, Harold and Gerald Jay Sussman with Julie Sussman. *Structure and Interpretation of Computer Programs*. Cambridge, MA: M.I.T. P, 1985.

"The Ae'lanoic Rosette." 23 May 2013. http://www.kickstarter.com/projects/617502838/shadow-of-the-eternals/posts/489456?ref=email&show_token=9accd5ce6222bf94 23 May 2013.

Age of Conan Wiki. http://aoc.wikia.com/wiki/Magic 3 August 2012.

Agrippa, Cornelius. *Three Books of Occult Philosophy*. 1651. Trans. James Freake. Ed. Donald Tyson. Woodbury, MN: Llewellyn, 2012.

Almar's Guide. http://almarsguides.com/eq/general/spells.cfm 2 August 2012.

Almost Human Ltd. *The Legend of Grimrock*. 2012. PC.

Anders, Charlie Jane. "The Rules of Magic, According to the Greatest Fantasy Sagas of All Time." 8 December 2011. http://io9.com/5866306/the-rules-of-magic-according-to-the-greatest-fantasy-sagas-of-all-time 6 March 2013.

Anderson, Dean and David H. Thornley. *Cthangband*. http://www.visi.com/~thornley/david/cthangband/.

Anderson, Dean. *Hellband*. Windows PC. http://hellband.net/.

Arkane Studios. *Arx Fatalis*. JoWood Productions/DreamCatcher Interactive, 2002. Windows and Xbox.

—. *Dishonored*. Bethesda Softworks, 2012. Xbox 360, PS3, Windows.

Arneson, Dave and Gary Gygax. *Chainmail*. Lake Geneva, WI: Tactical Studies Rules, 19.

—. *Chainmail*, 3rd ed. Lake Geneva, WI: Tactical Studies Rules, 19.

—. *Dungeons & Dragons: Rules for Fantastic Medieval Wargames Campaigns Playable with Paper and Pencil and Miniature Figures*. Lake Geneva, WI: Tactical Studies Rules, 1974.

—. *Advanced Dungeons & Dragons Player's Handbook*. 1st ed. Lake Geneva, WI: TSR Games, 1978.

Atlus. *Persona 2*. Atlus, 1999. PlayStation.

—. *Shin Megami Tensei III: Nocturne*. Atlus, 2003. PlayStation 2.

Babcock, Jay. "Magic is Afoot." *Arthur* 4 (May 2003). http://arthurmag. com/2007/05/10/1815/15 May 2013.

Baker, Richard. *Player's Option: Spells and Magic*. Lake Geneva, WI: TSR Games, 1996.

Bakker, R. Scott. *The Darkness That Comes Before: The Prince of Nothing, Book One*. New York: Overlook Press, 2004.

—. *The Warrior Prophet: The Prince of Nothing, Book Two*. New York: Penguin, 2008.

Barker, Clive (@RealCliveBarker). "@SoundOfElegance Yes.All the magic in my books is part of a single massive system. It is best summarized by the words that open G.A.S.S...." 14 September 2012. Tweet.

—. *The Great and Secret Show: The First Book of the Art*. 1989. New York: HarperCollins, 1999.

—. "The Hellbound Heart." New York: Harper Perennial, 2007.

Barnes, Emrey, *The Book of Shadows*: *The Player's Guide for Mage: The Ascension*. Stone Mountain, CA: White Wolf, 1993.

Barton, Matt. *Dungeons and Desktops*. Wellesley, MA: AK Peters, 2008.

Bay 12 Games. *Dwarf Fortress*. Windows PC. http://www.bay12games.com/.

"Beginner's Guide to Roguelikes." http://www.kathekonta.com/rlguide/intro. html31May2013.

Benton, Mike. *Superhero Comics of the Silver Age: The Illustrated History*. Dallas, TX: Taylor Publishing, 1991.

Berger, Peter. *The Sacred Canopy: Elements of a Sociological Theory of Religion*. 1969. Toronto, Ontario, Canada: Anchor, 1990.

Bethesda Game Studios. *The Elder Scrolls III: Morrowind*. Bethesda Softworks, 2002. Windows and Xbox 360.

—. *The Elder Scrolls IV: Oblivion*. Bethesda Softworks, 2006. Windows, PlayStation 3, and Xbox 360.

—. *The Elder Scrolls V: Skyrim*. Bethesda Softworks, 2011. Windows, PlayStation 3, and Xbox 360.

The Binding of Isaac Wiki. "Tarot Cards." http://bindingofisaac.wikia.com/wiki/ Tarot_Cards 20 September 2012.

BioWare. *Dragon Age: Origins*. Electronic Arts, 2009. Xbox 360, Windows, and PlayStation 3.

Black Isle Studios. *Planescape: Torment*. Interplay, 1999. Windows PC.

Blizzard. *World of Warcraft*. Blizzard, 2004. Windows.

Blow, Jonathan. *Galstaff*. 2007. Windows PC.

Blue Sky Productions/Looking Glass. *Ultima Underworld: The Stygian Abyss*. Origin Systems, 1992. DOS.

Bonewits, Isaac. *Authentic Thaumaturgy*. 2nd ed. Austin, TX: Steve Jackson Games, 1998.

Borgstrom, Sean R. *Nobilis: The Game of Sovereign Powers*. London: Hogshead, 2002.

Bridges, Bill et al. *Mage: The Awakening*. Stone Mountain, CA: White Wolf, 2005.

Brooks, Frederick P., Jr. *The Mythical Man-Month: Essays on Software Engineering*. 1975. Anniversary ed. Boston: Addison-Wesley, 1995.

Brough, Michael. VESPER.5 2012. Windows PC.

Brucato, Phil and Stuart Wieck. *Mage: The Ascension*. Clarkston, CA: White Wolf, 1998.

Brust, Steven. *Taltos*. New York: Ace, 1988.

Capcom. *Haunting Ground*. Capcom, 2005. PS2.

Capybara Games. *Superbrothers Sword & Sworcery EP*. Capybara Games, 2011.

Carroll, Bart and Steve Winter. "Alumni: Deck of Many Things." 22 April 2010. 9 July 2013. http://www.wizards.com/dnd/Article.aspx?x=dnd/4alum/20100422.

Carroll, Peter J. *Liber Kaos*. York Beach, ME: Samuel Weiser, 1992.

Carroll, Peter J. *Liber Null & Psychonaut: An Introduction to Chaos Magic*. York Beach, ME: Samuel Weiser, 1987.

Chick, Don. 1984. "Dark Dungeons." http://www.chick.com/reading/tracts/0046/0046_01.asp 13 June 2013.

Chumbley, Andrew. *Azoëtia*: *A Grimoire of the Sabbatic Craft*. Cheshire, England: Xoanon, 1992.

Coberly, Bill. "Magic Needs to Be Mysterious and Unpredictable in Games." Nightmare Mode. 24 July 2013. 20 June 2013. http://nightmaremode.net/2012/07/magic-needs-to-be-mysterious-and-unpredictable-in-games-21543/.

Codrington, Robert Henry. *The Melanesians: Studies in Their Anthropology and Folk-Lore*. Oxford: At the Clarendon P, 1891. http://archive.org/stream/melanesiansstudi00codruoft#page/n5/mode/2up.

Colantonio, Raphael and Harvey Smith. "Empowering the Player in a Story-Rich World: Co-Directing *Dishonored*." Game Developer's Conference 2013.

Cook, David et al. *Tome of Magic*. Advanced Dungeons & Dragons 2nd Ed. Lake Geneva, WI: TSR, 1991.

Cook, Monte, Jonathan Tweet, and Skip Williams. *Dungeons & Dragons Player's Handbook*: *Core Rulebook I*. Renton, WA: Wizards of the Coast, 2000.

Crawford, Chris. *Chris Crawford on Interactive Storytelling*. 2nd ed. San Francisco: New Riders, 2013.

Crowley, Aleister. *The Confessions of Aleister Crowley*: *An Autohagiography*. 1969. http://hermetic.com/crowley/confessions/ 15 May 2013.

Crowley, Aleister and Hymenaeus Beta. *The Goetia: The Lesser Key of Solomon the King*. Boston: Red Wheel, 1997.

Crowley, Aleister with Mary Desti and Leila Waddell. *Magick*: *Liber ABA, Book 4, Parts I–IV*. 2nd rev. ed. San Francisco: Weiser Books, 2012.

Crowley, Aleister. *Aleister Crowley: The Order of the Silver Star*. Red Cab Records, 2011. CD.

Davies, Owen. *Grimoires: A History of Magic Books*. Oxford: Oxford UP, 2009.

Davis, Erik. "Calling Cthulhu." http://www.techgnosis.com/chunkshow-single.php?chunk=chunkfrom-2005-12-13-1057-0.txt.

Delano, Jamie et al. *John Constantine: Hellblazer*. Issue 11. DC/Vertigo: November 1988.

Doull, Andrew. "Designing a Magic System," Parts I–XV. 3 May 2008 http://rogue-likedeveloper.blogspot.com/2008/05/unangband-magic-system-part-one.html 12 Aug 2012.

Drake, Shannon. "There's a Lot More to Tell." *The Escapist*. 29 August 2006. http://www.escapistmagazine.com/articles/view/issues/issue_60/356-Theres-a-Lot-More-to-Tell.2 4 July 2012.

DreamWorks Interactive. *Clive Barker's Undying*. EA Games, 2001. Windows, Mac, PS2.

The Dungeonmaster. Dir. David Allen et al. Ragewar Productions, 1984. Film.

Dyack, Denis. "Ken and Denis Discuss the Magic System of Shadow of the Eternals." http://www.kickstarter.com/projects/617502838/shadow-of-the-eternals/posts/49368429May2013.

Erikson, Steven. *Gardens of the Moon: Book One of the Malazan Book of the Fallen*. New York: Tor, 1999.

Event Horizon Software, Inc. *The Summoning*. SSI, 1992. DOS, Amiga.

Fireproof Games. *The Room*. Fireproof Games, 2012. iOS, Android, Kindle Fire, Google Play.

Fisher, David. *Suveh Nux*. Z-blorb.

Frazier, James George. *The Golden Bough: A Study of Magic and Religion*. 1890.

From Software. *Demon's Souls*. Sony, 2010. PlayStation 3.

—. *Dark Souls*. Namco Bandai, 2012. Microsoft Windows, PlayStation 3, Xbox 360.

—. *Eternal Ring*. Agetec, 2000. PlayStation 2.

FTL Games. *Dungeon Master*. FTL Games, 1987. Atari ST.

Funcom. *The Secret World*. Electronic Arts, 2012. Windows.

Gaiman, Neil. *The Sandman*: *Preludes and Nocturnes*.

Gaudo, Michel and Guillaume Rohmer. *Maléfices*: *Le jeu de rôle qui sent de soufre*. Jeux Descartes, 1985.

Gordon, Joan. "Reveling in Genre: An Interview with China Miéville." Science Fiction Studies 30.3. November 2003 http://www.depauw.edu/sfs/interviews/Miévilleinterview.htm 5 May 2013.

Grant, Barry Keith. "Video Games: The Eighth Art—Blog #34." 21 June 2007 http://www.ign.com/blogs/silicon-knights/2007/06/21/video-games-the-eighth-art-blog-34 15 May 2013.

Grasshopper Manufacture. *Killer7*. Capcom, 2005. PS2, GameCube.

Grey Area. *Shadow Cities*. Grey Area, 2011. iOS.

Gygax, Gary. *Advanced Dungeons & Dragons Player's Handbook*. 1st ed. Lake Geneva, WI: TSR, 1978.

—. "The *Dungeons & Dragons* Magic System." *The Strategic Review* 2.2 (April 1976).

—. *Master of the Game*: *Principles and Techniques for Becoming an Expert Role-Playing Game Master*. London: Perigee Trade, 1989.

—. *Men and Magic: Dungeons & Dragons Vol I*. Lake Geneva, WI: TSR, 1974.

Heinsoo, Robert, Andy Collins, and James Wyatt. *Dungeons & Dragons Player's Handbook*: *Arcane, Divine, and Martial Heroes*. 4th ed. Renton, WA: Wizards of the Coast, 2008.

Hesse, Herman. *The Glass Bead Game*. 1943. New York: Picador, 2002.

Hickman, Tracy and Margaret Weis. *Dragonlance Adventures*. Lake Geneva, WI: TSR, 1987.

Howard, Jeff. "*Demonik* and the Ludic Legacy of Clive Barker." The Workshop on Integrated Design in Games. Dakota State University. 5 November 2010.

—. "Howard's Law of Occult Game Design." *100 Principles of Game Design*. New Riders, 2013.

—. "Magic Systems in Theory and Practice." Lecture. M.I.T. Gambit Game Lab. 9 April 2010.

—. "Occult Game Design: An Initiation into Secrets and Mysteries." GDC Online 2012.

—. *Quests: Design, Theory, and History in Games and Narratives*. Wellesley, MA: AK Peters, 2008.

Howard, Robert E. *The Coming of Conan the Cimmerian*. New York: Random House, 1932.

Hubbard, John. "Wizardry I–V Spells." http://www.tk421.net/wizardry/wiz-15spells.shtml.

Huizinga, Johan. *Homo Ludens: A Study of the Play Element in Culture*. London: Roy Publishers, 1950.

Ice-Pick Lodge. *The Void*. ND Games, 2008. Windows.

Infocom. *Enchanter*. Infocom, 1983. DOS.

Inkle Studios. *Steve Jackson's Sorcery!* Inkle Studios, 2013. iOS.

Interplay Productions. *The Bard's Tale*. Electronic Arts, 1985. DOS.

Jackson, Steve. *Sorcery!: The Shamutanti Hills*. New York: Penguin, 1983.

King, Stephen. *Danse Macabre*. New York: Penguin, 1981.

Koenig, Becky. *Color Workbook*. 3rd ed. Upper Saddle River, NJ: Prentice Hall, 2010.

Konami. *Castlevania: Dawn of Sorrow*. Konami, 2005. Nintendo DS.

Konami Computer Entertainment. *Silent Hill 2*. Konami, 2001. Microsoft Windows, PlayStation 2, Xbox.

Koster, Raph. *A Theory of Fun for Game Design*. Scottsdale, AZ: Paraglyph P, 2005.

Kuhn, Thomas S. *The Structure of Scientific Revolutions*. 1962. Chicago: U of Chicago P, 1996.

LaVey, Anton Szandor. *The Satanic Bible*. New York: Avon, 1976.

Laycock, Donald C. *The Complete Enochian Dictionary*: *A Dictionary of the Angelic Language as Revealed to Dr. John Dee and Edward Kelley*. 1978. Red Wheel/Weiser: San Francisco, 2001.

LefflerWebDesign. *Goliath: The Soothsayer*. 2008.

Legend Entertainment. *Death Gate*. Legend Entertainment, 1994. DOS.

Le Guin, Ursula K. *A Wizard of Earthsea*. 1968. Bantam: New York, 1975.

Leiber, Fritz. *Swords and Deviltry: The First Book of Fafhrd and the Gray Mouser*. 1970. New York: ACE, 1979.

Leitch, Aaron. *Secrets of the Magickal Grimoires*: *The Classic Texts of Magick Deciphered*. Woodbury, MN: Llewellyn, 2005.

Lévi, Eliphas, trans A.E. Waite. *Dogme et Rituel de La Haute Magie, Part II: The Ritual of Transcendental Magic*. 1896.

Lionhead Studios. *Black & White*. Electronic Arts/Feral Interactive, 2001. Windows/Mac.

Looking Glass. *Thief: The Dark Project*. Eidos Interactive, 1998. Windows.

Lovecraft, H.P. "Supernatural Horror in Literature." http://www.hplovecraft.com/writings/texts/essays/shil.asp.

—. "The History of the Necronomicon." http://www.hplovecraft.com/writings/texts/fiction/hn.asp.

Lucasfilm Games. *Loom*. Lucasfilm Games, 1990. DOS.

Luck, George. *Arcana Mundi*. 2nd ed. Baltimore: Johns Hopkins UP, 2006.

MacLeod, Mindy and Bernard Mees. *Runic Alphabets and Magic Objects*. Woodbridge, Suffolk: Boydell P, 2006.

"Magic of *Dungeons & Dragons*." http://en.wikipedia.org/wiki/Magic_of_Dungeons_%26_Dragons 25 September 2012.

Mars Volta, The. *The Bedlam in Goliath*. Universal Motown Records, 2008.

Martin, George R.R. *A Clash of Kings: Book Two of a Song of Ice and Fire*. 1999. New York: Bantam Books, 2011.

—. *A Feast for Crows: Book Four of a Song of Ice and Fire*. 2005. New York: Bantam Books, 2011.

—. *A Game of Thrones: Book One of a Song of Ice and Fire*. 1996. New York: Bantam Books, 2013.

—. *A Storm of Swords: Book Three of a Song of Ice and Fire*. 2000. New York: Bantam Books, 2011.

Marvelous AQL and SCE Japan Studio. *Soul Sacrifice*. Sony Computer Entertainment, 2013. PlayStation Vita.

Mentzer, Frank. *Dungeons & Dragons Player's Handbook*. Lake Geneva, WI: TSR, 1983.

Mercury Steam. *Clive Barker's Jericho*. Codemasters, 2007. Windows, PlayStation 3, Xbox 360.

Métraux, Alfred. *Voodoo in Haiti*. 1959. New York: Pantheon, 1989.

Middleditch, Sean. "Representing Magic Skills." http://roguebasin.roguelikedevelopment.org/index.php?title=Representing_Magic_Skills 31 May 2013.

Midway Games West. *Gauntlet: Dark Legacy*. Midway Games, 2000 and 2002. Arcade, PS2, Xbox.

Miéville, China. *Perdido Street Station*. New York: Dell Rey, 2000.

The Mindscape of Alan Moore. Dir. Dez Vylens and Moritz Winkler. Shadowsnake, 2005. Film.

Montfort, Nick. *Twisty Little Passages: An Approach to Interactive Fiction*. Cambridge, MA: MIT P, 2005.

"Moons of Krynn: Moon Tracking Chart." Dragonlance Nexus. http://www.dlnexus.com/fan/rules/11899.aspx 23 May 2013.

Moorcock, Michael. *Elric of Melnibone*. 1972. New York: Berkley Publishing, 1987.

—. *Elric: The Stealer of Souls*. Chronicles of the Last Emperor of Melniboné, Vol I. New York: Del Rey, 2008.

Moriarty, Brian. *Perlenspiel*. http://www.perlenspiel.org/.

Mulder, Ben. "Magicka Infographic." 9 February 2011 http://lmc.gatech.edu/~bmedler3/?p=639 3 March 2013.

Newitz, Annalee. "China Miéville explains theology, magic, and why J.J. Abrams hates you." http://io9.com/5605836/china-mieville-explains-theology-magic-and-why-jj-abrams-hates-you 11 Aug 2010 3 August 2013.

Nihon Falcom. *Sorcerian*. 1987. Sierra Entertainment, 1990. DOS.

Nihonen, Anttii. "Magic and runes." 14 October 2011. 3 July 2013. http://www.grimrock.net/2011/10/14/magic-and-runes/.

Ogmento. *Paranormal Activity: Sanctuary*. Ogmento, 2011.

Origin Systems. *Ultima IV*. Origin Systems, 1985. Apple II.

—. *Ultima V: Warriors of Virtue*. Origin Systems, 1988. Apple II.

—. *Ultima VI: The False Prophet*. Origin Systems, 1990. Apple II.

—. *Ultima VII: The Black Gate*. Origin Systems, 1992. DOS.

—. *Ultima VIII: Pagan*. Origin Systems, 1994. DOS.

Petersen, Sandy and Willis Lynn, et al. *Call of Cthulhu: Horror Roleplaying in the Worlds of H.P. Lovecraft*. 6th ed. Hayward, CA: Chaosium, 2005.

Piccione, Peter. "In Search of the Meaning of Senet." *Archeology*. July/August 1980, pp. 55–58. Excerpted online http://www.gamesmuseum.uwaterloo.ca/Archives/Piccione/index.html.

—. *The Historical Development of the Game Senet and Its Significance for Egyptian Religion*. Doctoral Dissertation. University of Chicago, 1990.

Pinch, Geraldine. *Egyptian Mythology: A Guide to the Gods, Goddesses, and Traditions of Ancient Egypt*. Oxford: Oxford UP, 2002.

—. *Magic in Ancient Egypt*. 1994. Revised ed. Austin: U of Texas P, 2006.

Plotkin, Andrew. *Hadean Lands*. Work in Progress.

—. *Hadean Lands* Kickstarter Page. http://www.kickstarter.com/projects/zarf/hadean-lands-interactive-fiction-for-the-iphone/posts?page=1.

—. Interview. 7 January 2011. http://www.adventureclassicgaming.com/index.php/site/interviews/622/ 5 August 2012.

Rare. *Taboo: The Sixth Sense*. Tradewest, 1989.

Reality Pump. *Two Worlds II*. TopWare Interactive, 2010. Windows, Mac, Xbox 360, PS3.

"Re: Crowley's Influence on Wicca." 4 August 2010. The Cauldron: A Pagan Forum. 26 May 2013. http://www.ecauldron.net/forum/index.php?topic=6321.0;p=7.

Reed, R.D. 21 October 2010 "China Mieville and D&D." Cyclopeatron http://cyclopeatron.blogspot.com/2010/10/china-mieville-and-d.html 5 May 2013.

Regardie, Israel. *The Golden Dawn*. Woodbury, MN: Llewellyn, 2002.

Rein-Hagen, Mark et al. *Vampire: The Masquerade: A Storytelling Game of Personal Horror*. 3rd ed. Clarkston, CA: White Wolf, 2000.

Robertson, Pat. "'Demonic' *Dungeons & Dragons* Literally Destroyed People's Lives." *The 700 Club*. CBN.com. Television. 18 April 2013 http://www.youtube.com/watch?v= Ifwc_y_S3BY 13 June 2013.

Ryan, Marie-Laure. *Narrative as Virtual Reality: Immersion and Interactivity*. Baltimore: Johns Hopkins UP, 2003.

Saffer, Dan. *Designing Gestural Interfaces: Touchscreens and Interactive Devices*. Sebastopol, CA: Morgan Kaufman, 2008.

Sanderson, Brandon. "Sanderson's First Law." February 2007. 24 June 2013. http://brandonsanderson.com/article/40/Sandersons-First-Law.

—. *The Way of Kings: Book One of the Stormlight Archive*. New York: Tor Fantasy, 2010.

Schaefer, Peter. "Excerpts: Rituals." 28 May 2008 http://www.wizards.com/dnd/Article.aspx?x=dnd/4ex/20080528a 25 September 2012.

Schell, Jesse. *The Art of Game Design*. Burlington, MA: Morgan Kaufmann, 2008.

Schwarz, Rae. "The Tattoos of CONSTANTINE." BellaOnline: The Voice of Women http://www.bellaonline.com/articles/art29085.asp 6 March 2013.

Sernett et al. *Tome of Magic: Pact, Shadow, and Truename Magic*. Renton, WA: Wizards of the Coast, 2006.

Shea, Robert and Robert Anton Wilson. *The Illuminatus! Trilogy*. New York: Dell, 1975.

Short, Emily. *Damnatio Memoriae*.

—. *Savoir-Faire*.

Siembieda, Kevin. *Palladium Fantasy Role-Playing Game*. 2nd ed. Taylor, MI: Palladium, 2000.

—. *Rifts Book of Magic*. Taylor, MI: Palladium, 2003.

Sierra Entertainment. *Betrayal in Antara*. 1997. Windows PC.

Silicon Knights. *Eternal Darkness: Sanity's Requiem*. Nintendo, 2002. GameCube.

Simogo. *Year Walk*. Simogo Games, 2013. iOS.

—. *Year Walk Companion*. Simogo Games, 2013. iOS.

Simon. *Necronomicon*. New York: Avon, 1980.

Simtex. *Master of Magic*. Microprose, 1994. DOS.

Sir-tech Software, Inc. *Wizardry: Proving Grounds of the Mad Overlord*. Sir-tech Software, Inc., 1981. DOS.

Skinner, Stephen. *The Complete Magician's Tables: The Most Complete Set of Magic, Kabbalistic, Angelic, Astrologic, Alchemic, Demonic, Geomantic, Grimoire, Gematria, I Ching, Tarot, Planetary, Pagan Pantheon, Plant, Perfume, Emblem and Character Correspondences in more than 777 Tables*. 2nd ed. Woodbury, MN: Llewellyn, 2009.

Snellman, Juho. "Programming Roguelike Magic." http://roguebasin.rogue-likedevelopment.org/index.php?title=Programming_Roguelike_Magic 31 May 2013.

Spinnaker Software Corporation. *Nine Princes in Amber*. Telarium Corporation, 1985. C 64, DOS, Atari ST, Apple II, MSX2.

Square Product Development Division 4. *Vagrant Story*. Square, 2000. PlayStation.

Stoker, Bram. *Dracula*. 1897. New York: W.W. Norton, 1996.

Stolze, Greg and John Tynes. *Unknown Armies: A Roleplaying Game of Transcendental Horror and Furious Action*. 2nd ed. Roseville, MN: Atlas Games, 1998.

Stratton-Kent, Jake. *Geosophia: The Argo of Magic*. Encyclopedia Goetica Volume II. Bibliothèque Rouge. Kindle edition. Scarlet Imprint, 2010.

—. *True Grimoire*. Encyclopedia Goetica Volume II. Bibliothèque Rouge. Kindle edition. Scarlet Imprint, 2010.

Swan, Rick. *The Complete Wizard's Handbook: Advanced Dungeons & Dragons Player's Handbook Rules Supplement*. Lake Geneva, WI: TSR, 1990.

Swink, Steve. *Game Feel: A Game Designer's Guide to Virtual Sensation*. Burlington, MA: CRC Press, 2008.

Tecmo Koei. *Spirit Camera: The Cursed Memoir*. Nintendo, 2012. Nintendo 3DS.

Templum Nigri Solis. *Between Spaces: Selected Rituals and Essays from the Archives of Templum Nigri Solis*.

"The Eight Circles of Magic." http://www.uo.com/archive/ultima6/magic.html.

Thibault, Daniel U. and S. John Ross. *GURPS Grimoire: Tech Magic, Gate Magic and Hundreds of New Spells for All Colleges*. Austin, TX: Steve Jackson Games, 1994.

Toady One, Rainseeker, Capntastic. "Dwarf Fortress Talk 7.2." http://www.bay12g-ames.com/media/df_talk_7_transcript_2.html.

Toltilo, Stephen. "Should the iPad Ouija Board Have a Mind of its Own?" *Kotaku*. 8 April 2010. 21 June 2013. http://kotaku.com/5512828/should-the-ipad-ouija-board-have-a-mind-of-its-own.

Tweet, Jonathan and Mark Rein-Hagen. *Ars Magica*. 5th ed. Roseville, MN: Atlas, 2004.

—. *Dungeons & Dragons Player's Handbook*. 3.5 ed. Renton, WA: Wizards of the Coast, 2003.

Twelker, Eric. "Master of Horror Clive Barker Discusses Undying." http://www.amazon.com/gp/feature.html?ie=UTF8&docId=134969 14 May 2013.

Ubisoft Montreal. *Assassin's Creed*. Ubisoft, 2007. PlayStation 3, Windows PC, Xbox 360.

Ultima Online Guide. 6 April 2012 http://www.uoguide.com/Spellbook 2 August 2012.

"Ultima Presented as a Series of Occult and Ritual Actions." Renfusa: A Blog of the Secret Motions of Things 20 July 2012 http://www.renfusa.com/2012/07/ultima-presented-as-series-of-occult.html 17 June 2013.

Vance, Jack. *Tales of the Dying Earth*. 1950. New York: TOR, 2012.

Wasserman, James. *Art and Symbols of the Occult: Images of Power and Wisdom*. Rochester, VT: Destiny Books, 1993.

Watson, Ross. *Dark Heresy: The Radical's Handbook*. Roseville, MN: Fantasy Flight, 2009.

Weil, Fréderic, Fabrice Lamidey, Sam Shirley, and Gregg Stafford. *Nephilim: Occult Roleplaying*. Oakland, CA: Chaosium, 1994.

Weis, Margaret and Tracy Hickman. *Dragon Wing: The Death Gate Cycle, Volume 1*. New York: Bantam Spectra, 1990.

Weise, Matthew. "Dishonored: World Building 101." Outside Your Heaven. 21 October 2012 http://outsideyourheaven.blogspot.com/2012/10/dishon-ored-world-building-101.html 14 May 2013.

—. "Looking Glass Studios Interview Series, Audio Podcast 2—Dan Schmidt." 21 March 2011 http://gambit.mit.edu/podcasts/lgs/podcast2_lgs_schmidt.mp3 13 May 2013.

—. "Game Prescription: Vagrant Story." Message to Jeff Howard. 14 May 2013. E-mail.

—. "The Rules of Horror." *Horror Video Games: Essays on the Fusion of Fear and Play*. Ed. Bernard Perron. Jefferson, NC: McFarland & Company, 2009.

Wells, Dominic. "David Lynch: The Road to Hell." 9 July 2013 http://www.dominicwells.com/2010/09/stylish-new-look/.

Westcott, Wynn. *The Chaldean Oracles of Zoroaster*. 1895. Wellingborough, UK: Aquarian P, 1983.

Wigdor, Daniel. *Brave NUI World: Designing Natural User Interfaces for Touch and Gesture*. Burlington, MA: Morgan Kaufman, 2011.

Willis, Lynn. *Stormbringer: Fantasy Roleplaying in the World of Elric*. Oakland, CA: Chaosium, 2001.

Wizarbox. *Gray Matter*. dtp entertainment. Windows PC, Xbox 360, 2010.

Wright, Bradford W. *Comic Book Nation: Transformation of a Youth Culture*. Baltimore, MD: Johns Hopkins UP, 2001.

Yid Yang. "Death Gate Review." Mobygames. 4 July 2008. 22 June 2013. http://www.mobygames.com/game/dos/death-gate/reviews/reviewerId,6226/.

Ylinen, Topi. *Zangband*. http://www.zangband.org/.

Zelazny, Roger. *Nine Princes in Amber*. *The Great Book of Amber*. 1970. New York: Avon Eos, 1999.

Appendix A: A Magic System Worksheet

Express the system in the most clear and focused way possible, highlighting what is unique and interesting about your game's particular way of casting spells, working enchantments, and/or summoning spirits.

Answer the following questions in a brief, high-level document. You can break down each of its component parts according to the principles discussed in depth throughout the book.

1. What is unique about your magic system? What is its overriding theme condensed into a nutshell, its elevator pitch that you could give in 2 to 3 sentences?

2. To what kind of world does this magic system belong?

   Is the world high-fantasy (in which magic is common and powerful, such as Middle-Earth or Melnibone) or low-fantasy (in which magic is rare and often regarded with suspicion, as in the *Conan* stories or *A Game of Thrones*)?

   Post-apocalyptic

   Horror (Lovecraft)

   This can be an actual, preexisting fictional world from someone else's IP, or an original world of your own creation. Make sure to describe the world concisely, since your focus is on creating the system.

Lay out a description of your world in abstracted and systemic form. World-building is a term frequently used in creative writing, especially in science fiction and fantasy, and it overlaps with the concept of narrative design as first described by Eidos' lead game writer Mary deMarle. Narrative design refers to the process of bringing together game mechanics and game story to create a cohesive world.

Remember that the heart of magic is symbolic correspondences, so the building of your world may often consist of realms, planes, and spheres of existence that are more schematic and symbolic than physical. Digital games add exponential possibilities for world-building, since they can keep track of tens of thousands of objects, variables, and states, each of which can be manipulated through your game's magical language, provided that it is co-extensive with the world it describes and alters. The development of such a rich world and a corresponding language to describe it requires the most clear-headed rigor and planning, and is probably best done on paper before being implemented in digital form.

3. What are the themes of this world that need to be expressed in and through the system?

Examples include, but are not limited to:

Perception vs. Reality

Dwindling resources

Brutality

Light and beauty

Playfulness

4. What is the magical vocabulary and grammar of this system?

Vocabulary (spell effects/actions)

Grammar (rules for how spells effects and actions are combined)

Any actual linguistic elements (runes, sigils, glyphs)

What aspects of the simulated world do these words and grammatical structures manipulate?

5. Mode of input (gestural, verbal/incantatory, material/ingredient-based)

   What does the player do?

   What does the player character do?

   How different or similar are these actions?

6. Schools of magic

   What are the domains over which the spells operate?

   > What objects are governed by these domains?

   > What attributes do these objects have?

   > What states can these objects be in?

   > Can these states be assembled into larger state machines?

   What are the classes of spell effects?

   From what planes or domains do the spells originate?

   Is there a natural color-coding or iconography for these schools?

7. Pie graph of schools of magic

   Construct a radial diagram or pie graph representing the relationship of the schools of magic (i.e. their oppositions, alliances, how they counterbalance each other).

8. High-level overview of the rules/steps of casting a spell.

   How calculate spell effects? (random numbers, dice pool)

   Ability modifiers

   Penalties

   Resources (mana, Vancian memorization)

9. Detailed flowchart for casting spells

Flowcharts are at the heart of developing a magic system because they illustrate in rigorous, step-by-step form the process of casting spells. Flowcharting a magic system is analogous to programming one, since at its core programming is a form of symbolic logic that breaks down complex processes into smaller, modular parts. Many visual programming environments are essentially flowcharting tools, such as the Unreal Development Kit's Kismet. Kismet allows level designers to connect nodes representing events in a world (such as opening a door or setting off an alarm) with conditions that trigger these events or connect them with one another (such as a player passing through a zone or firing at a target).

One way of modeling such a system is a state machine, in which parts of the system are represented as devices that can be in a finite number of states. For example, a traffic light is a state machine that can be in the red, green, and yellow states.

Spellcasting, especially ritual spellcasting, can be effectively represented as a flowchart, sometimes representing the system's component state machines.

The software development meta-language called UML (unified modeling language) is also essentially a flowcharting methodology designed to represent the deep structures of complex processes.

1. What are the phases of a spell?

2. Where does the player make choices?

3. What are the consequences of these choices?

4. When does the process repeat/loop back?

10. Representative spell list

    Name

    Effect

    Duration

    Radius

    Footprint

Appendix B: Timelines

B.1 VIDEOGAME MAGIC TIMELINE

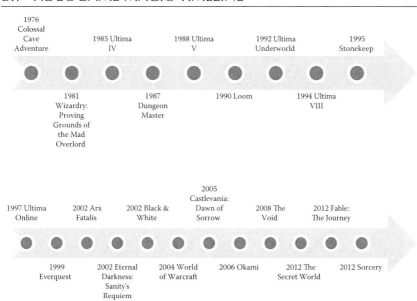

B.2 TABLETOP GAME MAGIC TIMELINE

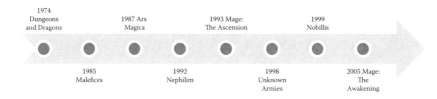

B.3 FICTIVE MAGIC TIMELINE

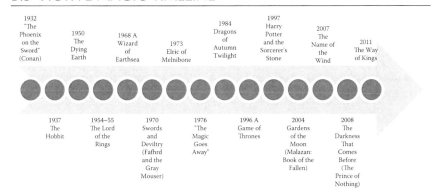

1932
"The
Phoenix
on the
Sword"
(Conan)

1950
The
Dying
Earth

1968 A
Wizard
of
Earthsea

1973
Elric of
Melnibone

1984
Dragons
of
Autumn
Twilight

1997
Harry
Potter
and the
Sorcerer's
Stone

2007
The
Name of
the
Wind

2011
The Way
of Kings

1937
The
Hobbit

1954–55
The Lord
of the
Rings

1970
Swords
and
Deviltry
(Fafhrd
and the
Gray
Mouser)

1976
"The
Magic
Goes
Away"

1996 A
Game of
Thrones

2004
Gardens
of the
Moon
(Malazan:
Book of the
Fallen)

2008
The
Darkness
That
Comes
Before
(The
Prince of
Nothing)

B.4 OCCULT MAGIC TIMELINE

1531 Cornelius
Agrippa
publishes
Three Books of
Occult
Philoosphy

1875 Birth of
Aleister
Crowley

1581 John Dee
and Edward
Kelley begin
skrying

1888 Order of
the Golden
Dawn
Founded

Index

Printed and bound by CPI Group (UK) Ltd, Croydon, CR0 4YY